My Kingdom of Books

First impression: May 1999

Cover photograph by Julio Donoso

Typeset in 11/16pt Bembo

ISBN: 0 86243 495 5

Published and printed in Wales
on Munken Print acid-free and partly recycled paper
by Y Lolfa Cyf., Talybont, Ceredigion SY24 5AP;
tel (01970) 832 304, *fax* 832 782, *isdn* 832 813
e-mail ylolfa@ylolfa.com
website www.ylolfa.com;
casebound in Wales by WBC Book Manufacturers,
Bridgend CF31 3XP

My Kingdom
of Books

Richard Booth

with Lucia Stuart

ACKNOWLEDGEMENT

Producing an autobiography seemed to be an increasingly unrealized and unachievable ambition. For this reason I am extremely grateful to Lucia Stuart, my stepdaughter, who became a co-author. Only through her love and conviction has it been possible to articulate my beliefs.

In addition, for twenty years my publisher, Robat Gruffudd, has supported my battle against the overpaid officials who claim to be reviving Mid-Wales. Although I am not a Welsh speaker, I know that I can rely on a strong core of Welsh-language support.

I am enormously grateful to them both.

FOREWORD

GREAT BRITAIN, WALES, HAY-ON-WYE can seem like looking down the wrong end of a telescope. To see a small town almost entirely dependent on books, by the yard, the kilo, the containerful, the mile, is to see a commerce and a passion which has spread further and further afield. Will there even, perhaps, be a book heaven, one vast library in the sky with cumulus cloud shelving and erudite angels, their wings folded in concentration? Who knows? With Richard one expects the unexpected, and a lot of fun it is.

Back to earth, this particular book of autobiography is about the obsesssion of Richard Booth, who as rightful king of the RSPCB is bent on freeing the printed word back into happier times.

Richard is a man I am delighted to have met in Wales and Paris. His astonishing optimism comes through in these pages as do his championship of reading itself, his courage and his scholarship, all combined with an energetic and imaginative business sense and, thank god, a lively sense of humour.

He lives in a youthfully humorous world of castles and kings, but his real life is still a successful struggle and a passionate adventure.

MAXIME DE LA FALAISE

Chapter One

The Birth
of a Book Town

"Nobody reads books in Hay-on-Wye."

"I've got a shop for sale for seven hundred pounds," said the vet in Hay-on-Wye. The building was Hay's Old Fire Station, in a good position on the main road coming in from Brecon. The year was 1962. Impulsively, I decided to buy it and open a shop.

I had shelves hand made with tenon joints and lovingly finished with several layers of white paint. They were far more expensive and less efficient than they should have been; unfortunately I was a victim of the pride of rural craftsmen. The town surveyor gave me a fireman's helmet to put on the bracket outside and the doctor's sister, Mrs Hamilton, agreed to run the shop. Everyone was to be kept provided with beer from The Blue Boar pub opposite.

I thought I would sell antiques to supplement the income from my first love, second-hand books.

"What's this?" asked a customer, hoping for an explanation of the intricacies of a Chinese root sculpture.

"It's thirty bob," I replied.

After the first week of trading it was pointed out to me that a miniature wooden port barrel in the window was brand new, and available from the local pub.

Antique dealers viewed my beginning with some interest. My parents were livid. Their despair was increased by my complete lack of business sense. "Get yourself an accountant," they urged. I did, and the episode ended with a writ for his fees.

"Richard is ruining us," my mother announced to anyone who would listen, horrified that her only son had become a small shopkeeper. To open a bookshop in a sleepy market town appeared lunacy.

"Booth won't last three months. Nobody reads books in Hay," was the commonly held opinion in the town.

I was a newcomer. My family had moved to Hay after the death of a distant relation and had rebought Brynmelin which formely belonged to my uncle and aunt, William and Kit Booth. My father had made a sudden decision which profoundly affected the course of my life. He sold our comfortable house in Surrey – nothing could stop him fleeing the golf clubs and businessmen – for the house that had been a shelter during his poverty-stricken years in the army.

Brynmelin was a drafty, rambling mansion within walking distance of Hay-on-Wye. It lies at the end of a leafy lane called Cusop Dingle, home to the last fairies seen in the British Isles. It was also referred to as 'The Golden Mile' because of the number of large houses inhabited by professional people. One of them, set back from the road, belonged to a solicitor called Herbert Armstrong, the last man to be hanged in Britain, for poisoning his wife with arsenic.

Brynmelin is partially obscured by tangled woodland. A bleak silence is pierced by the cawing of rooks. Behind the house, beyond the croquet lawn and rhododendron bushes, the Black Mountains reach towards the sky like a runway. The house was built in 1893 by a Canadian who saw great opportunities in the local lime-kiln, brickyard and slate quarries. However, all his dreams and chances of wealth vanished after London brick swamped the market, and he committed suicide. In fifty years of residence my uncle never climbed up to the glass observatory at the top of the water tower where the tragic deed was perpetrated.

Willie Booth retired to Brynmelin in 1903, after the Boer War. A vain man, the house was a showcase for his sporting triumphs. He spent his time fishing for salmon in Wales or shooting stags in Scotland and

Northumberland. In the hall, which smelt of polish and linseed oil, there were rows of antler horns. Black-framed photographs of Willie, sporting an enormous handlebar moustache and proudly brandishing man-sized fish, were hung for all to admire. Relics of Edwardian luxury were strewn in every room: horseshoes mounted in silver to make inkwells, magnificent, thick leather suitcases, and a glass-fronted game called 'Get the Balls in the Nigger's Eyes'.

In contrast to my uncle's aggressive pursuits, my aunt Kit, the daughter of a wealthy Birmingham brewer, kept a bird garden and provided one of the last sanctuaries for the red squirrel, which she would feed by hand. I met her as a small boy and she gave me twenty-five pounds, a huge amount in those days, but Willie and Kit gave generously and freely to all who needed it. Quite rightly, they regarded the state's attempts to regulate their charity as gross impertinence. 'One of Lloyd George's damn insurance stamps,' Willie had scribbled across an envelope I found in his desk.

For my father, moving into Brynmelin represented an ideal; the Booths were to re-establish a rural existence. For both of them it signified a rejection of society. Hay was a small rural town, a horse and cart still delivered blocks from the sawmill and market day brought small farmers down from the hills. It offered a social life to which they felt they need not adapt.

In the fourteenth century Hay-on-Wye was larger than Birmingham. In the nineteenth century it was a relatively prosperous town with a hundred shops and a busy railway service to Brecon four times a day. The 1960s saw the small market town decline. School children, farmers' wives and geese still went about their business, unaware of the impending threat from the lorry-drawn cargo destined for new supermarkets. But for its market and the determination of its people it might have suffered the fate of the nearby Norman town of Aberllynfi and disappeared into the green fields. Every few days another shop would close. The fine grocer called Maddys, whose family had owned land there since the sixteenth century, knew the writing was on the wall. I hoped that, surrounded by mountains and with a small population, Hay might be saved from the nightmare of industrial retailing.

One of the few shops that managed to survive was William Mayall the jewellers. As a champion watchmaker in the Army, Mayall had been responsible for the maintenance of thousands of watches during the Second World War. A gentle and intelligent man, his small shop in the market square is impervious to modern fashions.

Secluded in Brynmelin, my mother met very few people. In Surrey my father had shared the reading of the lessons in church with a bank manager; now he was chatting happily with the vet and the old men who remembered Willie. He regarded his new home as his Elysian fields.

My initial excursions into local society were not auspicious. I started dating a respectable girl called Anne Miles whose father, Colonel Miles, was a friend of my father's. I took her to The Mason's Arms. "Gentlemen don't take ladies into pubs like that," her father sternly informed me afterwards. He then gave me a piece of advice which must have related to his traditional regimental world. "You've got to build yourself a squash court," he told me with a friendly wink. A few retired Army acquaintances of my father still lived in the area. One day a General Frisby invited us to a cocktail party. After a few drinks, I addressed him as General Busby and became further disgraced.

At this time I was an awkward, immature and outspoken undergraduate and soon achieved a disastrous reputation among the people of Hay. In a rural society xenophobia is easily aroused. I was largely helped by one man whose genius enabled me to be accepted by the locals. When my parents realized that the problems of living in Brynmelin were harsher than they had estimated, they advertised for more staff. The successful applicant for the post of Gardener/Handyman was called Frank English. One morning I came into the kitchen, where he was sitting at the table drinking a steaming mug of tea. Cigarette smoke curled around a large, beak-like, magenta nose. Thin legs were twisted into a spiral and anchored to the floor by a pair of old Army boots.

"I've got an appalling headache," I announced.

"Go and dig the garden," he said.

"I don't dig," was my immediate response.

This short conversation showed our respective attitudes to life. Just out of university, I was a third-rate aesthete. My personality, weakly constructed from a life spent in Oxford and Surrey, disappeared in the face of Frank's extraordinarily clear view of human existence. Life was simply work and drink, and occasionally a bit of sex. From that moment a life-long friendship began.

Frank had known my father in the Army before I was born. He was a natural iconoclast and had deserted three times in the 1930s. He had even deserted my father's own regiment in India. I was in a youthful, anti-Army mood and appreciated his stories.

"The Guards Division were magnificent," he said, referring to the race to release troops trapped at Arnhem. On patrol in the middle of the night he had once come face to face with a German, but in the interest of safety both had ignored each other.

Frank's first achievement was to wean me from The Crown Hotel, where the majority of the so-called upper class of the area drank. It was not without its attractions. A beautiful, squint-eyed ex-chorus girl called Lady Borwick would dislodge even the smallest copper saucepans off the beam in the saloon bar with her astoundingly high kicks. Owen Jones drank in The Crown. He sold a Hereford bull to Argentina for a record two hundred and fifty pounds, an amazing price considering hill cottages could be bought for a hundred pounds. Owen's deals financed his consumption of gin. In time the corned beef trade with Argentina withered through competition with Charolais cattle and Owen died, at the age of thirty, from a destroyed liver.

Hay had eleven pubs, rather fewer than the thirty-five at the beginning of the century. It did not take me long to notice that Frank's knowledge of the town's pubs and families was encyclopaedic. He made a point of knowing exactly who was related to whom. In a town where eight hundred of the twelve hundred inhabitants were called Davies, this was quite a feat. Knowledge is power and Frank was respected locally. "You can have anything you want at any time," said Cliff Metcalfe, an old shopkeeper who lived above his shop. Frank woke him up, banging on the shop door at four o'clock in the morning to ask for ten Woodbines and a small tin of baked beans.

After Frank took a right hook from a Crown drinker for swearing in public, he introduced me to the working-class pubs. "Meet Jean," he would say, taking me to The Old Black Lion, "She's famous for knocking down the local police sergeant." Jean was married to a railwayman called Tom Beattie and was an ardent protector of the youth of the town against an over-zealous police force. Bill Powell was a butcher famous for his faggots, which he took around the pubs, and for his unhygienic distribution of them after he had been to the Gents and forgotten to wash his hands. Albert Powell ran a bookies from The Wheatsheaf and for over sixty years his sister Lucy has occupied The Three Tuns, the oldest licensed premises in Hay. Her father pressed their own cider, which he sold for threepence a pint. It cost half the price of beer, which was half the price of Scotch. The large breweries levelled the price of all three, destroying the local scrumpy tradition.

Inside her pub, cats still thread through chair legs in the half light, embers hiss in the grate and Lucy's bright eyes peer over the bar like a country mouse.

"Did I tell you that the Great Train Robbers came in here? The five of them!" Lucy was fond of telling the story. "They parked their car, a very smart shooting-brake, just outside. They paid for their drinks with a five-pound note. You didn't see many of them around. They were on the run you see. I think they were hoping to buy a property round here and they probably thought they could hide out among the hills."

Although there was a nationwide hunt for the men in August 1962, there was no question of exposing her customers. "It's all very well being patriotic, but it's no good being patriotic and dead," she concluded. A week later, it was reported that one of them had been seen coming out of a barber's shop in Abergavenny.

"So then I knew I must have been right," Lucy said.

Her melodic voice is a bubbling Welsh stream that carries stories like leaves in the current. She has enchanted her customers over the years.

"Will you marry me, Lucy?" Frank would ask, not infrequently. "I'll think about it, Frank," she would reply.

Frank taught me that ten pounds spent in a Hay pub was more appreciated than a hundred pounds in a London night-club. At The Half Moon the publican refused to serve drinks after time but, as an ex-Army sergeant, he rose early and would happily supply any drinker who had made it through the night. His wife served wonderful faggots and peas in cracked dishes with pewter spoons for a few pence on market days. Real vigour emerged on market day – hundreds of small farmers poured into the town and drank themselves silly.

"This shows I'm still a virgin," announced Bill Brown. Removing his uncircumcised penis from his trousers and balancing an egg on his head, he would walk across the pub. He lived on the hill in eighteenth-century squalor.

"I'll get you anything you want," he would say, "Eggs, vegetables, chickens, anything!" All the farmers knew that he would steal to supply these orders but they tolerated this as he was a popular character. Behind the bar there was a photograph of Bill smiling jovially, his monumental body as curved as the rolling green hills behind him.

Ken and Violet Jenkins of The Mason's Arms were special favourites of Frank and myself. The labourers who drank there did not talk much but sat quietly around the fire putting hot pokers into their cider to take the chill off it. The pub was warmer and more comfortable than their lodgings. Ernie Chambers had been at Dunkirk but was not quite certain what or where the English Channel was. He believed that a horse ride would bring him to London; nobody told him that it was a hundred and fifty miles away. Tom Preece was an ex-forester who refused to pay his National Insurance each year. To roars of laughter he would explain that the food was better in prison and the accommodation more comfortable than anything he could find in Hay. Prison was his annual holiday. His landlady had two mentally defective, incestuous children. Her daughter hardly spoke, and her son regularly drank sixteen pints of cider, after which he beat his wife and sister. In The Mason's Arms, all were tolerated without complaint.

I was moving in a peasant society where all pride was in manual work. Vernon Meredith was a wild-haired bulldozer-digger with a moustache like a Cossack general. "The best people in the world are bulldozer drivers," we sang dancing around the pub at three in the morning. He did a job that a hundred labourers used to do. In those days I did not realize that the agricultural economy was being destroyed by the greed of industry. Bill Cooke was a hard-drinking lorry driver in blue overalls. He used to take radiators from Llanelli to the Austin Morris factory in Birmingham, and seven-foot high loads of lavatory paper from South Wales to Liverpool.

"Does it get boring doing the same runs every day, Bill?" I asked him.

"No," he replied, "you can see the seasons changing in the fields."

Thrown into the toughest part of industrial society, bloody-minded union officials would sometimes keep him waiting for twelve hours at factory gates. Bill was a country boy at heart and talked lovingly of the time he 'took a hundred rabbits' on the hill above Hay with his ferrets. His beautiful, blonde wife June, who looked like Marilyn Monroe – only two stone heavier – provided the perfect antidote to his wit in the pub. We would drink until the early hours and at five in the morning several heavy lorries would crunch out of the car park.

"I'm very worried about the amount of money we're getting from the fruit machine in The British Legion," the manager of Barclays Bank confided to me. Lorry drivers earned a lot and spent a lot. Hay was a changeover point between South Wales and the Midlands. Bill Cooke would relax after fourteen hours on the road with the glittering symbols of the fruit machines. Other drivers would work day and night in forty-eight hour stretches to buy a three-piece suite for their socially ambitious wives.

As Frank methodically undertook odd jobs around Brynmelin he chain-smoked Woodbines and professed to stick to bottles of Whitbread when working, instead of going onto 'the hard stuff'. Nevertheless, he was an alcoholic and, as is not unusual with heavy drinkers, catastrophe struck. His career with my parents was brief. He returned very late one night from the pub and there was a fire in his bedroom. When the inevitable moment came for his dismissal, my mother confronted him.

"I've never seen anyone in that state. You came home and set the bed alight!"

"No, Mrs Booth," Frank replied, "I came home stone-cold sober, and when I got into it, the bed was already on fire."

My mother, Frank remarked, had lived an extremely sheltered life if she had reached the age of fifty-five without ever having seen anyone drunk. With my father, who was similarly secluded in the loyalties and prejudices of the Army, she formed an alliance that denied or criticised most of the realities of the outside world.

My relationship with my parents was deteriorating. I appeared to be wasting my expensive education. As soon as I graduated from Oxford, they insisted upon the career that made my grandfather so spectacularly successful and apprenticed me as an accountant to Bolton, Pitt and Bredon, the family firm. Only a few weeks were enough to persuade me that I did not want to work in the City of London. Buying a small shop in Hay-on-Wye meant that, instead of playing a minor rôle in a major business, I could play a major rôle in a minor one.

Chapter Two

Books for the Book Town

"You can always sell a good book."

"Come and work for me, Frank," I said, following his dismissal. Much under the influence of his wit and charm, I thought a working association would be beneficial. Frank was diffident about his skill as a carpenter but told me that, unlike the professionals, at least he tidied up after the job. Thus he began a twenty-year occupation building bookshelves. I always paid him in cash, whereupon he would lavish every penny on the pubs within a day or two.

To find stock I took out an advertisement in *The Western Mail*: 'Libraries purchased, any quantity from a single volume to a whole library.' The first response came from a merchant seaman called John Parker who ran the Albany Auction Rooms in Cardiff. He was selling a library that belonged to the Catholic Archbishop of Cardiff, Bishop Hedley, and appeared overwhelmed by the hundreds of volumes of seventeenth- and eighteenth-century theology and sets of *The Catholic Record Society* that had come into his possession. I completed the purchase only to discover that the leading Catholic bookshop in London would have nothing to do with them. Theology has one of the worst reputations in the book trade, but I have always found it fascinating. The Mormons put on white gloves to read books, the Plymouth Brethren ask to be buried with them and the Christadelphians buy books about natural disasters.

When Bishop Hedley's library arrived in Hay, the immediate problem I faced was the sheer physical effort of carrying such a vast number of heavy books upstairs in the Old Fire Station. Frank and a small boy called Delwyn Davies staggered up the narrow staircase with them. Frank became enamoured with Delwyn, claiming that his winkle-picker shoes and prowess on the fruit machine made him sexually irresistible.

My success as a bookseller was built against the background of manual work. I was thrown into the society of diggers of ditches, labourers and woodmen. Rural pride enabled us to do a job others would have spurned. Pride in manual work, I believe, is the basis of any traditional rural economy. I hold a good manual worker in higher esteem than any intellectual. Working with just a few country labourers, I ended up possessing books of greater intellectual variety than all the universities in the British Isles put together.

Bishop Hedley's library brought me into contact with my first 'runner', a man called Newcombe. A runner buys from one dealer and sells to another. Newcombe arrived on the train with his bike and posted his purchases in neat parcels to Thorntons, an Oxford theological bookseller who bought everything he sent. "You will grow out of me," he pontificated. Full-time running is a precarious existence and often does not last more than five years because sources are exhausted or a supplier decides to sell direct to the dealer. In the USA a runner is called a 'scout' and the distances they have to cover are far greater. David Magee, in *Infinite Riches: The Adventures of a Rare Book Dealer*, describes the typical scout as 'an original, happy-go-lucky man who laboured hard for no vast return'. I think this was an optimistic description inspired by the romanticism of California. A runner is more likely to be a man whose ego needs boosting. He probably lives in a wretched little bed-sit with an overweight, middle-aged girlfriend, any romance being centred around a bottle of gin.

John Moss thought runners highly knowledgeable and introduced them as necessary and important members of the book trade. Whenever I was in London I drifted into his second-hand bookshop, Oppenheim and Company, at the bottom of Exhibition Road. Looking like an unkempt schoolmaster, loquacious and opinionated, he zealously introduced me to the lore of the second-hand trade. The shelves immediately behind his desk were a honey pot for swarms of dealers whose abilities to spot the under-priced book led Moss to formulate the endlessly repeated maxim, 'you can always sell a good book'. Jargon abounded: 'Americana', 'Australiana', 'misbound', 'defective', 'that's early for it'. "Come and have tea at Joe Lyons," he would say on favoured occasions. An old man, he would regularly repeat a story about literary rarities being found by dealers wishing to relieve themselves because old books had been in universal use as lavatory paper before the real thing was invented. Years later, in a Saratoga bookshop in New York State, I enhanced John Moss's mythology by discovering a valuable Italian Fascist periodical in the corridor of the Gents. The first glimpse told me that Mussolini was a better graphic designer than a politician. I bought it for seven dollars fifty. It was worth far more. Even today, shortage of space in bookshops means that the bathroom is often a precious storage area.

John took me to see a dealer who was selling his theatre stock in the West End. He had an extraordinary range of playbills, theatre programmes, celebrity photographs and several thousand volumes of the *Illustrated London News*, *The Theatre* and *The Graphic*. Before the age of the photocopier, he was a sort of retrospective press or cuttings agency for his customers. Today his razor-blade would be doing hundreds of pounds worth of damage but in the 1950s he was providing a service. Gradually, long runs of *Illustrated London News* disappeared from the market. *Punch* was more common but it had not yet achieved popular appeal, which made it an exciting prospect for the book dealer. Fifty-volume runs cost about ten pounds and the edition covering the Prince of Wales's visit to Canada in 1863, for example, contained about forty pounds worth of prints.

Like many of the London dealers, John Moss could not hold large numbers of books. Even a taxi load would create chaos when his shop was crowded. I was prepared to buy in bulk; it was the only way I could compete with the London trade and its supporting cast of runners. Sotheby's, Christie's and the prestigious shops of Cecil Court did not attract me. I was not an expert or a specialist, nor was I able to manipulate the large sums of money which these establishments needed. With youthful enthusiasm, I commandeered lorry-loads of books from the paved streets of London to the muddy, sheep-blocked lanes of Wales. Never before had a small Welsh town seen such large numbers of books. 'Welsh Mecca for Celtic Studies,' wrote *The Western Mail* in an article that brought thousands of Welsh book-lovers to Hay. Publicity appeared an effective aid to selling all the books I had. It was later that I realized the truth: the media are the devilish High Priests of Western civilization, hungry for human sacrifice.

Far too many books were arriving in the town. We had to weed the shelves and throw them away by the ton. To sort the books I employed a thin man called Philip Worsley and his thin wife whose figures suggested they had been physiologically affected by the science-fiction in which they dealt. Their passion was single-minded and much of the non-science-fiction that they came across was thrown away. Some of the discarded books were gems: out of a rubbish sack fell a rare volume about the scandalous sex life of Queen Charlotte in 1828.

I found there were dealers who specialised in what other dealers discarded. Prominent among these was 'Chalky' White, whose black Homburg and coat suggested the third bearer of a very humble undertaker. He was the first dealer to move to Hay, buying a shop from me in Market Street and emblazoning it with the words 'Michael White & Sons'. This was somewhat hopeful: his sons did not share his enthusiasm

23

for books and his wife remained in London. He was an expert on Catholic theology, the Oxford Movement, G.K. Chesterton and almost anything to do with the Roman Catholic World. Chalky brought distinction and a higher class of customer to Hay. His clients were loyal and serious collectors who would spend hundreds of pounds on the right books. He would send them tightly-worded lists which were calculated to minimise all costs, as was his habit of reusing even short bits of string.

Newcombe, the runner, suggested I hire Mike, a beautiful young Indian boy who began to push books around Hay in a pram. After a few weeks he made a decision which was to become the curse of employment in Hay: it just was not an interesting enough place to live. After the homesick Mike returned to the Indian colony in south London, I employed John Berridge. John had a short goatee beard and a slightly pompous manner but was a very good bookseller, immediately persuading a county lady to give a generous sum for a set of Swinburne. My greatest early patron was my sister Mary whose husband, Deryck Healey, owned design studios in London, Johannesburg, Tokyo and Australia. Mary loved fine books with coloured plates and spent lavishly.

Geoffrey Aspin was a lecturer in French at the University of Liverpool. Like many university lecturers he had taken up dealing part-time, specialising in French literature, Gustave Doré, Bibles and antiquarian books. He was extremely meticulous and customers who requested his first catalogue continued to receive the next ninety-nine. I took him to dinner and by morning he had decided to move to Hay. Installed in Castle Street, he provided two of the most vital elements in a Book Town. Firstly, he lovingly restored his fine seventeenth-century shop, packing the windows with the literary curiosities that give Hay such an enticing, bookish appearance. Secondly, like Chalky White, he had many erudite customers.

Geoffrey made regular excursions to Sotheby's to buy books and to visit good London restaurants. During one of his periodic jaunts the bitter weather caused broken pipes. He returned to find his collection of Corneille, the seventeenth-century French dramatist, ruined. The white vellum books were worth a fortune and the collection had been superior to that in the Bibliothèque Nationale in Paris.

Harry Benz made himself a fortune from the post-war collapse of the country house. He was a legend in the South Wales trade. "I'll give you a fiver for the old tent pole, lady," Harry was reputed to have said upon seeing a valuable ceremonial Maori totem pole. A brilliant Jewish dealer, he gained entrance to large houses by claiming that he was religiously persecuted: nowhere could he find a Kosher chicken. When he had gained his host's confidence by buying a suitable bird at a high price, he would move on to their antiques.

"A good dealer will have the owner running all over the house trying to find stuff to sell them," explained Harry.

He advised me to advertise for books; they were like linen or jugs in that they led one to affluent houses. 'Knockers', those dealers who visit houses without an appointment, were often very successful. Harry thought enormous opportunities lay ahead of me in this field. "Nobody 'knocks' for *books*," he said, "they're undervalued by the antiques trade. Follow the river, boy! All the best houses are along the rivers." I fantasised about country houses with a large celestial and terrestrial globe at either end of the library.

I bought my first country-house library from the Bourdillions of Llwyn Madoc, a distinguished family whose history included a friendship with de Gaulle, who had stayed there during the Second World War. The recently-married heir wished to sell off some vast calf folios, which he no doubt considered darkened the room, and replace them with a vellum-bound set of Delphine classics, whose golden-white bindings Frank strove to improve by cleaning them with milk. This library gave me a vital start in Wales and other country-house libraries followed.

"Dynevor here," announced a voice on the telephone. "Can I please speak to Richard Booth?"

"I'm afraid he's gone for his Dynevor," said Frank. The quip was taken in good spirit.

Lord Dynevor was a shabbily-dressed, idealistic youth who wished to dispose of thousands of his ancestors' eighteenth-century books. In the grounds of the estate was the ruin of a pre-Norman castle, one of the most valued sites in Wales. As with many large houses, much of the economy of neighbouring Llandeilo used to depend upon the family. Now all had changed and the present Lord gave himself over to promoting modern American jazz. He was painting his enormous eighteenth-century library royal blue and gold so that the neighbouring inhabitants could enjoy the musical talents of Cleo Laine and Johnny Dankworth. He was ahead of his time in forecasting that Jazz Festivals were going to replace the traditional culture of rural Wales.

Perhaps the finest library that I ever saw in a Welsh country-house was at Nanteos near Aberystwyth, where George Powell, a homosexual squire, had romped with Swinburne. As a monument to turn-of-the-century prosperity, a magnificent stuffed bear, brought from the wastes of Siberia by members of the family, loomed large in the shadows of the entrance hall. The library dated from the seventeenth century and the books were in mint condition. There was a pristine collection of three-volume novels and a first edition of *Lady Audley's Secret* worth a four-figure sum. Removing them from the solid oak, glass-fronted bookcases, I realized that an era was coming to an end.

Everywhere I saw country houses struggling miserably for a new form of life. The owner of a grand Irish house said to me, "I am sorry that we cannot ask you to lunch; my wife and I are sharing a tin of sardines." Trying to survive on an estate for generations is a difficult and painful operation. "You can always tell when the owners are in financial trouble," said Taxi Davies, my driver, " – they start cutting down the trees in the drive."

Many of the grand houses had become schools or were promised rich pickings by the Government on becoming tourist attractions or nursing homes. So miserable was one female owner of a country house which became a new tourist hotel along a Scottish river, that Taxi claimed he had made love to her in the hotel telephone box. Searching for a culprit, I identified tourist boards, quangos and local government as the enemy. Wisdom was moving from the community to the bureaucracy.

Country houses provided only a small proportion of my purchases. Although the idea was to buy every book I could, I also bought fifty pairs of Staffordshire dogs, the standard pottery ornament for a Victorian home. I was an incorrigible buyer, quickly learning that the worst mistake one could make was not to buy anything.

'You can never give too much for a private library' was an adage of the trade.

In remote rural areas books were often regarded as worthless and volumes which would fetch a high premium elsewhere would be sold for very little. One dealer cultivated the squirearchy by joining the local natural history society. This tactic proved successful and he met the perfect squire with a magnificent library. He tentatively asked the owner how much he wanted for it. "The price of a couple of bitches," had been the reply, frequently repeated throughout the trade.

One of the great joys of second-hand bookselling is that one can research values after purchasing. Inscriptions, pamphlets and rare first editions can be bought in total ignorance; the relationship with the seller is more important than scrutinising the books. Negotiating deals needed acting ability and I decided that my best persona would be that of a gauche public schoolboy who did not know what he was doing. "Gosh, what do you think they're worth?" was a comment I made more often than I care to remember.

Despite Frank constructing a special spotlight over my desk, hoping it would witness the inscription of enormous sums, I was inexperienced and apt to sacrifice bargains through my ignorance and haste. I was reluctant to undertake the meticulous scholarly work needed to get the highest prices for my books. In order to continue buying voraciously I sold my stock quickly, figuring that if a dealer got a bargain from me he would return. A particular sacrifice I remember was a three-volume edition of Jane Austen's *Sense and Sensibility* in publishers' boards, before it was properly bound. I sold it for £200. Even in those days that was about £1,000 too cheap.

Frank was more astute. His views had been formed in the hard school of human experience. A customer arrived claiming to be an international bookseller. He drove a Jaguar and wore a mauve blazer. "Nobody who looks like that is ever remotely honest," said Frank. His instinct was correct: when 'Good Appearance' departed it was found that he had stolen a valuable book by slipping it under his pile of purchases.

Wales was a booksellers' wilderness in the late 1960s and I had the field almost to myself, not least because a jocular fifty-year old bookseller called Kyrle Fletcher was run over by a motorbike. For example, a shop in Caernarfon belonging to a nationalist called Morris had been inherited by a less commercial nationalist called Jones. He had a chapel four feet deep in dog turds and damp books. First editions of Dafydd ap Gwilym from the eighteenth century were in good supply. I simply piled up the books and gave whatever I wanted to pay for them. Similarly, I bought a garage-full of books from Williams Bros. of Carmarthen. It contained, among others, several copies of *Archaeologia Cambrensis* and Grant Francis's *Copper Smelting in Swansea*.

The bibliophile elder brother had died and the younger wanted five hundred pounds for the lot. With youthful confidence I knocked him down to under a hundred.

"There is never any good gear in a house with an illuminated bell-push," Alan Mobey warned me. Hundreds of times we visited the minor streets of Cardiff and found objects which depicted the dignified home of the petit bourgeoisie: antimacassar-covered armchairs, a set of Scott, *The Pilgrim's Progress*, a Bible with chromolithic-coloured plates, and a potted plant. 'You can never refuse a cup of tea,' was another adage of the trade. In a day I could drink ten.

One day I received a letter in a feeble, scrawled hand from a Mrs Evans who wanted to sell her books. I arrived at her address and rang the bell. The lace curtains twitched and the door opened slowly. "Can I see Mrs Evans?" I asked politely. I was shown into the room where she lay. Mrs Evans had just died.

Welsh books are generally thinner than Scottish and Irish books. This is because Cardiff, the Welsh capital, was a nineteenth-century creation. Earlier Welsh publishing was a small, decentralized activity. The Scots and the Irish published in their capitals as early as the sixteenth century and the books grew in weight and size. Big books are generally bad books in the second-hand trade because they are unlikely to vanish in the course of time and are not small and hard to find. "Doorstopper," said an effeminate bookseller, touching a large, antique vellum-bound folio disdainfully with his foot. At this time, however, I did not understand many of the natural laws of bookselling.

The first Welsh books were published in Newcastle Emlyn, Trefecca and Carmarthen and were never much thicker than a lady's cigarette case. I like to think of Hay-on-Wye as part of a Welsh tradition because it is only a few miles from Trefecca, where followers of John Wesley produced some of the most beautiful publishing of the eighteenth century. The pages of books from the Trefecca press are so thin and delicate as to be translucent and the sepia print so small that it could be stamped on a matchstick.

On one occasion it became apparent that we were going to bid against Quaritch, the great antiquarian bookseller in London. The focus of our attention was a large library in the Countess of Huntingdon's country house at Trefecca. Such was her belief in Wesley that she had devoted her life and property to improving the fortune of his followers. All eighteenth-century books written in Welsh are very valuable unless published in London or Oxford. I wanted this library and Frank was sympathetic to the cause. He offered to go to the elderly keeper of the library straight way. After a few pints en route he proposed to knock at the door and, smelling strongly of beer, say, "I'm from Quaritch, lady. Can I have a piss?" There was no need to put Frank's plan into action. When Quaritch looked at the library they handed it over to me, declaring that it was too large and many of the books were damp.

Despite buying a Linguaphone Welsh-language course, I never got much further than being able to say, "there is bread and butter on the table", and I never really mastered the detailed research necessary to deal in Welsh-language books. But I know that 'Rhydychen' means it was printed in Oxford and I can roughly estimate the value of a Welsh-language book by its physical appearance. Welsh was scarcely spoken in Hay, even on market day. But Owen Morgan, a small man in a head-brace, translated the inscription on the side of my van into Welsh: 'The leading second-hand and antiquarian bookshop in Wales'.

The first Welsh word I needed to know was 'trysorfa' (a volume of selected prose and verse). Owen helped me to sort the first Welsh-language books, all temperance works of the 1830s and 1840s. We came across hundreds of biographies of Welsh ministers of the late nineteenth century. Many were neatly bound in the sheepskin which was often used by travelling binders. Each preacher prefaced his devotional work with a proudly-posed photograph of himself.

"What the hell can I do with these, Owen?" I asked.

"You can write 'A History of Welsh Hairstyles between 1860 and 1900'," he replied.

I could only wonder at the language which had inspired hundreds of preachers, most of whom the modern clergy neglect entirely. Spurgeon's theological writings were in great demand. A theologian told me that his sermons, if laid out page to page, would reach from here to the moon.

Handling so many books, I reached rather unorthodox conclusions. Napoleon was the most important figure in the development of a Welsh tourist trade, I pontificated. He made it too dangerous to visit the picturesque beauty spots of Italy and so, between 1780 and 1820, travellers discovered the glory of Wales instead. The 220 Welsh Tours published in the eighteenth century, which first inspired the use of the word 'tourist' in Anglo-Welsh books, were most desirable objects.

Over beers in The Great Western Hotel in Abergavenny, Owen became a great friend. He had risked his life in the Spanish Civil War taking gold through fascist lines to La Pasionaria. Left for dead after a gas attack in the First World War, he had special philosophical attitudes.

"What do you think of the class war now, Owen?" I asked him.

"There is no class war now," he said. "There is only war against the officials."

Chapter Three

"Up the 52nd and at 'em!"

Major General William Booth

My father slowly accepted my career in the book business, but it saddened my mother. Her attempts to dissuade me only hardened my resolve. Bereft of her family, the only life she had known before and after the War, she was increasingly withdrawn and miserable. This may have been the result of a growing illness; she collapsed in tears one day and was found to have cancer. My mother died in 1969 without seeing a glimmer of sunshine. Surprised at the rapid decline of her health, which occurred at a very pressurised moment in my early career, I bitterly regret that we were not reconciled. She could not accept that I was rejecting the opportunities and contacts of my privileged upbringing in order to live in an area where they counted for nothing, and I failed to communicate that my decision was based on a genuine moral conviction. She was buried in Cusop churchyard under an unusual modern headstone with a large hole in the centre. Her death caused me to reflect on my childhood.

I was born in 1938 during the Munich crisis, the prelude to the Second World War. My sister Mary had preceded me in 1936 and my sister Joanna was born in 1940. My father gave her the nickname 'good old Jo Stalin' in memory of the Russian troops who rebuffed the Germans on the Eastern Front. He hated Germans and had good reason to. His first military experience was at the second battle of the Somme, where seventeen out of twenty-one of his fellow officers were killed. The Regimental Sergeant-Major saved his life by finding suitable shelter amid the gunfire.

My father's military career ended during the Second World War. As a member of the Pioneer Corps he took part in the liberation of several thousand Jews from the concentration camp at Belsen. A polite and unshaven Rudolf Hess was brought before him and explained that he had been following orders. Later in life my father would explode in fury if anybody suggested he buy any German product. His most charitable analysis of the German people was that they were "awful bloody fools for having followed Hitler in the first place".

My first childhood memories are of looking for poisoned sweets dropped by German aeroplanes as we walked to school, and of the bumps in the road to slow down speeding American Jeeps. In my family I was closest to my sister Mary. Together we enjoyed the excitement of war. From our back lawn we could see vignettes of rural England, such as prisoner-of-war farm labourers clubbing rabbits or fleeing, petrified, from the combine harvester.

My parents' house in West Wittering, Sussex, was on Britain's front line against Hitler. There were fields of telegraph poles to prevent gliders landing and the beach was mined. Concrete blocks, barbed wire and gun emplacements waited for the German invasion. It was forbidden territory; I had to be content to play on the pebbles of a small, muddy cove. Physically unattractive in my round spectacles, I could have passed for an ugly son of Himmler. Near to our house, on a patch of waste ground, was a dummy airfield. It was hoped that this would confuse the enemy bombers. The Germans dropped large amounts of silver paper to deceive the radar and these frequently landed on our house. Black-outs and curfews were strictly observed. Mary's incautious visit to the lavatory without closing the curtains was supposed to have resulted in immediate aerial retaliation.

At the time of Dunkirk, after a battalion of his regiment had been captured, my father was certain that England would be invaded and warned my mother accordingly. "They're coming," he said, telephoning in a state of panic from the Isle of Wight. We became war refugees that moved northwards from Sussex to my grandmother's house in Surrey, where we remained for several weeks. As this was a comfortable estate with its own dairy producing delicious butter and cream, it was a worthy exercise in its own right. When we returned home, my father took me for long walks along the beach to discuss military strategy. We looked for objects which could be of use to ship-wrecked survivors and landscape suitable for building gun sites. In the background were the rolling green hills of the Sussex Downs, populated by the occasional windmill or crashed aircraft. To me the main benefits of peace would be proper sand in which to play and the end of sweet rationing.

With the arrival of my third sister Anne, in 1944, we moved to a village near Henley-on-Thames, where a friend of the family had an unoccupied farmhouse. I began a miserable career at a day-school which served innumerable lunches of corned beef and lettuce. I was expelled for conducting ballistic experiments with half bricks aimed at the headmistress's dog.

It was hoped that boarding school would cure such peculiar behaviour. I was dispatched to Bilton Grange Preparatory School, a Victorian mansion which the Prince Consort had turned down as an official residence. Fine mahogany cases of fragile birds' eggs – curiosities from an earlier age – were used to distract us from the departure of our parents. My mother wept as she said goodbye to me at the school gates. I was guided into an oak-panelled room large enough to engulf over a hundred small boys in grey shorts and proceeded to watch the school authorities struggle to construct a semi-perfect unit of Imperial youth.

Sport, and a place at a prestigious public school, motivated the 120 boys crammed into the school. The headmaster, Arthur Machlin, was a thick-lipped, semi-literate thug whose well-muscled wrists allowed him to play low-par golf and give us painful canings. His deputy, the English master, left under a cloud for hurling wooden blackboard dusters at his pupils, as did the senior master for 'necking' with an amorous infant in the cricket pavilion. Another fat and deformed master invented a form of torture called a 'Summy's Special', which involved twisting the short hairs on the back of our necks. Discipline was to be further instilled through the dubious inspiration of films celebrating Second World War heroism. *For Theirs Is The Glory* showed how paratroopers had fought the Battle of Arnhem, and *The Overlanders* was about Australians rescuing cattle from the Japanese advance. These films could only be seen if one had obtained fewer than five black marks; I was saved by default from a brainwashing. Like a herd of young pigs, squealing and protesting ineffectually, we were beaten and bullied in the right direction. The school was riddled with snobbery. We were indoctrinated with the theory that only the lower classes played soccer. A place in the First Fifteen saved my school career from total ignominy.

"Can I learn to play the violin?" I asked my father. He roared with laughter and told me it was an occupation only fit for girls; cricket was for boys.

My godfather, Lieutenant Colonel Richard Bannister Crosse, conscientiously visited me once a term and I was given a specific budget to spend on sweets. Crosse, after whom I was named, had been my father's Commanding Officer in the First World War. "Wear a belt as well as braces," was his tip for success in life, but any benefit from such sound advice was outweighed by my family's experience of sharing a house with him, and particularly the strong antipathy my mother felt due to his influence over my father.

At first the arrangement appeared perfect. He had inherited Raven's Oak, a secluded mansion whose modest servants' quarters were more than adequate for his simple needs. We lived in the rest of the house, which was furnished exactly as it had been in Crosse's mother's time. Long rows of nineteenth-century copies of *Punch* filled the passage between our two halves. An old man in braces, Crosse would sing, "D'ye ken John Peel?" as he smashed old 78 records, having discovered that yesterday's music was today's perfect fire-lighter. In the overgrown garden I learnt to shoot with a .22 rifle, drilling the Highland dancer on packets of porridge oats. An utterly dedicated soldier, Crosse was the only Commanding Officer who refused to take even a day's leave in the First World War. "It was not in the regimental tradition to take a day's leave in the Crimea, and it is not now," he proclaimed. He also refused a promotion, feeling it was more important to stay with his men. My father would have been the first to follow him into the breach. Raven's Oak was regularly visited by a stream of elderly regimental admirers. Soldiers received uncritical devotion and my earliest ambition was to be one. I regretted that the War was ending and, with it, my chances of fighting. Despite this, and perhaps due to my mother, I had a sceptical streak.

"Do British soldiers ever shoot each other in battle by mistake?" I asked an aunt.

"Don't be ridiculous," she replied.

Crosse was a passionate historian of his regiment, writing a short history of the Oxford and Bucks Light Infantry from 1741 to 1922 for its younger members. My father, whose family had been in the same regiment since the battle of Waterloo, was to do the same, taking fifteen years to write the Oxford and Bucks volume for the Leo Cooper series of Regimental Histories. "Up the 52nd and at 'em!" was the regiment's war cry, and it would be an inspiration for the way I chose to lead my life.

My father was at a loss after the War. He was too old for the Army, the only life he knew, and he proved too inflexible to work in one of my maternal uncle's cereal factories. His years in India had isolated him from the realities of the world. He would not concede that Britain was no longer the most powerful nation and never adjusted to the country's switch of allegiance from Army officers to businessmen. His last job was in administration at an army depot in Warrington. He lived in the past, dreaming of the days when the Booths had been wealthy landowners in South Yorkshire. Even our golden Labrador was called 'Brushes', after the house on the Yorkshire estate where one of my ancestors lies buried next to his horse. My father's nostalgia was heightened because his own father appeared to have lost everything.

William Henry Booth relinquished his Yorkshire estate and went to live in Argentina on becoming bankrupt in 1889. En route he met my grandmother, Gwendolen, in St. Louis. They had two sons and a daughter in Argentina and my father, the youngest child, was born in England. Shortly after moving back to England, William abandoned his young family and went to live in Paris. Although he only had a small bed-sit, he would regularly appear at the races, immaculately dressed, with a beautiful actress on his arm. One day he bet that he could walk from the Carlton Hotel, Paris, to the Royal Hotel, Nice. He arrived after two months and was photographed for *The Tatler*, triumphant in his walking boots and plus-fours. Feeling a little worse for wear he went to see a doctor, who told him to take more exercise.

Aunt Viva was the only person who spoke to me about him. "Your grandfather loved snooker," she said. "He was an excellent player, more or less a hustler." Knowing very little about him made him a hero to me. I had an unrealistically romantic picture of him walking down tree-lined Parisian boulevards with a soft-skinned mistress on his arm. He died alone in Paris without ever returning to his family. His wife survived by running a boarding house in South Kensington. I remember her, in a high-necked Victorian dress, from a faded photograph of about 1900.

Hers was probably an even harder existence than that of her famous literary grandfather Captain Marryat, who fought naval battles in the Napoleonic Wars. That he had spurned a knighthood as a mark of public opposition to William IV's authoritarian belief in the advantages of flogging was a sacred part of the family history.

My grandmother encouraged my father to enter a good marriage, lead a moral existence and make a prosperous life. She found him an apprenticeship as a motor mechanic in London but the manpower requirements of the First World War and friendship with Richard Crosse allowed him to escape this uninspiring trade and enter the family regiment. He was posted to India where, even on an Army Officer's meagre income, he could afford servants and half a dozen polo-ponies. But my Aunt Viva was not convinced of the benefits:

"Your father went to India a sensitive young man who knew Keats by heart, and returned talking of Wogs."

"We machine-gunned a goat to show the natives it wasn't sacred," he said about a campaign in Burma. Whether or not he regarded this as normal military behaviour, I do not know.

My parents met in India when my mother was on a chaperoned tour of the country. She was under strict instructions from her parents not to become engaged: Army officers frequently had poor private incomes. My father was nearing forty and both his career and domestic life were demanding a quick marriage to someone who could rectify the appalling injustice of not having a private income. The young Elizabeth Joanna Pitt was everything he desired. She lived in a large manor called Broadlands in Surrey with three sisters and two brothers. Her father, George Pitt, was President of the Institute of Accountants and commuted regularly to London. As a director of Yardley's perfumiers he was able to leave his twenty-two grandchildren a private income for which I, for one, was extremely grateful. He died from a heart attack in the Dorchester Hotel shortly after my parents' wedding.

To my father's private contempt, both of Elizabeth's brothers were in civilian employment during the War. Although he disapproved of wealthy city capitalists, he was prepared to compromise. For the Pitt family it was possibly a highly diplomatic move to align themselves with a fighting officer. My mother had enjoyed a sheltered life in suburban England and my father came from a sheltered life in the officers' mess. Somehow they agreed a suitable treaty and, building their lives around the family, their marriage lasted until my mother's death at the young age of fifty-seven.

Despite my parents appearing happy and close, I now realize that they were ideologically opposed and unsuited for the task of preparing me for the modern world. Differing influences meant that the family split. The two elder children, Mary and myself, sided with the Army. I wanted a military career and all Mary wanted as her inheritance was the Regimental sword. Joanna and Anne were more interested in share certificates. Although Anne married a Gurkha officer, her father-in-law had been prominent in the City and financial interests predominated. Regarding our schooling my parents were of one accord. We were all doomed to the misery of a post-war educational hysteria. The purpose of education, my father told me, was to enable us to build better radar to shoot down German aeroplanes. An enthusiasm for beating the Germans was replaced by one for educating the young.

1935. My parents – at one point I was the only blot in a close marriage.

Perhaps the origins of my later ambitions – me sitting on top of the world.

Lieut. Colonel H.Booth, 1806-1830.

William (Willie) Booth, 1888-1957. Perhaps too sybarite, but the first Booth at Brynmelin.

Three military Booths who overshadowed my childhood and early adolescence

My father c. 1951. The Last Booth to paper over the cracks of declining militarism.

Kit Booth. The daughter of Sir John Holder, an economic lifeline for the Booths. You can see from this photograph why people came to Mid Wales to fish.

Willie Booth. He spent his time fishing in Wales or shooting in Scotland.

My father and Lt. Col. Richard Crosse. Rather than being an obedient heir to my two military fathers, I became twice as rebellious.

My mother, Mary and myself. I can still remember the blue sky, haystacks and beaches of Sussex.

Richard Crosse's house, Raven's Oak, Cheshire. No photograph symbolises my background better than this one – small landowners loving their horses, perhaps more than their wives.

Chapter Four

A Confusing World

Hugh Vickers

"Buggery is delicious."

Rugby School had a very clear idea of schoolboy achievement. The brightest boys went to Oxford and Cambridge, the next most intelligent looked for professional qualifications in law or accountancy, and the thickest read Geography and went into the Army. The 1945 Socialist Government further undermined the public schools' remit to provide heroes for the Empire. With an acute understanding of our petty snobbery they decided that the Officers' Training Corps was too elitist a name and must now be known as the 'Combined Cadet Force'. This organization, rather than training me for future military employment, alienated me. Plagued by hay fever, I deserted one warm day in summer. Finding my absence went unnoticed, I did the same in winter. It took two years for the authorities to catch up with me.

Taking the same action was a cherubic-looking boy called Hugh Vickers. When he first saw me I was eating cold baked-beans from the tin with a protractor. He became my closest friend at Rugby. Hugh's father was Sir Geoffrey Vickers, the school's only Victoria Cross in the First World War and a personal friend of the headmaster. Despite these connections, Hugh loathed the Establishment and was soon expelled from the Cadet Force. 'Hugh Vickers is a disgrace to The Queen's Uniform' was posted prominently on the Cadet Force notice board. Hugh was delighted. He used some of his time in detention to tape-record the passionate advances of a homosexual master in a study where beautiful silk cushions had been placed in anticipation. This Hellenic occupation was to lose the school two successive Head Boys.

"Buggery is delicious!" Hugh remarked in a particularly precocious moment. Though I once opened an airing cupboard to find the son of a distinguished Far Eastern general engaged in an erotic act, I never achieved Hugh's sophistication. I was to leave a heterosexual and homosexual virgin.

The headmaster, Sir Arthur Fforde, practised a kind of religious philosophy which involved reading from Christian explorers like Sir Arthur Grimble in *A Pattern of Islands*. "To get out of a rut, you have to get into one," was one of his favourite sayings. I believe he was fairly out of touch with what happened in the school.

"You belong to the upper five per cent of the country," one master would regularly inform us. I am sure I was in the bottom five per cent of that upper five per cent. Rugby School was unctuously breeding a body of bureaucrats which Imperial Britain, let alone an increasingly non-Imperial Britain, would have found hard to absorb. Bankers, lawyers and accountants strolled confidently out of the school gates while nobody paused to consider who would actually create the wealth. I did not participate in any of the school's many activities, such as the theatre, the Training Corps and the choir. I even failed to be chosen as anyone's 'fag' and suffered the humiliation of being appointed a mere 'passage fag', responsible for sweeping the corridors.

At home, my mother was slowly learning that my father's military ideals only related to a period of war, and she found close proximity to Richard Crosse difficult. The *Punch*-lined corridor quickly took on an atmosphere akin to that of the Berlin Wall. My father had more in common with Richard Crosse than with my mother, who did not share their wide literary and intellectual interests. Only occasionally did the older man's views differ from those of my father. "Who are the greatest troops in the world?" I asked him. "The Germans," he said without hesitation.

"Richard Crosse is a homosexual," stated my father, explaining that theirs was a psychological and not a physical relationship, though I am sure that he was able to take a more objective view of the matter than Crosse himself. When he spoke to me about the subject, I am sure he had absolutely no idea of the extent of my Athenian education at school. After 'lights out' in the dormitory the favourite activity was called "cock fighting", and even our breakfast cornflakes were referred to as "last year's circumcisions". Crosse and my father's shared experience of war and their similar beliefs and ambitions sealed the two men's friendship. It lasted until 1973, when they died within a week of each other.

Rather than being an obedient heir to my two military fathers, I became twice as rebellious. I could not relate to the ethics that dominated their life. My father had the absurd loyalty which I found in all his military friends. When, for example, General Sir Frank Messervy was arrested for indecent behaviour with a little girl in Hyde Park, the military counter-intelligence stated that it was the young girl who had corrupted the General; he could not be blamed because he was a man who knew no fear.

My private battle against the adults in the family shattered, in turn, the natural affection I should have felt towards my two younger sisters Joanna and Anne. My mother kept a clear focus on her priorities. To her, Richard Crosse was an anachronism. She opposed him instinctively, holding him responsible for my father's decision to reject the secure employment offered by her family. Her quiet determination resulted in a move to Surrey, close to my aunts and uncles, who could not consider existing more than an hour's drive from Harrods. Our new family home was in Worplesdon, between Guildford and Woking, which proudly proclaimed itself the national seat of mixed doubles in golf. My father stumbled around the course with a rusting, badly-painted golf cart and clubs which were shortly to become antiques, ignoring the gleaming equipment of his neighbours. Snob or not, he refused to adapt to convention.

It was in Woking that my father decided my future by taking me into a second-hand bookshop run by an ex-Guardsman called Edward Fineron. Fineron loved books, which he had collected by bicycling around the suburbs of Woking before the War. He dispensed bargains to all those who wanted them. The great classics were available for threepence; leather-bound eighteenth- and nineteenth-century books were a few shillings. By the age of fourteen, and largely through the influence and advice of Edward Fineron, I was a book-collector.

"You'll finish up as a second-hand bookseller," he prophesied, and would not be shaken from this opinion. He said the same of another of his young customers, and in both cases he was right. I treated his forecast with adolescent disdain. The Army or the City appeared far more prestigious careers and Rugby School did not consider that people could be shopkeepers. Nevertheless, wandering into a second-hand bookshop was one of the few alternatives to the tennis courts and golf clubs of Surrey. Subliminally I learnt the first lessons of second-hand bookselling. Every bookshop creates a museum of the unsaleable, from popular theology to outdated novelists and political biographies. The most vital lesson taught me what to avoid buying. When occasionally broke, I had to sell books back to Fineron and I realized the enormous profit margin he made. One day I discovered a volume of eighteenth-century pamphlets in a town junk-shop and sold it in London for a thirty-five shilling profit. At the same time, some of Hugh's friends were financing a life of considerable luxury by stealing books from the Bodgkin Bequest, a fine antiquarian collection left to Rugby School by an idealistic old boy. "You can be a second-hand bookseller anywhere in the world," Fineron told me. If one advertised in catalogues it did not matter where one lived.

"A good bookseller is judged by his catalogue," he said, proud of his carefully-compiled lists of his best discoveries. Although in my future career as a bookseller I would buy far more books than I could catalogue, it was a remark I never forgot.

I spent two years visiting Fineron's shop before he dangled an issue of *Clique* before me. The trade magazine was used only by dealers and was on no account to be shown to a member of the public. I did not fully appreciate this breach of commercial secrecy because I was as yet unaware of the huge premiums paid for a wanted book. He explained how members of the trade used *Clique* for 'fishing'. This was a tactic of advertising for a valuable book and hoping that members of the trade would respond with a quotation below the market price.

So pleased was my father with my passion for books that he constructed a special room full of shelves next to the kitchen. My erratic school career was redeemed by the breadth and depth of my library. I coveted books, both to read and because they were beautiful objects with decorative covers and fine illustrations. Also I hoped people would be impressed by what I owned. I was a passionate but not particularly intellectual reader. I recall devouring the work of Arthur Ransomeunder the bedclothes by torchlight. Occasionally I read a book recommended by Tosswill, my tutor at Rugby. His plump and dishevelled German wife looked like a War refugee and the room where our essays were marked was hung with washing. Devoted to English literature, Tosswill recommended Gibbon and Macaulay and I almost blinded myself by reading the 1,000 page stereotype editions still available from the nineteenth century.

My father wanted education to make his son and was desperate for me to take the right steps on the right ladders at the right time. But my career at Rugby came to an abrupt end when I was caught cheating. I am not certain whether I felt more unhappy about my own failure or for the misery I caused him by not conforming. Deemed incapable of displaying the responsibility which Rugby esteemed so highly, it was suggested that I continue my education at Miss Hobbes, a crammer in Guildford preparing boys for Oxford and Cambridge Universities. This was to increase my knowledge of the book trade as Guildford was one of the most prestigious centres for second-hand bookselling in the country.

Three well-known dealers were Thorpe, Traylen and Fletcher. Thomas Thorpe was a descendant of the eponymous sixteenth-century bookseller. His vast, rambling hall taught me an advantage of the large bookshop, which is that you do not have to talk to the owner. An undisturbed browse can be followed by a secret departure. Although his business was uncommercial and poorly organized, it somehow carried the several hundred year old name into the twentieth century. Thorpe's shop became my weekly Mecca and I bought a finely bound set of Zola from a hidden foreign language room for a few shillings a volume. Charles Traylen was a maestro who was still buying in Sotheby's aged over ninety and Keith Fletcher, who also had a shop in Cecil Court, provided a kind of sophistication not generally found in the provinces. Nevertheless, despite the riches of Guildford, my real home was Fineron's shop, where I would linger for hours with my master and slowly expand my collection of books. I bought a set of *The Yellow Books*, which Fineron regarded as one of the great monuments of English thought, and some fantastical drawings by Sidney Sime, whose museum was nearby at Worplesdon.

I found my new educational environment infinitely preferable to Rugby. For the first time I met females of my own age. Social life meant necking at a nearby beauty spot. A beautiful, demure redhead called Caroline Ward became my first unrequited love. My closest relative was my cousin David Gill, whose parents sported chromium golf clubs and a new Bentley. The majority of my friends came from wealthy business environments. I met a blonde beauty called Elizabeth Matthew whose father, as editor of *The Times*, had a spectacular country house, a gleaming Rolls Royce and dispensed infinite cases of champagne. It was my first experience of the wealth of the press. Even my richest uncle, who complained that a badly-parked bicycle did more damage to the door of his new Bentley than some people earn in a year, could not match this.

The car was the great romantic symbol of the era. We knew exactly how each model differed. The Consul, the Zephyr and the Zodiac were the three most popular makes of Ford. The most coveted possession of every youth was a sports car which opened doors to sex, excitement and prestige. My cousin David and I failed to make his small Austin capable of a hundred miles an hour and it ended up a dismembered wreck on the beach. Tragically, I remember meeting Mike Hawthorn, the world motor-racing champion, in the pub on the day before he was killed when driving too fast down the Hog's Back near Guildford. Even the local beat poet wrote about a car crash with a few gruesome lines about 'a bloodstained clutch'. Cars pointed the way to the pleasures of London; a night visit to Leicester Square and Soho was a great adventure.

Secretly, my father was harbouring a resentment towards the priorities of Surrey. "He calls himself a Wing Commander, but all he did was command barrage balloons!" he remarked angrily about a neighbour who wished to capitalise on the post-war prestige of those who had helped to protect the Empire. His dislike of suburbia could also have been explained by his anti-German sentiments. In Surrey he encountered anti-Semitic attitudes which could well have been expressed in Bavaria during the Nazi period. "How can you bear to play with a Jew?" I was asked about my tennis partnership with my friend Charles Lewis, whose family flouted Anglo-Saxon sensitivities not only onaccount of their race, but by owning a Rolls Royce and a flashy Ford convertible.

In London my father's sister Viva represented an exotic world neither suburbia nor the Army could provide. Like him she had narrowly escaped the poverty of her background. Before becoming a successful dressmaker she had been secretary to Augustus John. Round faced, dark haired and Spanish-looking, Viva was pretty enough to inspire John to take out his penis, lay it on her desk and say, "I bet you've never seen one as big as that!" In the late 1920s she married William King. He was the Keeper of China at the Victoria and Albert Museum and used to throw small stones in the basement at pieces of china that he particularly disliked.

They had a wide circle of literary and artistic friends, such as James Pope Hennessy, the biographer of Queen Mary, Dylan Thomas, Norman Douglas, for whom Willie was literary executor, and Angus Wilson, who used them as prototypes in one of his novels. Viva complained that Willie flirted outrageously with head waiters, and he was indeed gay. Instead of protesting, she gathered a gay circle around their home in Thurloe Square. She tolerated and liked the wealthy eccentrics and homosexuals of the museum world. The head of the Queen's Guard would go to Viva's parties in a dress with inflated bosoms as 'Aunt Mabel', and Cecil Gould, Keeper of Venetian Pictures at the National Gallery, was known to his friends as 'Gouldilocks'. The youthful Knight of Glyn was Keeper of Furniture at the V & A and insisted that his title be used, but he was known as 'the pink nightie' at Thurloe Square. Her parties were generally Sunday soirées and could range from her offering her last bottle of vodka to a couple of drunken gays who often exploited her hospitality, to a full-scale event attended by celebrities such as John Lennon, Shirley Bassey, Peggy Guggenheim and even Aubrey Beardsley's mother.

By the time I knew Viva the days of the Rolls in its private garage had passed and financial hardship forced the sale of her Reynolds portrait and fine porcelain in order to continue entertaining. Her eclectic knowledge and brilliant wit made her the ideal hostess at cocktail parties. "The earliest French Letter was found in a book!" she told me. "It was made of fish skin and kept hidden by a noble Lord in a hollowed-out novel." Willie's death did not put an end to my aunt's socialising; in fact she was rather relieved when he died. He often collapsed after drinking and had to be collected from police stations. My father, who held the same attitude towards drinking as an eighteenth-century Methodist, also suspected his sister of excessive vodka consumption.

I achieved a place at Oxford after my father made a personal plea to Merton College. Trying to conform to accepted standards in the remaining months before I was to go up, I agreed to become an articled clerk in my grandfather's firm in the City. The only good thing about this was that I was to live in a small flat at Viva's house in Thurloe Square. Like her own mother, she was taking in lodgers to survive, including a New Zealand schoolmaster nicknamed 'Miserable wet wank'.

In the head office of Trust Houses in Shorts Gardens, Drury Lane, I sat in the Accounts Department checking the returns of the two hundred or so establishments controlled by the group. The chain had been started by a philanthropist to provide decent hotels which were not dominated by their bars. Now, however, most of their profits were drawn from that source. Never had they possessed a less conscientious clerk. I ticked all figures regardless and played with the knees of the attractive female clerk opposite. I subscribe to the psychological theory that sexual activity is the inevitable response to the unnatural environment of the office. It was an utterly uninteresting occupation, a view which the internal auditors themselves seemed to share. One weekend several of them were sacked for concealing pound notes in their socks whilst running the special bar the hotel group organized for Derby day.

I found life in the City totally unacceptable. When, after three weeks, I said I wanted to leave, the elderly chief auditor apologised for not putting me in a more interesting location. It was kind of him but perhaps naïve. I abandoned the city hastily and contemptuously, and with the instinctive knowledge that I was absolutely unadaptable.

Chapter Five

Torn Loyalties

Kyril Bonfiglioli

*"More rich young men walk down that streetthan any other
street in Europe."*

By the time I reached Oxford, National Service was no longer in force but a large number of the college members had still been through this 'maturing' experience. I felt no need to penetrate this gregarious and confident beer-drinking group and retreated into a small set of friends. We decided to form the WOL club, an organization whose purpose now escapes me. The most prominent member of the group was Lennox Money. He was long, sandy and sleek like a greyhound on tranquillisers. His passions were foreign girls, architecture and fine Persian pottery. He studied all three with devotion. Although he had not even an 'A' Level when offered a place at university, his admission was an inspired decision, though ultimately his scholarship was probably too diverse to be acceptable in Oxford. (I remember that he and I were interested in the girlfriend of an eminent T.S. Eliot scholar who was reputed to have breasts joined in the middle.) Lennox and I both had cars and would drive up the Banbury Road to St. Clare's English Language School, where beautiful foreign girls fluttered out of the gates like butterflies. In the week of his finals, faced with the choice of dating an exotic girl called Maite or getting a degree, he unhesitatingly chose the former. Lennox has remained an invaluable friend. Another close friend was William Armstrong, but we could not ignore his Catholicism and were disdainful of Nescafé-drinking Catholic intellectuals. Somehow we could not forget our prejudices. "I was taught in my childhood to beware of flowers, trees and mountains," said Lennox, referring to Berg, Bloom and other Jewish surnames.

Our studies were dull compared to extra-mural undergraduate life. Patrick Cavendish, who became a pioneer publisher of the hobby magazines often advertised on television, devoted his energies to punting girls on the River Cherwell. Sexual intercourse had very little to do with his academic curriculum. Similarly, an old Etonian called Patrick Campbell saw Oxford as an environment where one needed musical relaxation and spent hours playing the guitar. Eventually he decided his first two years at Oxford had been totally wasted and left to take up medicine. Farouk Bharucha was an Indian friend whose father had been President of the Bombay Social Exchange. He divided his time between the River Club and the Savoy. Clad in a dark blue coat with velvet collar, he had a Rolls Royce with a private number plate, FHB1 ('Fucking Horrible Bastard').

After Oxford, Farouk invited Lennox and myself to travel around India with him, which we did by means of ancient Dakota aeroplanes. Lennox's antiquarian enthusiasms amazed Farouk and myself and contrasted with our more languid approach to life. He clambered enthusiastically up every hundred-stepped temple we visited, earning himself the nickname 'Harry Pioneer'. At a tea party with Nehru's sister I dropped a priceless porcelain cup, and rounded off the trip by falling ill after a visit to the Tatangear Steel Works. I was in a critical condition and had to have an operation in Delhi. As I passed out under the anaesthetic I thought the end of my life would be spent gazing at the crowd of turbaned Sikh doctors looking down at me. All in all the trip was not a success and I returned to England with a huge hospital bill in my pocket.

I entered Oxford with the best intentions but did not keep them for very long. I instinctively turned away from the academic world, the Oxford Union, the Sports Club and the Radcliffe Camera, the great library central to the lives of all undergraduates. Too intimidated to enter, I bought or borrowed the necessary books and occasionally used friends' notes, which proved more useful than my own rambling researches. The Oxford libraries were impressive monuments to culture, in many cases dating from medieval times, and they will no doubt remain invulnerable to the threat of technology. But the nineteenth century brought their graceful accumulation of learning to an end. Since the invention of stereotype printing in 1820, and faced by the subsequent plethora of publishing, they have only been able to choose drops from the ocean of world scholarship. My college library could barely accommodate the books donated by alumni. In any case, fate seemed to keep me out of them, while my interest in second-hand books grew and grew.

Blackwell's, the University booksellers, thought they could help their business and Oxford's intellectual life if they extended long credit to undergraduates. My circle of friends suspected that this was not pure altruism, as Oxford University Press books were very expensive. Hugh, whose father was a friend of Sir Basil Blackwell, was taken to task by the distinguished Oxford patrician for running an account roughly approximate to the Irish National Debt. The strongest objections to Blackwell's came from a brilliant scholar of our generation called Jeremy Cato. He stole a rubber stamp from the Bodleian library and furtively stamped all the expensive art books on the shop's display table. More often than not, university cities are a bad place to look for second-hand books. There are plenty of resident academics quick to snap up bargains. Blackwell's, with their close ties to the University Press, were primarily interested in new books. Sackfuls of their unwanted stock were dumped in The Turl Cash Bookshop, where the bald proprietor, known derisively as 'elephant ears', struggled to build a business. He tried to supplement his income with hand-coloured steel engravings of the Oxford colleges ripped from various books.

Cheltenham had better bookshops than Oxford. Alan Hancox ran an excellent bookshop from a basement on one of the main promenades. He boasted of an earlier triumph when he had bought an unopened publisher's parcel from the loft of Thorntons in Oxford. It contained first editions of Oscar Wilde's *The Newdigate Prize Poems*, published in 1872 and written when he was still an undergraduate. As with Fineron, I became both Alan's customer and his pupil. Still naïve, I had a quarrel with him when I discovered he was selling remainders even more expensively than Oxford shops. Remainders are a constant temptation to booksellers. Easy to come by, their predictability alienates a more discerning customer. More irritating than the remainders was the unrelenting sound of classical music drifting through Alan's shop. I don't think the human mind can stuff itself with two kinds of culture at the same time. I wanted to devote all my energies to the books.

As at Rugby, my main stimulus at Oxford was provided by Hugh Vickers. "There's a fabulous David Cox for sale in Little Clarendon Street. Go and buy it," he told me. The shop belonged to Kyril Bonfiglioli. Bonfiglioli was the James Bond of antique dealing. Whether considering a silver whisky flask or the poems of Kipling, his passion and knowledge conveyed itself to those around him. 'Good kit' was his term for anything that emerged from the distant past to win his approval in the present.

An ex-sergeant in the King's African Rifles and an Army sabre champion, he had defeated a field of 10,000 to win an adult scholarship at Balliol College and had then been a research assistant at the Ashmolean Museum in Oxford. Too poor to continue in academia with a wife and children to support, he opened his first shop without being able to pay the rent. Bon's attitude was that of an Army sergeant. He viewed education without the unsophisticated reverence which had been my own experience. The dons who sunned themselves by the River

Cherwell had "swollen bellies and shrivelled privates". He gained a devoted circle of admiring undergraduates, not one of whom had ever awoken to four-foot piles of elephant dung outside a tent in Africa. I fell hopelessly under his spell. Sipping his favourite Scotch, he would hold court until the early hours of the morning.

"I had a child by a black girl," Bon would remark to undergraduates who were just on the point of tremulously losing their virginity. "I used to send her a pound at Christmas until I lost the address. Her bottom was like two small boys fighting under a blanket." Although these comments may seem coarse and cynical, there was another side to Bon. He had an encyclopaedic knowledge of English literature and of Kipling in particular. Edward Fineron, a private in the First World War, had begun my enthusiasm for dealing and now Kyril Bonfiglioli, an ex-sergeant, was to develop it. Their literary enthusiasms were similar to my father's. Thus my earliest mentors were all ex-Army officers who had become deeply immersed in a passion for books. The armed forces contain many avid bibliophiles due to the enforced leisure of security duties. They contribute hundreds of regimental histories and magnificent colour-plates to the literary world. Every base of the British Army subscribed to Blackwood's Magazine, *Maga*, making it the most widely-read periodical in the world.

I had greater respect for Bon's knowledge than the education prescribed for me at Oxford. He had a far more entertaining approach to the modern world. Gauguin was known as 'Guggins' and B.W. Leader, an important nineteenth-century English artist, as 'Bleeder'. Pictures bought from him for a few pounds leapt in value in later years. He was a dangerously persuasive dealer with a semi-hypnotic quality when charming and bewitching his undergraduates.

"More rich young men walk down that street than any other street in Europe," Bon said, gazing out of the window like a hunter tracking prey. One day he detected an approaching customer who had just returned from abroad. Swiftly, he put a red 'sold' dot on an ugly, unsold picture. "I kept this for you, Alan," he said. "I knew you'd want it." He made the sale.

Ministering patiently to the household was his wife Margaret, whom many regarded as a kind of saint. She was a graduate of Lady Margaret Hall and a distant relative of Pasternak. At least one of Bon's elderly assistants fell passionately in love with her. "Do sleep with my wife," Bon would say, "It will do her a power of good." To do all the manual jobs he employed a six-foot homosexual in a deerstalker called Sandy who had an equally ostentatious and irritating Irish wolfhound. Bon's method of dealing came from a past age. During and just after the Second World War, when antiques were cheap and in enormous supply, it was possible to fill a shop with every kind of antique, curio and picture, and to have a catholic attitude towards anything old. Dealers jammed their shops and storage areas so high that they were inaccessible to the public. Profit could be made by keeping antiques instead of selling them, as enormous prices became plausible after a few years of inflation. After the War, specialisation became increasingly important and Bon's breadth of interests may have prevented him from being as successful as less talented dealers.

Guided by Bon's expertise, I learnt how to smash the frame off a picture without breaking the glass, how to clean and restore paintings and make a reference library of minor nineteenth-century landscape painters by cutting out advertisements from the *Connoisseur* magazine. Every aspect of the dealing business fascinated me. I watched how he negotiated with the Smiths, a crowd of dealing gypsies who dressed as if they were on the committee of The Country Landowners Association, and from whom Bon bought a rare Richard Wilson and an unrecognised

Titian. Two Swedish dealers would call regularly and ask for "empty landscapes", by which they meant paintings without figures. Later they would be cut in two to make a pair and little children would be painted on each, perhaps playing on the grass in the foreground, to enhance their value. I had ambitions of becoming a picture dealer. But despite several trips to study pictures at the National Gallery, which Bon said would give me an eye for quality, I failed to recognise subtleties, such as whether an oil painting had been overcleaned. I was happiest with my first love, books. Drinking with Bon in The Eagle and Child, learning shove-ha'penny and enjoying Indian restaurants for the first time, I drifted into a circle of dealers. In the same street as Bon was an old picture dealer called Johnny Spurling. "If I can con an old lady out of a Canaletto, I can retire for life," was one of his favourite phrases. Next door were two antique dealers, A.J. and Joan Stuart-Mobey. She was beautiful, highly sexed and Jewish; he was a schoolmaster who had discovered that he could buy cupboards in Oxford sales for a pound and sell them to landladies for a tenner. The added 'Stuart' conferred greater social credibility. Bon once boasted gleefully how Joan Mobey masturbated him under an enormous brass plate in the back of the car while her husband drove them to a sale.

Oxford and the educational system were largely ignorant of the boom in the second-hand market which swept the country. Despite the expansion of post-war bureaucracy, universities were providing more graduates than could be employed in traditional rôles. As a result, antiques, second-hand cars and building restoration were becoming significant employers of graduates in rural areas. Whether one enters the trade by haggling for bargains in markets or by bidding enormous sums at auctions, second-hand dealers rely on experience rather than training. I am happy that qualifications are regarded as unnecessary for bookselling. Real education is gained by exploring beyond the paths chosen by teachers. Nevertheless, in America the Universities of Colorado and Columbia now run courses for second-hand booksellers and, in England, Peter Miller of the Provincial Book Fairs Association is trying to interest the University of York in similar schemes. To me they seem highly illogical. I imagine standardised aspiring booksellers spending two years being taught that they should be earning as much as lawyers.

Foyle's bookshop in London boasted that they could find any book for a customer. Bon asked the assistant for *Caxton's Game and Play of Chess*, published in 1477, one of the rarest and most valuable books in the country.

"I think we can find it, sir," said the assistant.

"In that case, I'd like two."

Bon drew my attention to the under-priced reference-book market. Zwemmer's in Charing Cross Road stocked Williams's standard work on early English watercolours as a remainder for two pounds. A few years later it would fetch a hundred.

"Science-fiction," he claimed, "is the only significant form of modern writing." Previously I had regarded it as a minor literary quirk of H.G. Wells and Jules Verne. In those days there were very few science-fiction books on the second-hand market, but Bon's prophecy was correct, and in the next few decades it grew to become one of its biggest and most profitable branches. Today there are feminist science-fiction writers, and a science-fiction dealer in Los Angeles specialises in Lost Worlds.

Bon expanded ambitiously, leasing an art gallery in the Turl from Lincoln College for an absurdly low rent and persuading Saunders, the last independent bookshop in the town, to sell out to his consortium. He immediately dumped all the modern poetry, which he said made no difference to his profitability. My ambitions seemed to coincide with his. I would travel all over the country looking for stock. I bought a new Jaguar in which, grossly overloaded, I would screech off for Oxford leaving a hundred-yard trail of sparks behind me.

When Bon's father died I was shunted to a business he owned in two derelict cottages in Eynsham, near Oxford. It quickly became apparent that I did not have the patience to keep such a small, quiet shop open. Back in Oxford, proximity to Bon was making things difficult. Sleeping on his couch was becoming less attractive; he was constantly surrounded by a group of undergraduates, dealers, customers, children and a wife. As he expanded his empire, no rôles were defined nor records kept. There was no better man for buying an unrecognised Titian but there was scarcely one less competent to run a large business. Always insecure, he was constantly looking for rich sponsors, although he did not actually need them. "If only I had been born with £5,000," he would moan. He eventually received the backing of Christopher Lennox-Boyd, a wealthy member of the Guinness family.

I began a chaotic, three-dimensional existence between Hay-on-Wye, Oxford and London. I bought the Old Fire Station in Hay, thinking it would be useful to have a Welsh base from which I would search for antiques, pictures, books and 'good kit' for Bon to sell in Oxford. Although he gave me a collection of bee-keeping books to sell, even he was highly sceptical about the shop's potential.

Chapter Six

On the Road

Ex Commando, Paddy. He killed sixteen Germans and could cook a good breakfast.

"Some men simply are not made for marriage."

Although I was beginning to feel at home in the pubs of Hay-on-Wye, it was only when I became the owner of Hay Castle that my fate in the town was sealed forever. Whatever difficulties I faced, never would I leave my town and my castle, which symbolised my attack on centralized authority. As soon as I heard that it was for sale I wanted to buy it. My decisions when buying books, property or dating girls were always very opportunistic. Behind its magnificent Norman walls I could shelter from my parents' objections to nocturnal female visitors and store as many books as I could buy.

"The council wouldn't give a thousand quid for it in 1946," said a local business magnate called George Keylock, after its then owner, Mr Tuson, died in 1971. Nobody was showing an interest in the property. Tuson showed me around the Castle shortly after my family had moved to Hay. The frail old man barely had the energy to remove a dead jackdaw from the floor.

There is probably a greater density of castles along the Welsh border than anywhere else in Britain. Hay had two. As the stealing of dressed stone has been an occupation of the townspeople for centuries, piece by piece, some of the castles have disappeared. The one I purchased looked like a piece of unprotected cheese at which mice had been nibbling. A large Jacobean mansion adjoins a crumbling tower and keep, originally built as a frontier post by Norman invaders. It had been the scene of many a great, bloody battle and for military reasons had been in almost continuous disrepair since its construction in the twelfth century.

Mr Tuson had married into the Studt family, the 'fairground aristocracy' of Wales, who owned Aberystwyth and Llandudno piers. One of his regular duties was to fill his large Rover with bags of sixpences from fairground games. When I moved in, the ground floor still contained fairground skeletons: twisted golden pillars from the carousel and a horse with a chipped mane and peeling red nostrils.

Hay Castle has suffered three serious fires. The first was in 1231 when its owner William de Breos and his wife Maud lost favour with King John of England, who then set fire to the Castle and the town. The second, in 1939, destroyed one of the finest seventeenth-century oak staircases in Britain. A legend was attached to it. One day, a housekeeper discovered a murdered body on the stairs. Shaking with terror, she dropped a bunch of keys into the pool of blood seeping from the corpse. Despite repeated scrubbing, the bloody imprint of the keys had remained through the centuries. The third fire was in 1978 and, as I shall relate, was my responsibility.

Although the River Wye meanders through the valley two hundred feet below the Castle, a view of the river was not, apparently, considered important. Even the houses in the town do not look directly upon the beauty of the river. The Castle garden slopes in tiers down to the walls, where an arched door opens onto Castle Street. On the south side, between the beech trees on the lawn, are glimpses of a fine oak forest and the hills overlooking The Golden Valley. In autumn the leaves from the Castle's trees descend on the town and an old council worker called Greenway used to sweep them up. I have always owned a pair of peacocks that wander around the grounds. Their vibrant, blue-green plumage sparkles against the grey stone. Sometimes they grow restless and fly over the wall into the path of an astonished tourist; at other times they have been found stoned or strangled by spiteful youths.

I entrusted Frank with the decoration and the maintenance of the

Castle. His first priority was to find a man who was 'good with a hook', the local term for a sickle. Cutting the long grass on the central lawn was easy; less so was the fifty-foot bank surrounding the Castle, a breeding ground for three-foot high nettles and old Coca Cola tins. After Hay's young lovers had taken their summer walks, the easiest fate for an uneaten bag of chips was to find itself flung onto the Castle bank. One of Frank's hardest tasks was removing a fourteen-foot deep jackdaws' nest from the attic. Its extraordinary growth had been due to twigs constantly falling down the chimney. "I played Beethoven in the fireplace below, very loudly," he said. "It's the only way to get rid of them." As labourers began working in the grounds I explored the potential for storing books in the outbuildings and the cobbled stables.

Although I have barely smoked a joint of marijuana in my life, the Castle became known as a drug-taking centre of sin. Rising ostentatiously from the centre of the town, it affords little privacy to its occupants. Through the windows the Georgian staircase can be seen crossing several floors like that of a doll's house. One spectacle occurred while Frank was decorating. He was attacked by a fellow employee who had been concealing a fury subsequently released by swallowing pints of Guinness as if they were egg cups filled with lemon tea. Two paint-splattered policemen had to chain him to the railings to restrain him.

One day my father arrived and beat my bedroom door with a stick. I was in bed with someone whose husband was studying economics at Oxford in order to help the Third World, an occupation to which I did not grant the slightest credibility. Often in Bon's company, I regret that I imbibed his sexual attitudes. "I have made the basement of my gallery into a knocking shop," he told me enthusiastically. The Castle made a much better knocking shop. I was not successful with the local girls; my conquests were more likely to be customers, historians or anyone else who arrived in Hay.

I never gave regular parties at the Castle but occasionally we had Booze, Bands and Bonfire nights. During one of these Hugh climbed to the top of the Castle wall brandishing his wine glass. Stumbling drunkenly, he fell into the portcullis shaft. The fall would have been thirty feet, but the shaft narrowed and his body became wedged between the thick stone walls. Hugh's life was saved by his enormous stomach. The Hay Fire Brigade discussed his fate for an hour before he was finally extracted by a passing potholer. "I've got an arse like an orang utan," Hugh said.

As well as maintaining the Castle, Frank was its Public Relations Officer as he talked to curious locals in every Hay pub.

"I think Richard Booth is a Swedo," said the Mayoress, who would carry a Christian Dior coat over her arm to make sure everyone saw the label.

"No, Mrs Birch," said Frank, pulling her leg, "I think he's British." 'Swedo' was the nearest her accent could get to the word *pseudo*.

Frank persuaded some of the working classes out of the pubs to the Castle, where he would hold court. Building an enormous fire, he would make everyone feel at home. If they were too drunk to get home they could always spend the night there.

The Castle overlooked The Mason's Arms where visiting booksellers, no matter how indecorous their behaviour, were received tolerantly by Violet Jenkins. City book-dealers appreciated the tranquillity of rural life and would drink until the money ran out.

When I first came to Hay there were four butcher's shops. One butcher had lost his arm in the First World War but was renowned for his ability to poleaxe a beast with his left arm and kill it immediately. Another was an alcoholic who would thunder on the door of The Half Moon at seven in the morning. Whatever their faults, the quality of Hay meat was superb. Elwyn Jones, the bull breeder, refused to sell to any butcher who would not hang his steers for ten days. Whether it was 'meat and two veg' in Hitchcock's café or a sizzling joint of roast beef at The Crown Hotel, the production of beef and lamb was central to the economy of the town. Drinking a bottle of Whitbread in The Mason's Arms one day, I was asked to help pull a beast into the slaughterhouse next door. There were few health regulations but nobody suffered from eating Hay meat. I love the hard crackling of an orchard pig and cannot eat the white, watery pork sold in supermarkets. Today there are no slaughterhouses in Hay; stringent government health regulations have forced their closure. Animals with whom we have lived for thousands of years have disappeared into intensive units.

I had a much-loved sheep-dog which I named Maggs after the Berkeley Square bookshop. She raced around the lawn with great velocity but my housekeeper took it upon herself to have her put down and then promptly resigned. Faced with the insoluble problem of my domestic ineptitude, I decided to get married.

"She's easily the best wife you're likely to get," observed Frank of the fair, oval-faced Elizabeth Westoll. She was working as an assistant to Lennox Money in his antique shop on the Pimlico Road. Animated and enthusiastic, Elizabeth was enjoying London life after a country upbringing. Her family were part of the Cumbrian rural establishment, kind, decent people whose disapproval of the arrogant commercialism of The Cumbrian Tourist Board was an inspiration to me. Elizabeth's family outnumbered mine by a hundred to one at the small Cumbrian church where the wedding took place. We spent our honeymoon in Egypt, where Elizabeth bought some Nubian musical instruments.

Elizabeth loved the Castle and would have made a perfect wife, but she was not to know that she was marrying a kind of monster. Nearly all my friends were hard-drinking eccentrics for whom alcohol was the only release from a society they could not adapt to. If any other person was responsible for the failure of my first marriage it was a dealer called Richard Gilbertson who, during our early married life, frequently invited himself to stay with the excuse that "Booth needs a good catalogue". True or false, he remained at the Castle. He appeared at noon in a Paisley dressing gown and, in a hyena-like voice, would proceed to bore us with endless details about the Romantic poets. Elizabeth also had to tolerate dinners with an inebriated Owen Jones during the few months before his gin-sodden liver finally killed him. Drink, lorry drivers and exclusion from respectable society made the collapse of our marriage inevitable. Like a saint, Elizabeth stayed married to me for nearly a year. Ultimately she had every reason to leave. Elizabeth's mother wisely summarised the situation: "Some men simply are not made for marriage."

Bonfiglioli had not bothered to come to my wedding. He was beginning to regard dealing as a great waste of his middle years. "Why should I be interested in making money?" he said. "I've already done so." Work interfered with his strong predilection for whisky. The doctor tried to be firm. "You've got lots of dead liver cells floating around in your blood," he told him, but Bon did not care enough to do anything about it. With a new girlfriend, Judith, he eventually retired to Carnforth Sands in Lancashire to write novels. I heard that she would lovingly make him anchovies on toast at two in the morning. It seemed absolutely appropriate. I did not see him again, and learnt several years later that he had died in a detoxification unit in a Manchester hospital

A neglected food warehouse in the centre of Hay became my second bookshop. There was an explosion of dust when even the lightest book was dropped on the floor. My father, now a widower, came to the warehouse with his little dog Sam, trailing on a lead. He liked putting the works of ancient theologians in alphabetical order.

I spent a lot of time on the road. I would depart at five and stop for a dawn breakfast in an all-night café. Cardiff was a regular destination. On the return journey, tired from a day's work, I had to negotiate twenty miles of twisting and unlit roads between Crickhowell and Talgarth. One day, I gave the son of the local surveyor a lift back from Crickhowell. Pausing to tune the car radio, I ran into the back of a large lorry. The boy was killed. It was a tragedy for which I cannot forgive myself, and was made greater by the fact that his father had helped me to set up at the Old Fire Station and had given me the fireman's helmet to put over the door.

"Get a chauffeur or you'll kill yourself," said Frank. He proposed Taxi Davies, "arguably the best lorry driver in the world". Taxi was an attractive personality, boisterously roaring with laughter at his own jokes. He would assess the potential of a country house by talking to the servants in the kitchen, and entertained me with endless stories about two local tarts called 'Gelignite' and 'Dynamite'. But, like a horse, he always returned home faster than he went out, and I needed someone who could survive away from Hay. Norman Radcliffe became my new chauffeur and friend. He had been one of the first British soldiers to serve in Kenya and the last to leave. In the decline of the empire he had seen much of its brutality as he controlled the police in the struggle against the Mau Mau. Together we travelled throughout the British Isles. Whether in a council house in Birmingham or a manor house inNorfolk it was impossible to predict the enthusiasms of private purchasers. I have visited every town in the British Isles except Greenock in Scotland, which for some reason never produced any books for me.

Once a week the chiropodist who owned The Lamp Press came to

Hay in a chauffeur-driven car to purchase any book that would spread the word of God. Theology was attracting wealthy buyers. In Wales I could buy 1,500 volumes for three pounds. Nevertheless it was subject to Pareto's Law: ninety per cent of the value of the stock is in ten per cent of the bulk. The chiropodist's assistant, an ex-sergeant, would put the books in piles for me to accept or reject their offer. "The kiss of death for a Lamp Press book is when it is written by a female author," he said. This proved true, although Catholics occasionally collected biographies of nuns. Today things have changed and Lampeter, a town fifty miles away in Cardiganshire, has a feminist theological conference.

It was my father who first made contact with Tom Loome, a quiet, black-bearded German-American who, as a brilliant graduate from St Mary's College in Oakland, California, was studying at Tübingen University. My theology department, full of large, rotting calf folios, some of which had begun to turn to dust, amazed and intrigued him. Archivists from the National Library in Canada came to buy the letter book of a Governor General who was one of the Herberts of Abergavenny and had led the Red River Rebellion. Tom also found rare pamphlets by Loisy, Von Hugel and Tyrell as well as a precious edition of *La Vie Spirituelle* by Père Joseph, Richelieu's mentor. At this time the Jesuits were centralizing their books in London in order to achieve university status, a policy which meant the decimation of most of their libraries throughout the country. Tom researched the Jesuit library which I bought from Heythrop in Oxfordshire. Father Courtenay at Heythrop had given a smile of relief when I offered him a series of post-dated cheques. Meticulously, Tom categorised everything that came into our possession. Three months later I received a cable from the National Library in Canberra, Australia, offering £14,000 for the collection. I caught a plane the next day. Preparing to immerse myself in the culture, all I could remember was that the kangaroo is the only animal, apart from a human being, which makes love face to face.

Australian universities were springing up like towns in a gold rush. The National Library felt it should also serve parts of the Far East which they believed had neither the foresight nor the resources to build libraries. The Jesuit collection was desirable because their missionaries had been active in the area. Talking to the Australian National Librarian, I realized that only a very small percentage of the books would be read. When I raised this, she said, "We're building for the future." Money was no object and the Library was proud of its contacts. "We're next door to the Treasury," I was told. Any amount of money requested was available.

The library at Canberra Polytechnic was run by Victor Critenden. He told me that their current project was to trace those who arrived in Australia on the first and second fleet of ships. He was bitterly anti-Aborigine, complaining that they smashed up the houses the Government gave them. One of the oldest human societies on earth was threatened by a civilization of National Library builders.

The Book Purchasing Officer of the National Library, Peter Saunders, suggested I speak at the Australian Library Conference and I gave a long speech about my dear friend 'Doggie' (Clifford Hubbard), whom I have always revered as an inspired specialist dealer. Doggie visited Hay frequently to indulge in his passion for collecting second-hand dog books, which he sometimes swapped for his wife's delicious Bakewell tarts. In appearance he resembles a dimpled Einstein, and in the dog world he would be a spaniel with a ripple of hair over his ears and a generous moustache. In his career as a superior book-dealer Doggie saw a profitable niche in the second-hand market: dog books. The top floor of his house is reinforced with iron girders to support the quantity he has accumulated. He wrote 'bibliodographies', introduced Miniature Breed histories, attended dog shows and travelled the world lecturing.

The only Hungarian word he knows is for 'Kennel Club' and he can recite the name of every dog that appears in Agatha Christie's books. Clifford became a world authority on a subject he himself created. Last time we had lunch together he spoke about Conan Doyle's *The Hound of the Baskervilles*. "Even if Holmes hadn't emptied his pistol into him, I believe the dog would have died from phosphorous poisoning. You see, he was dabbed all over with phosphorescent paint."

At the Australian conference I tried to explain that such specialist dealers had perhaps a more important role to play than the trained librarians who at this time were considered the lights to illuminate the world.

My belief in specialist bookselling was further reinforced when I stopped in the USA on the way home from Australia. I visited The Gambler's Bookshop in Las Vegas. They had hundreds of books, from casino thrillers to serious volumes about mathematical theories of probability. I believed in private culture, but institutions were keeping me going. I went on to Los Angeles. Many dealers enter the second-hand book trade in their late middle-age. Bill Dutton was one. His Hollywood factory had supplied custom-made brassières for the likes of Rita Hayworth and Pola Negri. We toured the factory, passing between long lines of seamstresses bent over mounds of pink satin which would enable American women to emulate the physical magnificence of their celebrities.

Over the years Bill had turned a book-collecting hobby into his main business, but he could not help thinking like a businessman.

"To what do you ascribe your success as a bookseller?" I asked.

"I've got a car park," was his immediate and refreshing reply.

Staying with Bill gave me my first taste of America. Having a gun was like having a toothbrush. Books that were ordinary in Europe became magical treasures. I felt that Bill, with his beautiful and supportive wife Thelma and their happy children, represented the entry of The American Dream into the second-hand economy.

When I returned to Wales I started attending auctions. Bon had warned me against entering 'the ring'. "Just bid for what you want and you'll be successful," was his unheeded advice. 'The ring' was an arrangement by which dealers agreed not to bid against each other. Smaller dealers were paid off by the bigger ones from London and Birmingham. In remote areas along the Welsh Borders we met as friends and tried to manage the sale for mutual benefit. Although possibly illegal, the ignorance of the auctioneer made the racket possible. Auctioneers were the unattackable establishment. At an auction in a Carmarthen hotel, a corrupt conspiracy of antique dealers had evidence gathered against them by two undercover police constables snogging on the sofa.

Sales began to bore me. They took two days, one for viewing and one for bidding, and this was frequently lengthened by a ceremonial ordeal of tea and sandwiches at the end of which the senior dealers made complicated assessments of who owned what from the ring. The passion for dealing was enormous. One dealer had a heart attack and was carried from the room still bidding. My friend Wean Morgan's dealing was motivated by a hatred of the Birmingham dealers. "They would kick a volume from a set under the piano and tell the auctioneer it was incomplete," he would say in fury.

Dealers were also scornful of interfering academics who, being salaried, were under no pressure to sell. In the early 1970s a dealer called Turkey was seen at salerooms masticating a piece of wet cotton. He would lay it along the most valuable plate in an antiquarian book and extract it furtively. "It's imperfect, sir," he would announce to the baffled auctioneer, who was never able to refute this villainous deed.

Wean suggested I visit the National Library of Wales, which stands like a Roman palace overlooking Aberystwyth. David Jenkins, the Keeper of Printed Books, proved to be a tremendous ally. "There are two hundred and fifty workingmen's libraries in Wales," he told me. These libraries were closing and the National Library could only take a small percentage of the books.

Like chapels, miners' libraries were a spiritual part of the small Welsh valley towns. In fact, every working-class social centre was obliged to have a reading room in order to gain a bar licence. When Karl Marx arrived in South Wales he thought the workers the most educated he had seen. The miners and steelworkers represented the largest and best organized labour force in the world and their passion for education produced excellent libraries. There can be no doubt that such facilities played a rôle in the growth of socialist politics and the formation of Labour governments. As part of their struggle against Fascism, pits even produced their own newspapers to offset the influence of the capitalist press. David Jenkins was eager to find copies of some of these miners' newspapers for the National Library's archives.

"Aneurin Bevan spent more time in here than anyone else," I was told when I bought Tredegar Working Men's Library. A glass-fronted case of dark oak held handsome volumes showing that the mine owners wanted the miners to appreciate books as much as they did. They had donated copies of Wilkins's *History of the Iron, Coal & Steel Trades* and *A History of Merthyr Tydfil*, bound in Moroccan leather. Apart from the orange books of the Left Book Club and a vast amount of unpalatable verbiage from the pages of *Hansard*, the books were about the Wild West, railways, travel and exploration in the nineteenthcentury. Flicking open the nearest book, I read that Hannington of Uganda was the last Anglican bishop to be eaten by cannibals.

Ferndale was the most valuable miners' library I purchased. It contained a complete set of *The Dictionary of National Biography* and magnificent travel books. I rescued the contents of one small library from the scrap-heap where it had been dumped by the local waste paper dealer. Slowly, every miners' library in South Wales disappeared, their demise preceded by the industry which had inspired them. I bitterly regret that I did not document their end. The libraries became snooker and TV lounges, or public libraries, and the miners' scholarly interests were replaced by cheap shelving and romantic paperbacks. Everybody assumed that a more educated Wales was being built with public resources. But the stock in a public library is chosen for the masses, not by them, and is a product of a bureaucratic conception of culture. The erudition of miners' and similar libraries, in which every book is of importance, is irreplaceable. Books from a public library which had been built at the same time as the miners' libraries, would have been largely a worthless mass representing debased tastes. I am not opposed to the principle of public libraries, but the rare and interesting books they contain are invariably stolen, sold or disposed of due to lack of money or space.

"If you want to make money, list books and circulate them to new universities," said R.B. Dale, a private collector of considerable persistence. "They're building up their libraries." All second-hand booksellers were looking to exploit this profitable market. It was a common dictum that 'the private customer is a waste of time'. I did not admire universities but I could not ignore institutions such as York, Surrey and Hull, who would order just about anything with scholarly pretensions. I must confess that I abused the goodwill of some university librarians and sold at least one collection of which I am extremely ashamed.

The poet Philip Larkin was Librarian at Hull University. He sent me a request for English literary periodicals of the nineteenth century. These had lain forgotten for years but were now regarded as a treasure trove by Literature departments. Periodicals circulated in Canada, Australia and India as monuments of the British Empire. Some are very rare. George Eliot received £1,000 for writing *Romola* for the first issues of *The Cornhill Magazine* in 1860, and Thomas Hardy's first published work, *How I Built Myself a Home*, was published in *Chamber's Journal* in 1863. Over the years leather bindings would rot; hence periodicals such as *The Edinburgh Review* and *The Quarterly Review* became much harder to obtain in bound volumes. I often found myself with ten copies of the common volumes and none of the scarcer ones. University libraries wanted complete 'runs' of periodicals. Even if only a few volumes were missing, a run was worth considerably less. The University of Toronto decided to jump on this fashionable academic bandwagon and compiled a four-volumed, highly expensive *Wellesey Index of Victorian Periodicals*. Tony and Heather Jackson were responsible for organizing the bedlam of muddled Victorian periodicals, and managed, through their efficiency, to build complete runs in chronological order.

Trading in periodicals convinced me that I was onto a fortune but as they became rarer I had to shift towards library collections. Toronto had seventeen universities within a fifty-mile radius. One of them bought the library from Orebu Castle that belonged to Rosenorm-Lehn, the Danish Foreign Minister, for £28,000; I had paid £4,000 for it. He had been a poor minister but a wonderful collector, owning first editions of Holberg, the Danish dramatist, and several hundred pamphlets about the Schleswig-Holstein crisis.

My friend Jack Joram lived in Toronto, where he had a small shop in Queen Street. Having spent much of his life on a kibbutz, Jack was an idealist, but this was being taxed by conditions in the trade. The lavish, state-of-the-art libraries with enormous budgets rarely bought stock from small local booksellers. "You know what these librarians like, Richard?" he said. "They like travelling. They don't buy in Toronto but if something comes up in London, Frankfurt or Ghana... gee, they just get on a plane."

Jack did everything he could to help my early career. He put me in touch with a Canadian university to whom I sold the Library of Charles Bradleigh and a collection of nineteenth-century socialist literature containing the edition of *The Red Republican* in which *The Communist Manifesto* was originally published. Two years later, the library had still not put the collection into stock. I found university libraries invariably had a deadening effect on the culture of the book.

Canadian and Australian universities were very pro-British. They wanted to develop national identities by returning to their European origins, and buying British books linked them to the British tradition. Late nineteenth-century religious novels were almost unsaleable in Britain but were regarded as objects of great interest by Australia and Pacific countries, who were eager for collections of the first printed material to arrive on remote islands which had previously been inhabited by bare-breasted girls in grass skirts. One dealer sold a collection of books published by the Society for the Promotion of Christian Knowledge to Tasmania for thousands of pounds. American universities were buying books from Russia, China, Mexico and all over the world in a kind of manic imperialism. In any case, they were all in hearty competition with each other.

There are over two thousand Colleges of Education in America alone. With most academics putting their theories of teaching on paper, it was not a difficult subject to supply. I made rich pickings selling 20,000 books on the history, theory and practice of modern education to an Australian college. The British Government claims that democracy depends on education, so the deal could be seen as beneficial. I am more cynical.

Paul McNally, the librarian who made the purchase, was aware that the education system was bleeding rural areas of the young people who could offer much to a community if they were encouraged to remain within it. Local newspapers are full of beaming farmers' sons in academic dress, the first members of their family to go on to higher education. They are brought up to believe that their home town or village does not contain the opportunities for which their education has prepared them. I regard this manifestation of the brain drain as more important than the poaching of academics by richer countries. The object of higher education is to teach the son of the dairy farmer to work for the milk-marketing board. In reality rural areas need gardeners not soil scientists.

"If I see a book going to a university library, I tell them I won't pack it," claimed Ralph, a well-known dealer by the station in Swansea, in whose shop Dylan Thomas, Vernon Watkins and other Anglo-Welsh poets gathered to chat. Framed on his sitting-room wall was a bounced cheque from Dylan Thomas, together with one from me. "You've got to pay one day, boy," he said gently. Ralph's business depended on recycling books within the community but gradually he found his stock depleted and no books coming back. Universities were like giant vacuum-cleaners; treasured Welsh authors would disappear unread and unloved in an Arizona University. Ralph was unusual in fighting a guerilla war against academic purchasing. He had the vision to see that putting all the culture of the world in institutions was destroying national identities. At the time I thought Ralph foolish not to exploit a wealthy market. I now see that he was a prophet.

Travelling around Wales laid the foundations of my radical beliefs. It is a poor country and I saw its cultural traditions – literary societies, historical societies, theological colleges and country-house libraries – being sacrificed at the altar of centralized education. To what end? A university library which increases its stock from a quarter to half a million books will not necessarily increase the number of its readers. Numerous academics complained about 'the rape of Wales' but never considered their own responsibility for the destruction of the magnificent Welsh libraries I saw eroding before my very eyes. The massacre was quick and thorough. It stretched from Bala in North Wales to the Royal Institution in Swansea and through hundreds of fine libraries in between. A small percentage of the books went to the new Welsh universities but many more were sold to overseas universities with greater buying power.

It is now commonly accepted that the closure of the Bala College Library in 1969 was a major tragedy that could have been prevented by redirecting a fraction of the funding made available to, for example, the National Library of Wales. Because I made a good profit out of the purchase of Bala's collection I did not join in the subsequent outcry over the sale.

Driving to Bala from the south, I found the route was more tiring than if I had driven to Europe. It was very beautiful. I passed remote slate quarries and exquisite mountain scenery. The landscape reminded me of the truism that great spiritual revivals occur in the hills. When I arrived at Bala Lake I looked across the dark sheet of water at the enormous stone building housing 30,000 books. Here, protected from industrial Britain, the Methodists had formed a community which inspired the birth of the British and Foreign Bible Society. When Mary Jones walked over the barren hills from the Dysynni valley below Cader Idris to obtain a copy of the Bible in Bala, she became an inspiration, not only in Wales but throughout the Empire. In the nineteenth century the Bible was a vital tool of Imperial expansion. The work of the missionaries meant that Welsh culture spread throughout the world.

Inside Bala College's oak-panelled Library were row upon row of ancient books bound in the distinctive brown sheepskin of Wales. It would have rivalled the library of any Renaissance prince. Scanning the shelves, I saw the life's work of various nineteenth-century notables and works of the Protestant divines from the sixteenth century onwards, many in their original editions. By the end of the day this magnificent library had been dumped on the floor and sold for almost nothing. It was the equivalent of swapping the Mona Lisa for a couple of pints at Bermondsey Flea Market.

Because Bala was so remote I thought I might be the only dealer present. I was disappointed. There was a small cluster of buyers including James Thin, the well-known Edinburgh bookseller, and a tax inspector who collected sixteenth and seventeenth-century maps and precious Welsh books. Twenty years on, his garage is still full of books with the Bala stamp. The National Library of Wales managed to obtain Mary Jones's original Bible and a few other treasures, but rare Methodist periodicals describing early missionary visits to remote parts of the world went to New York. I bought the bulk of the books for a fraction of their real value. Packing boxes full of *The Hibbert Journal*, *Mind* and *The Expository Times*, I was exposed to the full force of a hundred years of philosophical theology. All of us had incredible bargains. The library was sold for a few thousand pounds; today it would fetch millions. It was the beginning of the devastation of Wales but, as a young dealer eagerly searching for books, I was not able to view the tragedy as I do now.

The University of Swansea eventually decided to commission studies documenting the disappearance of one of the proudest intellectual achievements of Wales. "They were ravaged by dealers," wrote one academic, without even having bothered to speak to me. But no academic I know scrambled over scrap heaps in the rain trying to save books.

Chapter Seven

The Quest
for Books

"There go the boys doing their duty."

At a cocktail party in Aberystwyth, I became aware that reality in Mid Wales was fundamentally different from reality in London. "I do wish we could come down here more often," a fashionable lady from South Kensington said to me, loudly.

"I don't care if she never fucking comes down," said a voice from under a paramilitary beret. Caio Evans, the self-declared Field Marshal of the Free Wales Army, partially funded his force with second-hand books inherited from his father, who had been an eminent mathematician. Although he doubtless alienated much of his support by bombings, threats to the investiture of the Prince of Wales and by carrying a photograph of decapitated Malayan terrorists in his wallet, he became a valued acquaintance. "If the police suspect you, boy," he said to me, "they check to see if the bonnet of your car is warm." The British Secret Service spread rumours about the IRA refusing to co-operate with him because of his amateur approach. Many in Wales hoped that a Celtic revolution would spread eastwards from Ireland to Wales but, despite some of Caio's Army spending a few months in prison and his valiant struggle for his country and its language, the sole battlefield remained the Emerald Isle.

In the early 1970s Norman and I were making an increasing number of trips down the A40 to Fishguard on the west coast of Wales. We began to realize that Ireland was nearer than England, both geographically and spiritually. Ireland is a land of Celtic myth. *The Book of Kells* was discovered under some dairy churns. Captain Cook's manuscripts were found in Ireland; they had been stolen by a dealer and hidden under some floorboards. A professor at Yale University was publishing twelve volumes of Boswell's papers from Malahide Castle. Who knew what treasures might emerge by placing a large request for books in *The Irish Times?*

"If you don't want to get your tyres slashed, don't wear GB plates," was advice frequently given before our intended journey. We hoped to receive favourable treatment by announcing ourselves to be Welsh.

Norman and I arrived at Rosslare at seven in the morning. Here was a country where small donkey carts still took produce to market. The pace of life was slow. "There are no transport cafés," Norman complained. Irish cafés had imitation lace table-cloths and served stew with a great quantity of potatoes. Expecting to find a very religious nation, we found a greater devotion to the holy relics of the Kennedy family. The cottage of the President's grandfather in Wexford was decorated like a shrine, with hundreds of images of the American 'Holy Family'.

I was inspecting books in a small shop in Cork when I heard sharp footsteps behind me. "I am Captain Feehan. Do you buy second-hand books?" On confirmation that I did we were taken to Cork Cathedral, where Bishop Murphy had established a large library at the beginning of the nineteenth century. It had once contained the first pamphlet printed in Australia. "I sold it to Dawsons for several thousand pounds," Feehan said. He now wanted to get rid of the bulk of the library. The towering columns of faded antiquarian books could themselves have built a cathedral. After an excited telephone call to the bank in Hay, we began loading. Undisturbed for nearly two hundred years, the fur of dust on the top shelves was so thick it was like touching a rabbit.

Captain Sean Feehan began his publishing house, The Mercier Press, in his spare time while in the Irish Army. His wife Mary was an editor and the two editorial assistants were both beautiful German countesses. Feehan was generous beyond all commercial considerations, insisting on taking several hundred pounds less for the books than I offered him and buying us lavish Guinness lunches at The Oyster Bar. He was a nationalist and this extended to his business. He was fighting a bitter battle against the British Law of Copyright and The British Museum. He thought it unjust that an Irish publisher had to give copies of a new book to all five of the copyright libraries in Britain, whereas Ireland only received one copy from British publishers. For the first time, I received an educational dose of anti-British sentiment. "We'll be up to help them," said Feehan's wife Mary, referring to the expected revolution promised by the violent events in the North of Ireland.

Sean Feehan became a close friend and supporter. His sense of humour was delightfully bawdy. He loved telling a probably untrue story of how Norman had tried to exchange Green Shield stamps for prostitutes on the Cork quays and how, on his first day in the Irish Army, he had come upon his Sergeant Major making passionate love to a jar of liver. He finished his career by publishing Irish regional joke books: *Corkman Jokes*, *Kerryman Jokes* and so on, finding it easy to compile them from his own casual conversations.

Feehan took me to Doneraile Court, one of the finest Georgian houses in Ireland and stocked with all kinds of treasures. Standing in the library was the seventeenth Viscount Kilmeandon and son of the Earl of St Doneraile. The story of the St Leger family would have made a splendid romantic novel. In the eighteenth century the family had been close personal friends with George III, providing a gallant general for the American War of Independence. They had been painted by Gainsborough, were experts on the new game of croquet and founded one of the most important horse races in the British Isles, The St Leger Stakes. In 1941 the sixth Viscount died without an heir, as did his brother in 1956. Nobody was able to trace Richard St John Leger, the next in line. Eventually he was found driving lorry-loads of misshapen lemons along the coast of California whilst his wife Nancy sold sandwiches from a small truck outside an ammunitions factory. Although they knew their family name was connected to Doneraile, when news came from Ireland that the house was rightfully theirs they were completely unprepared.

It was their son Dick whom I met in the library in the early 1970s. By that time the hard reality of life on the west coast of Ireland was apparent. It was hard enough to make a living, let alone maintain an enormous house requiring servants. Although the family received help from the Irish Georgian Society and Dick found work as a labourer on a neighbouring farm, they were unable to re-establish themselves. Even the new Countess began to miss the invigorating cash flow from her sandwich bar in southern California. Dick became my chauffeur and also a life-long friend. Dick and I had common interests. We were both young men who wanted to live in beautiful houses in the country. Second-hand books were to be our lifeline and we were prepared to work a fourteen-hour day looking for them. On our travels around Ireland we bought some precious nineteenth-century agricultural books from the tower of Adare Manor and several thousand pounds' worth of bibliographies from a man on a Dublin estate whose jacket was stuffed with wads of ten-pound notes. His fortune had been made by selling second-hand books in Irish supermarkets. Dick's modest charm was increased by the empathy everyone felt for the fate of his family, whose sacrifices ultimately failed to save Doneraile Court. The Earl and Countess relinquished their title and returned to California, and Dick was to follow in 1982. The house stood an empty and abandoned shell until the Irish Georgian Society campaigned for its preservation and began to restore it.

From Cork we took the road to Mallow, travelling behind a huge tipper lorry overloaded with swedes, which smashed around us like grenades on a battlefield. We met Cal Hyland, a bookseller who thought it demeaning to deal in non-Irish stock. He disregarded an eighteenth-century Johnson's *Dictionary* because it was not printed in Ireland. To Cal, the only important race in the world was the Irish, who fortunately bred fast and were widely appreciated in the United States. President John F. Kennedy was proud of his Irish connections. In the book trade this meant that departments of Anglo-Irish Literature were disproportionately large in American universities. Prices for rare pamphlets by Joyce, Yeats or Lady Gregory were high. The 1878 *Dublin University Magazine* which contained the first published work of W.B. Yeats was worth £1,000. Printing an Anglo-Irish catalogue was like printing money. Faced with a list of Irish ethnic gems an American professor would behave like a hungry child in a sweet shop.

The second-hand book trade has always flourished on the West of Ireland. In the early 1970s, Shannon Airport was to transatlantic passengers what Fiji was to transpacific travellers – an enjoyable free stopover. This most rural part of Ireland received plane-loads of wealthy Americans in whose honour a string of new hotels was built. Even after the stopovers ceased Kenny's Bookshop in Galway still flourished. Feehan mischievously claimed that some of his stock was acquired through his access to convent libraries. He visited the nuns posing as an altruistic scoutmaster who would be pleased to help relieve them of heavy tomes. Next door to his enormous shop Kenny had an art gallery to extract the maximum revenue from Americans making the pilgrimage to the Holy Land. He priced his books as if he were the king of Celtic bookselling, a position slightly weakened by his acceptance of a large grant from the Irish Development Agency. This enabled him to buy a binding machine, by which means pleasant old Irish books acquired ugly modern covers, an aesthetic nightmare which presumably did not matter if he was selling to universities overseas. Kenny's ambitions were supported by his wife Maureen, of whose beautiful brown eyes he wrote romantic descriptions in the front of his catalogues. United they fought off all intruders who sought underpriced books. Their Achilles' heel were their four sons. Maureen would ask two pounds per volume for a large set, and Kenny a pound, but the same set might be acquired for ten pence a volume from one of the less experienced sons.

The quality of stock in some of the Dublin shops was secondary to supplying the rich academic institutional markets. Day's Bookshop opposite the Dáil had been sold to a Captain MacGlinshy, Feehan's rival. The Overseas Development Bank invested thousands of pounds in MacGlinshy's Irish Universities Press, a name chosen for its bogus authority, which published British Parliamentary papers for enormous sums. MacGlinshy was incapable of running a second-hand bookshop yet, by riding the academic bandwagon, he became president of a million-pound business. His press was eventually liquidated along with an enormous property company.

The second-hand trade was changing. Dealers who quietly smoked Woodbines in backstreet shops were giving way to a new breed brandishing gold American Express cards. Once proud to sell books cheaply, they were now proud to sell them expensively. My Irish experiences, like my Welsh ones, helped make me an unacceptable eccentric. I held the view that the university was in a position of absolute power and that this power was destroying the second-hand book trade and many aspects of private culture.

Norman and I returned frequently to Ireland, where the welcome at the Oyster Bar was too good to miss. In 1974 we visited Belfast. "God shit on all Protestants," we heard a local inhabitant say as a strand of barbed wire was erected behind my Rolls Royce, which we had inadvertently parked close to the boundary separating Catholics from Protestants. Such fanaticism extended to the book trade. "I want only good books," Belfast theological booksellers told me fiercely. By this they meant impeccably Puritan commentaries, for no good book had ever been written by a Catholic. God had only spoken to seventeenth-century puritans, in original or reprint.

Violence was most likely to occur during the last weeks of a regiment's posting when troops knew they could settle old scores and escape revenge. "There go the boys doing their duty," muttered a public librarian as the window of a Woolworth's shop exploded into the street. "The streets were full of seventeenth-century pages," said a Belfast bookseller after a warehouse and a taxi rank were bombed. Broken-hearted, a small dealer called Kelly gave up when thousands of feet of his historic films were ruined by British troops sticking bayonets into his ceiling. Standing with my hands up in front of a nineteen year old with an automatic rifle, I realized that death could be the consequence of someone's whim.

Everywhere the atmosphere was electric. As in *The Lord of the Flies*, gangs of children were a chief danger, rampaging in the streets and setting fire to empty houses. In Green's bookshop there was a vast mound of earth where there should have been a staircase. We naturally assumed it was caused by a bomb but when I commiserated with the owner he told me it was woodworm. But even in Londonderry, and at times of extreme violence, we still managed to fill a container with books. By the mid-1970s, the small house-dealer with a lot of bargains was a very rare bird. A new type of dealer was emerging who would scour book fairs throughout Ireland. As the books became more difficult to find we stopped going.

It was successful dealing in Wales and the West Midlands that enabled me to buy a gleaming white Rolls Royce Phantom 6. It had a cocktail cabinet and a glass screen that separated the passenger from the driver at the touch of a button. I could sink into the leather seats and smoke my cigars contentedly. Between 1962 and 1968 the turnover of the business had risen from £6,000 to £100,000 a year.

"What you have to be aware of is the big C," said a life-insurance salesman from Allied Dunbar. Although I regarded life-insurance as an encouragement for people to murder wives and burn down houses, in this, his most carefully-rehearsed line, he was absolutely right. In the early 1970s my mother, my father and my elder sister Mary all died of cancer. Mary's death especially was a terrible loss. She was still in her thirties and left behind a husband, Deryck, and two young sons. Unlike my sisters Joanna and Anne, whose bourgeois pretensions meant that they lived in South Kensington and Oxford respectively, Mary remained in the depths of Wales and she was one of my best customers. The number of Booth graves in Cusop churchyard had more than doubled. After her death, my father's dreams of having a united rural family were shattered. In his great grief, Deryck moved to Essex, selling their house in Hay to my sister Anne and her husband. After this relations became strained. Frank said all families were *Schadenfreude*. As a bachelor, he still harboured resentment from his Army days when officers with families were given the less dangerous posts.

My parents were so influential that, after their death, I did not get an invitation to sherry for the next thirty years. My typical Christmas became watching John Wayne films with my friend Bill Cooke the lorry driver. One Christmas I spent mixing cement in front of the Castle. It was more enjoyable than going to church where I find the habit of having to stoop and kiss one's neighbour extremely distasteful.

The British Museum once argued that every book should be kept because someone, somewhere, might want it. I believe this argument is more applicable to a bookshop. I had my eye on another property in Hay, the old cinema. A confident piece of 1950s architecture, it had been lovingly cared for by its manager Desmond Madigan, who granted me a mortgage that was substantially lower than the bank-rate and substantial leeway in paying the deposit. Like many small cinemas in the area, its last gasp had been as a dance and bingo hall. In an immature act of exuberance I had once driven my Jaguar up the steps to watch the beautiful, wide-bottomed peasant girls jiggling vigorously in their tight, blue jeans. Now, with the thoughtlessness of youth, I ripped out the long rows of chairs, those silent witnesses to a million snoggings and ten million rustling crisp packets.

Frank built bookshelves which were to be "within easy reach of a five foot-two woman, without going on tiptoes". This was quite revolutionary commercial acumen for the book trade. Second-hand bookcases and tea chests which ripped one's trousers were traditionally used for large numbers of books. In his lifetime Frank built twenty-five miles of bookshelves. The Cinema was advertised as 'the largest second-hand bookshop in the world' and held 250,000 books. I held onto the position in *The Guinness Book of Records* for a brief year.

I needed staff for the new Cinema bookshop. "Prisoners are highly literate because they have nothing to do but read," Frank told me. From the Discharged Prisoners' Association I employed a manager called Tony Meagher who worked conscientiously and methodically for several years. My second experience of a discharged prisoner was less fortunate. John Clements boasted about how he jemmied up the floorboards of country houses but he appeared to be a good bookseller, establishing a productive connection with the John Jay Institute of Criminology in New York.

My delight was mitigated when I discovered he was filling a van with my books and selling them in Cheltenham.

An advantage of the second-hand book trade is that it contains a high number of displaced persons, especially Jews. It provides one of the few congenial occupations for men who, but for turmoil in their homeland, would undoubtedly have been pillars of the establishment. Magdashi of Edinburgh, Kellner and Koffler of Museum Street in London, Kraus and Johnson of New York, Hardy of Dorchester, Nothman of Covent Garden and Bon in Oxford were all first generation émigrés. The doyen of them all must be Hans Heinemann of Montreal, the famous publisher's grandson. After owning five bookshops in Shanghai and spending time in a Communist prison he opened the Mansfield Book Mart in Montreal. "The Chinese communists gave me a year of imprisonment for every bookshop I owned," he said. Having fled from Hitler's Germany, where book burning had made every second-hand bookseller into a minor criminal, Heinie now bemoaned the politics of Montreal, where in the early 1970s the Quebecois separatists were at their most aggressive. He now expected to become a refugee for the third time in his life.

Heinie was proportioned like a slightly swollen goose's egg. Behind him, of similar build though more of a duck's egg, was his assistant, a studious, intense German girl. "She will take over the business," announced Heinie proudly. Negotiating with a woman was unusual. In the 1970s ninety per-cent of the booktrade were male. The trade is a dusty business totally lacking in glamour and has remained dominated by men far longer than other professions. I can recall Mrs Leeming, whose husband permitted her to trade from his insurance office in Worcester, and Mrs Pinches, whose business 'Heraldry Today' is a credit to the international niche market.

Two other exceptions were my friends the Clifford-Wolf sisters, Rosamund and Antoinette, who owned The Square Orange Bookshop in Pimlico Road. They were pioneers in one of the fastest-growing fields of bookselling: bindings. Bindings are handsome, leather-bound books much sought after for their decorative value. The market was insatiable. Interior decorators, film sets, grand houses and country clubs all needed leather books to fill miles of empty shelving. From benders, which are thin books in publisher's calf, to thick vellum volumes, bindings represented thirty per cent of my turnover and we had more business than we could handle. We always put bindings on a top shelf above eye level and under good lighting, where they sparkle and appear more attractive than if the eye looks down upon the dust of a hundred years. Nothing glistens more than books that have been kept in pristine condition behind locked glass. These are what leather-binding dealers look for but rarely find. The bindings market was not always easy to please. An Arab prince did not consider fine leather encyclopedias as having any decorative value in his Mayfair flat; everything had to be old, and of the right quality and size. The film director Peter Greenaway ordered thousands of red, green and orange books for the death scene of a bibliophile in his film, *The Cook, The Thief, His Wife and Her Lover*. There is an overall aversion to theological black leather. I received an order for twenty tons of books written in 1820 for a film about Lady Caroline Lamb. I was meticulous about the dates but wondered if she would have possessed such beaten-up specimens. My own belief is that, as every politician broadcasts in front of a handsome row of them, books are more often subliminally advertised than washing powder.

International spies have been exotic members of the second-hand book trade. Colonel Kroger, the notorious Russian agent, found it was the perfect foil for receiving and dispatching small parcels in London. When the U2 spy plane was shot down over Siberia, its pilot Gary Powers was exchanged for the master Hungarian spy Colonel Abel, who was undercover as a distinguished antiquarian bookseller. Ian

Fleming, creator of the most famous spy of all, James Bond, used the profits from his best-sellers to invest in very fine antiquarian and second-hand books. He would buy the finest first editions of major books in the development of the world, like Darwin's *Origin of Species*. They would have to comply with his definitions of 'Books that have Started Something' or 'Milestones of Human Progress'. Fleming's was a Bond-like form of book collecting and remains the preserve of very rich men with considerable discrimination. I believe anyone can be a collector, but it is most suitable for the poor man as a means of getting rich. When Sir James Goldsmith asked me to stock his French chateau with books by major thinkers of his generation it was an example of upside-down book collecting. Profits should not accrue to the dealer but to the private collector, who may spend days and even years in second-hand bookshops.

The rôle of the second-hand book in charity fund-raising deserves a mention. Book-auction fund-raising for college libraries in the USA has become such big business that I have a friend who waits all through the night for sales to open. "How can you bear to handle such things?" said an antiquarian book expert watching the Castle's garage fill up with 200,000 paperbacks assembled from a *Blue Peter* Charity Appeal in 1975. But I found them fascinating, in particular seeing how Second World War factual history had been turned into fictional history by the insertion of dialogue, or wondering at the sheer number of books produced by Agatha Christie. There were sadistic Westerns, in which three rapes and five murders had been committed by page ten, and hundreds of Barbara Cartlands, the doyenne of romance. I used to think that romantic paperbacks were written in the same way as Mickey Spillane novels, for which undergraduates were given a few pounds to write lines like, 'He opened the door and she had nothing on but the radio'. The romantic paperback is the most difficult to sell. The type of cover which featured a sexually appealing doctor looking down a young nurse's blouse did not survive in the second-hand market. I was able to buy a thousand in the United States for twenty-five dollars. In shortest supply were green Penguins and those of high literary quality, and I suspected the load had been 'gutted'. Such books gave me a picture of post-War literature which I could not have obtained from any other source. I dispute the conventional book-trade snobbery that only the lowest form of dealer dealt in second-hand paperbacks.

The Cinema attracted customers ready to educate me in diverse esoterica. The most brilliant exponent was Dr Frank Lewis. "I believe I can be of considerable assistance to you," he suggested quietly when I met him by the sorting bay. I beheld a short fat man who was as ugly as a potato. In his youth, Frank had been a champion runner and gained one of the quickest Philosophy Doctorates at Oxford University. After his thesis, on The Medieval River System of Cologne, he had been offered the Chair of Medieval History at Bonn University by Ribbentrop, Hitler's Foreign Minister. "I refused on the basis that Wales was a more important country than Germany," he said. Now, hopelessly unable to look after himself or his interests, a worn and soiled suit documented his decline in the world. Drugs were a problem. On some days he swallowed handfuls of pills as if they were sweets, becoming passionately vindictive towards rivals and once going so far as to urinate into his pint on the Irish ferry, because he said that if he used the public urinal, the head waiter would make homosexual advances. But Frank had a profound impact on the business. His first innovation was to recommend Sunday opening. Looking up from *The Sunday Times*, he would greet all visitors to the business with displays of recondite scholarship.

"Have you got your Tamil University yet?" he asked a visitor from Sri Lanka.

"No sir, but we're trying," answered the visitor, who obviously appreciated Frank's empathetic approach to his culture.

"Do you know why Ceylon was the first country to have a female Prime Minister?" Frank continued, which baffled the visitor. "Because the constitution was written by two Welshmen, Sir Ivor Jennings and David Pryce Jones."

Frank always began his day by throwing away the Business section of the newspaper. The contempt with which this operation was performed is as clear to me now as it was twenty years ago.

"Tourism is the policy of the future," he said. "Mervyn Jones was at Aberystwyth with me. He's a very silly man. Tries to be nice to everyone, but he's probably worth seeing." So we clambered into the Rolls Royce and drove to Cardiff to have tea with the recently-appointed head of The Wales Tourist Board. Frank was right. The meeting was a great success and Mervyn became a strong supporter of the idea of a 'Town of Books'. This was a natural description for the small market town whose fire-station, castle, cinema and chapel were now filled with books. There were over a million of them on every subject under the sun. I had two dozen staff working on every aspect of the trade, from transportation, sorting and cleaning to buying, selling, cataloguing, binding and researching. However, I was in some financial difficulty, and was extremely glad to find someone in authority who was prepared to help. From pointing journalists in my direction to giving me a large grant, Mervyn did everything he could to help me, culminating in Hay being chosen as the Welsh venue for celebrating two hundred years of American Independence.

"You have given me three more years of useful life," Frank told me just before he died in lonely misery one cold day in his caravan. "You are the only genius I have ever met." His memory was a major motivation behind my future career.

1973. Hay Castle: my antiquarian bookshop.

I do not claim that the outdoor bookshops in Hay-on-Wye are as interesting as the left Bank in Paris.

Mr Mayall mending a watch in his shop in Hay. His expertise may well have helped to win the war.

Lucy Powell of The Three Tons. She has enchanted her customers for 50 years.

A pair of the local Hay Aristocracy, Bill and June Cooke.

Clifford Hubbard (Doggie). A revered dealer with an inspired specialist knowledge.

My Aunt, Viva King. Her homosexual saloon, including Norman Douglas and many distinguished writers, aroused the disapproval of my parents.

Lennox Money – the only friend who really understood I was a radical.

Me and Marianne Faithful. She told me to go to the 'City Lights' Bookstore in San Francisco. I did, but 20 years too late – the original vision of Jack Kerouac was replaced by glossy academic books.

Myself with Vicky del Rio, a passionate and impulsive girl I knew at Oxford. Unfortunately our marriage lasted only twenty-four hours.

Two of my passions: The Irish and the second-hand book trade. "Cork is the National Capital of Hay," I would enthuse to the bewildered tourist.

A Rolls Royce built of books.

'Bookhenge': I shudder to think of the value of the rare books in the foreground.

Chapter Eight

Fools rush in...

Frank English, the man who built twenty-five miles of bookshelves in Hay.

"Here's a rural town where the dustman talks like Freud."

After Ireland, my quest for books took me to the further reaches of Scotland, from the Outer Hebrides to Inverness and Aberdeen. In the nineteenth century, Scotland had the greatest concentration of literature in the British Isles. Edinburgh, Glasgow, Aberdeen, Perth and Dundee were all important publishing centres producing great literary journals such as *Blackwood's Magazine, Chamber's Journal, The Quarterly Review* and *The Edinburgh Review*. Scotland also had one of the finest education systems: thousands of poor students attended university with perhaps only a bag of oats and a box of kippers to sustain them each day. When Queen Victoria sailed up the coast for Balmoral, Scottish lairds lit bonfires on the beaches in welcome. Balmoral was just one of the magnificent Scottish estates which housed fine libraries. Even the medical library of Victoria's doctor warranted preservation by the National Trust.

Aberdeen was the best city for books in the British Isles. It had a flourishing local history society, The Spalding Club, and was a great seat of theological learning. Its nine-month winter helps to explain this impressive literary tradition. Books are always a success in cold cities, and Minneapolis is a comparable example in the USA. I explained this to a Spanish friend. "Yes," she said, "but in Spain we lie on the beach and make love." Aberdeen is built of granite and cobbles. The Rosemount Quarry was supposedly the largest man-made hole in the world; looking into it, half way down, seagulls were the size of a pinhead. At the time of my visit there was a dispute about whether it should become a tourist attraction or a rubbish dump, so solving the city's garbage problem for generations. I felt the controversy was a neat metaphor for the problems of rural areas like Hay, where tourism is given an economic rôle far beyond its ability to fill.

Auchinloss House, near Aberdeen, was so full of books that they piled up the stairs, into the kitchen and filled any available wall-space. The owner, A.C. Walker, could not stop buying grandfather clocks and I had to squeeze past one to get into every room.

"There's no rubbish," he said.

"What do you mean ?" I asked him.

"There's no fiction," was his gruff reply.

Walker had been a chemical engineer whose expertise had taken him around the world. From Singapore to Sidney, he bought books and posted them back to Aberdeen. On his death he wanted his wife to be able to use the rooms as they were originally intended. He provided cardboard chemical drums to protect his treasures on the long journey to Wales.

In Edinburgh, as in Dublin, bookshops were in decline. Ian Grant, who handled the great aristocratic libraries and published fine books, had yielded to the attractions of his loving female book-keeper and found a smaller shop. I once met him, in full kilt and bagpipes, looking for Jacobite bindings at an Antiquarian Booksellers' Fair in London. He was too much of a gentleman to profit from the hoards of bargain-hunters who boasted that they could make a day's wages buying under-priced books from him. Several of his employees started competing businesses of their own. It was a common remark in the trade that every bookseller in Edinburgh had been trained by Ian Grant.

Buying the stock of a distinguished firm or the library of a distinguished collector can be a very moving experience. Not being an expert on regional bookselling, the name Hugh Hopkins meant nothing to me until I went to his large house in Glasgow. All the great academic booksellers' catalogues were lovingly preserved along with dense catalogues from Quaritch, Henry Bohn and other giants of the trade. Finding it hard to sell second-hand books in the modern world and badly crippled with arthritis, the fifth generation of Hugh Hopkins sold me his reference books and wound up the business. I walked down the stone steps from his house feeling greatly saddened. The most exotic booksellers in Glasgow were a Pakistani bus conductor, Majid, who, peculiarly, amassed nothing but 'Volume I's from sets and periodicals, and an ex-actress called Sarah who would barter any amount of books for a bottle of gin.

My successes in the north of Scotland multiplied after I spent a journey to New York reading the Aberdeen and Inverness telephone directories. I wrote to any houses that appeared to be independent estates, asking if they had any books to sell. Scotland began to yield rich harvests, including the library belonging to the Reverend James Hastings, son of Charles Hastings, in Aberdeen. Charles Hastings was an Oxford don who won a worldwide reputation by compiling a thirteen-volume *Encyclopaedia of Religion and Ethics*. He was renowned in Oxford for stopping contemporaries in the street and asking them to write an article for his Encyclopaedia. As the editor of *The Expository Times,* review copies of books would drop through his letter box in their hundreds.

In 1900 Hasting's library had been the largest in Britain and required thirteen secretaries to keep it in order. Charles Hastings had worked with William Robertson Nichol, a friend of Queen Alexandra and regarded as something of an early Dr Johnson. They were fervent literary patrons, promoting J.M. Barrie and other Kailyard School writers who, by writing in the Scottish dialect, thought it was a method of inspiring the soul of the populace. The age of the Sermon was giving way to the age of the Novel. The scriptures became more palatable in the form of a religious novel. In this field, one of my interests was tracing the 123 novels written under three aliases by Mrs Burnett Smith.

Hastings's asthmatic son was chain-smoking on the sofa in an enormous house on Rosemount Terrace. He welcomed me kindly and said he would be glad to sell any number of books provided their absence "did not disturb the appearance of the place". Treasures sprang up before my eyes, including Hogarth Press pamphlets by Virginia Woolf, Edith Sitwell and T.S. Eliot. All the books were in mint-condition and I was able to remove 20,000 without breaching his stipulation. "Every bookseller has a bad back," Norman complained bitterly as he packed and loaded box after box of them with amazing fortitude.

Tom Loome saw the prestigious collection arrive in Hay. "You must sell it all together," he said. "Thousands of American libraries will want to own 'The Hastings Collection'." He received offers from three interested parties and sold the lot to a fundamentalist Christian group in California. Ambassador College had enough money to build two university campuses in America and one at St. Albans in England. It had its own radio programmes and published a magazine, *The Plain Truth,* which was given away at railway stations. American fundamentalism had a huge following and was still in its innocence when Garner Ted Armstrong, the son of Ambassador College's founder, was found to have bought himself a pair of cufflinks for £22,000. Fascinated by an establishment whose principal could raise $55m and travel in his own private jet, I accepted with alacrity an invitation to lunch in St. Albans. On arrival the librarian whispered to me, "I don't think your chauffeur would be happy eating with us". Dick St Leger good-naturedly went to the pub and I was shown into an oak-panelled dining room, where crystal glasses sparkled on the table. The hum of conversation was interrupted when the Principal raised a topic he clearly considered of significant general interest. "Do you think it would be cheaper to hire a car in Paris or to take my Mercedes across the Channel?"

Ambassador College became a regular customer, buying books whose dated scholarship was difficult to sell elsewhere. Shanon Turner's *History of the Anglo-Saxons*, Robinson's *Ecclesiastical Researches in The Holy Land*, and Pritchard's *Celtic Nations* all helped their research into the early history of races. When the College eventually ran into financial problems it was forced to sell the Hastings Collection.

Coups like the Hastings episode made me overconfident. I imagined I could continue to make profits indefinitely. One problem was finding good staff. Those who had a university education believed that opportunity lay outside small towns and those who did not often failed to understand the peculiarities of collectors. I needed staff who could both adapt to a rural area and compete in the book trade. I have always taken a rather anarchistic attitude towards recruitment. I once offered a job to a negro in a London telephone box with no knowledge of his background or qualifications, and I was also able to turn an ex-miner, an ex-bishop and the daughter of a local cleaner into successful second-hand booksellers. That said, jokes abounded about the ignorance of some bookshop staff.

"Where can I find Mrs Gaskell?" asked one customer in a Hay bookshop.

"I think she's away today, sir."

Someone searching for Mrs Henry Wood was directed to the Music department and one lady, on asking for Raeburn, was sent to the Cookery section. However, for nearly ten years, I was lucky enough to have a very good secretary called Julia Tomkinson. More sophisticated than anyone in the society in which she found herself, she kept my business affairs at a dignified distance from the chaos around me.

Major Norman Eggington had a pub at Ewyas Harold, a neighbouring village. He was something of a local legend. Chain-smoking and gulping beer from a two-pint pewter mug, he would zestfully turn a chattering skull into a marionette or extract merry tunes from a carpenter's saw used as a makeshift violin. The pub was affecting his wife's health, so he came to work in the bookshop. Neatly dressed in a grey suit, he dedicated himself to the business and greeted visitors with politeness and efficiency. He was adept at developing specialist markets and people would write to him from all over the country demanding books. Even if a small percentage of British bicyclists collected bicycling books, it was sufficient to create a dynamic market. 'Eggy' would answer each letter methodically. He was an optimist. "We will become the greatest bookshop in the world," he promised.

Eggy was joined by Michael Cottrill, known as 'Cotters', who after thirty years remains the longest serving member of my staff. He had become disillusioned with librarianship, and used his skills to set up sophisticated sorting systems. Through Cotters an amazing world of minority interests opened up to me. He was an avid collector of Beckford, Baron Corvo and Ludwig II of Bavaria. He compiled the specialist catalogues, dedicating one entirely to Samuel Beckett, printed in black with suitably grey covers. He even made a collection of Uranian verse, mostly schoolmasters writing about beautiful young boys playing football.

He had a passion for English literature and also for the literary celebrities who lived near Hay-on-Wye, such as Bruce Chatwin, Roland Matthias and Penelope Betjeman. Wearing the same drab, fawn anorak that has served him for twenty years, the service that he gives customers is the best in the country, and those searching for rare books can rely both on his knowledge and on his assiduity in finding them. "He's an extraordinarily talented boy," said Frank English.

I owe Eggy, Cotters and Julia an enormous amount. They could run the business on their own initiative and tolerated frequent mismanagement, while others came and went. Hundreds of my employees left to open their own shops. Trevor Mills's interest in antiquarian books was one of the purest I would find anywhere. He catalogued and annotated with loving care and had begun to create an extraordinary antiquarian department. Unfortunately, he left for Melbourne, Australia, to work in the state library there. Academic institutions were a magnet to those who wanted to fulfil intellectual ambition and be paid well for doing so; in the 1970s life within them was a kind of Mecca.

Many came to me looking for work. On one occasion the Bishop of Hereford appeared with a young protégé who he hoped could gain experience in the book business.

"I've got a little query..." he began.

"Bring him in," said Frank.

Although Frank spent his working life exposed to the biggest selection of books in the world, he never wanted to own them. He was interested in them as they related to his experience of life. Charles Duff's *The Handbook of Hanging* was a model he often referred to. A thin hardback with a black and white art deco cover, it contained descriptions of how hanging can go wrong. In Frank's eyes this was an unjust and barbaric practice conceived by illogical, conservative thinkers.

Hugh Vickers stayed for several months, but beyond consuming impressive amounts of cider, even by local standards, he achieved little. The Mason's Arms became as much a centre for drunken booksellers as for drunken farm labourers. "The trouble with Hay," remarked Frank, "is that whichever pub you go into you'll always meet someone from the business."

Dr Simon Nothman, known as 'the Doc', was a small, dark-haired man of Jewish origin. Still plump and prosperous from his professional days he was one of the wittiest men in the trade. "Good heavens, here's a rural town where the dustman talks like Freud," he said on bumping into Frank at the bottom of Brynmelin Drive.

In the 1950s the Doc had rejected a highly profitable practice in

Hampstead to print his own catalogues and publish minor works. His erudition equalled his enthusiasm. At the time I was very jealous of him. Although he knew less about books than me, the banks were prepared to lend him more money. He enlisted the help of a man called Jim Carter who could catalogue seven hundred books in an afternoon and drink two litres of wine at the same time, which in both cases was double the capacity of an ordinary human being. He catalogued 2,000 items by G.K. Chesterton which were sold to Hofstra University on Long Island. This made me even more jealous. One of Jim's inspired ideas was to launch a modern poetry competition and then sell all the manuscripts to an American university for a handsome sum.

The free-spending Doc was well-established in the trade and very ambitious. He wanted his first edition Antiquarian Bookshop and Twenty-Four Hour Bookshop to make Covent Garden the centre of London's second-hand book trade. For several years his exuberance and his credit from the Overseas Development Bank carried him through. But by the early 1980s, several hundred thousand pounds in debt, he fled to Ireland. "It's in the nature of Jews to flee," he explained. As a young man he had wandered around Europe at the time of the Holocaust. He narrowly escaped capture in Toulouse by pretending to be a member of the invading force and "arresting" a companion in the occupied café. He was in his seventies when a firm of Wall Street lawyers resurrected a $1m debt in England. He fought back valiantly and even secured a new mortgage for his home in Huntington, New York. "My address is 600 Park Avenue, Richard," he said. "What more could you want?"

A London taxi in Hay-on-Wye is an unusual sight. Inside was a tall, thin-lipped man called Jim Robson and a brunette who was someone else's wife. Jim was of mixed Irish-Dutch ancestry. His teens had been spent in South Carolina, where he once created a minor sensation by smearing his arm with tomato ketchup, dangling it out of the car boot and tuning his CB radio to the police patrols converging from all over the state. With long, blonde hair and persuasive charm he resembled a hero from a Scandinavian children's book. He turned out to be quite the opposite.

Jim came to work for me. Soon after his arrival I had a telephone call from Stechert Hafner, the largest bookstore in New York, whose stock was for sale. I picked a team of six staff to make the trip to America. None of us had been there before. We were a strange-looking group as we stood at the bottom of an antiquated, eight-storey building on East Twelfth Street, New York. Staring down at us was a magnificent bronze bust of the shop's founder, Otto Hafner.

In the nineteenth century Otto had been one of America's economic heroes. His shop served a nation rather than a town. He saw that all languages had a rôle in the melting pot of America, a fact that English-language chauvinism allowed many to forget. I did not realize, for example, that German failed to become the official language of the United States by only two votes. Or that, when Japan adapted to the modern world, Japanese doctors were educated in the German medical tradition using the German language, making *The German/Japanese Dictionary of Medical Terminology,* to some, indispensible, and only a taxi-ride away for New Yorkers.

Stechert Hafner opened its doors to the world's scholars, supplying books in every language and bringing culture from all over Europe into America. Their flagship was a catalogue listing some 5,000 dictionaries and grammars. But the store had been taken over by a publishing conglomerate and now accountants ran the show. The experienced 'old school' employees lost their jobs, although I did come across two elderly workers furtively whispering in Polish on the second floor. It was left to the money men to explain the *Updated Brazilian Encyclopaedia* to their customers. Meeting an unhappy-looking accountant just back from yet another abortive sales trip, I asked him whether it mattered that the company had had to write off half a million dollars in Stechert Hafner stock? Not at all, he replied. They had just published a book called *Jonathan Livingstone Seagull*, whose ornithological day dreams had made several million dollars.

Stechert Hafner had experience of supplying libraries worldwide and had branches in London, Frankfurt, Paris and Bogotá, but the company's expertise had waned after the Second World War. It had not adapted to the scams of modern publishing with the same opportunism as other large publishers. Institutional book-purchasing budgets were being milked by rivals churning out titles in cheap bindings especially for universities. The conglomerate which had bought Stechert Hafner did so in the hope that the most distinguished name in academic bookselling would open the floodgates to orders from rich new universities. Until then, the company had stood aside from the capitalist bonanza. Their stock had been of great quality, and could include a book with two hundred samples of rare Japanese woods, or an index to Latin names of plants neatly bound in light-green cloth. Their reputation depended to a large extent on the fact that they could supply anything out of stock. This entailed gigantic holdings and their New York base created such massive overheads that is was hardly surprising that the stock had turned from an asset into a liability. I allow myself to believe that Otto Hafner died from disappointment during the university boom.

Seeing the fate of Stechert Hafner, I feared that no bookshop would ever value quality of stock above the financial temptation of modern bestsellers. Before me were fine sets of Dante, Holberg and Schiller, and the company accountants were entirely happy to abandon them all for *Jonathan Livingstone Seagull*. I negotiated a rock-bottom price for Stechert Hafner's books. It was clear that, even in New York, no one wanted to put in the hours of manual labour required to shift them. However, even I underestimated the size of the task and was almost ruined by it. The expense of keeping six people in New York for several weeks, transport costs and the loss of profits in Hay all escalated. A generous loan from a girlfriend in Kentucky saved me from running out of cash completely.

The books had to be carried in an elevator dating from 1911, which stalled constantly. Tom Love, the Deputy Accountant, appeared in a crisp lavender shirt and white slacks, an amazing contrast to the years of filth and grime surrounding us. His meddling drove us into a frenzy and when he started trying to supervise the black workers clearing files from the top shelves, Jim Robson vented his feelings by urinating on his shoe. Tom felt something warm and wet on his sock and, swearing viciously, chased Jim into the street. I was later told that this had been a great public relations exercise and that the workers were cheering all the way.

This was a staggering picture of corporate America. When faced with important choices, Tom Love twirled a Decision Maker on his desk. Every time a door opened a different secretary would emerge. "You know, when a man dies, his finger nails keep on growing..." said my friend Jack Joram. "It's the same with the secretaries at Stechert Hafner."

I began boxing books which had come from the library of Professor George Vernadsky of Yale, who had collected Russian newspapers published in New York such as *Fresno* and *Scranton*. Russian bitterness had been one of the driving forces behind McCarthyism, but intellectualising had to be forgotten as we struggled to clear hundreds of tons of books in a city where a refuse skip cost a fortune. To make room for sorting and packing, we had to discard all the material which we judged obsolete and of no historical value. This applied mostly to medical journals. With cries of "Have a free book, mate!" Jim started giving them to New Yorkers on the street. A Japanese company removed loads by weight for waste paper but, in our haste, several precious publications also went east, including copies of *Annalen der Physik*, which had first published Einstein's Theory of Relativity and were therefore very valuable. The Latin American Consolidated Acquisitions Programme was stored in several gigantic bookcases which had to be placed in canvas trolleys and wheeled to the elevator. Under LACAP, Latin American countries had to supply an agreed quota of all books they published to the United States. There were inevitable problems. Guides to Venezuelan gas stations and other strange material arrived erratically at premium prices. American academics finally revolted but not before Stechert Hafner had accumulated 75,000 unwanted books which no doubt contributed to its decline. We did sell some of the Stechert Hafner stock to establishments in America, Canada and Australia, but the bulk had to be carried, in five forty-foot containers, back to Hay.

We divided our time between the apartment we shared together, the offices of Stechert Hafner, and The Captain's Table, a Greek restaurant with brown formica, chrome fittings and a glass showcase displaying food with exotic names. Our waiter told us that he had been mugged three times in the last six months. In our filthy old clothes we looked like muggers ourselves; even our sheets and pillowcases were grey with dirt. Jim relaxed by playing practical jokes. On one occasion I woke up to find someone in bed beside me. Gently, I pulled back the covers. It was the bronze bust of Otto Hafner.

Halfway through the trip the pressure had become so great that Norman went parachuting in New Jersey, and I went to see Charles Sanders in St Augustine, Florida. Sanders collected me from the airport in a Pontiac which had 400,000 miles on the clock and rubber on the floor in shreds;

to buy a new car would support the Yankee industrial economy he loathed. Tanned and fit, his military haircut recalled his days in the Korean War, when he had been evacuated as dead from a crashed helicopter. His battered helmet hung from the wall of his house and a picture of a gun on the front door warned, 'Never Mind the Dog: Beware of the Owner'. His wife Hokey cooked a traditional Southern breakfast of grits and bacon while Sanders consumed two cans of beer. Later, fed up with his womanising, Hokey was to run away with a sixteen year-old friend of her stepson.

St Augustine is a beautiful small town with a sixteenth-century castle jutting into the harbour. It struck me as a place which had rejected the American dream, with shrimp fishermen in small boats, a street full of craftsmen and a growing population of pot smokers. The town was established as a Spanish military post in 1585 and had been home to some of America's first printing presses. "If you find a book printed in St Augustine," Sanders said, "it could be the first book published in America, and worth several million dollars." When the South was cut off during the Civil War, hundreds of small presses expressed their outrage. Sanders collected Confederate imprints and had 6,000 examples: more than the Library of Congress. De facto, his radical position was established: he collected treasures better than the establishment at a fraction of the price.

Despite being a passionate Confederate with a liberal sprinkling of guns and flags throughout his house, he was an eccentric and had taken to smoking large quantities of pot in small cocina sheds with his friend, Art. Cocina is the fossilised coral from which St Augustine was built. Both stealing it and smoking drugs were Federal offences punishable by long prison sentences, but Sanders's dislike of the Yankees meant gnoring all the laws they attempted to impose on the South.

A very rich man, Sander's beliefs are easier praised rather than emulated. As a talented bookseller and collector, he had travelled thousands of miles supplying libraries. He owned a beautifully organized local history library which enabled him to get large sums for inconsequential guides to Palm Springs or sell a sixteenth-century History of Wales to Birmingham, Alabama at an enormous profit: there was a theory that the state had been discovered by the Welsh in the fourteenth century, and that the Native Americans speak a similar language.

Sanders told me that if one left a book outside, within three weeks it would be destroyed by silverfish: tiny, slithery creatures who would eat every scrap of paper. Ancient books from tropical silverfish countries – China, India, Africa, Ceylon – have not survived. "They even ate my leather jacket," said a dealer whose purchases were destroyed. Nowadays refrigerated libraries are often used in the South.

Both of us were handling more books than a dozen universities put together. We were in the front line, watching heavy political funding by officials who announced they were building a better world. We both interpreted LACAP as a Yankee tactic to help expand their domination of the world at a cost of a few million dollars. Sanders viewed the situation commercially. There were millions of dollars he considered it his duty as a Confederate to relocate. Knowing that Cuba had not participated in the LACAP programme, he said, "When the Bay of Pigs invasion was announced I took my Korean War battledress out of storage, and was going in behind the troops." He hoped to get his hands on the several thousand books published during the Castro regime which universities would have bought for whatever price he asked. Sanders's view was similar to mine: universities were established by Yankee imperial power and therefore there to be exploited. "Get their budget, Richard," was his simple advice.

As I did, Sanders drew on his experience as a second-hand bookseller to develop strong radical views. We knew that the ecological and rural world we lived in was declining. We suspected that Walt Disney would be turning in his grave if he knew how his empire was increasingly becoming a means of propaganda for multinationals. The latest addition to Florida's Disney World were displays showing the ecological benefits of underwater oil exploration. Yet Disney World had wiped out the natural habitat of the gopher turtle in Florida's precious swamplands. Sanders's backyard was a scrubland with intricate tunnels and lumps where he kept a sizeable colony of refugee turtles.

Near St Augustine was the St John's River. Here the American Fleet had been mothballed after the Second World War. Seized drug boats ranging from rafts to luxury yachts bobbed silently along the river bank. In a hut nearby lived Sanders's friend Baba, who celebrated my arrival with a roast alligator because several of his chickens had been disappearing. He gave me the skin as a present. I hung it up in Hay Castle and claimed it was the last crocodile shot in the River Wye.

Chapter Nine

The Swinging Seventies

April Ashley. April gets more beautiful as she grows older. She is now the most beautiful dowager duchess in San Diego.

"There's you, and there's Julie Christie."

I returned to New York with the alligator tucked safely under my arm to finish packing the half a million books from Stechert Hafner. Looking at them, I began to realize that in Hay-on-Wye we were not only competing with big city bookshops, but were now selling thousands of books unavailable anywhere else in Europe. America was to lead me to both opportunity and disaster, but at this time she was a rich foreign aunt whose pockets were full of sweeties.

Baltimore was my next destination, where Stanley Silverman of Silver Sales, a small, neat man in two-tone golfing shoes, had been an early pioneer of the porn industry. In the fifty years since the first prudish removal of pubic hairs from *Health and Efficiency* magazine, the sex industry had really taken off. "I was the first to go to Denmark," Stanley boasted. He had rushed to that porn dealers' Mecca because interstate regulations made it easier to import pornography than to move it around America. In the States, 'Danish bookshops' sell a few ordinary books as cover for the more absorbing enthusiasms of flagellants and sado-masochists. Stanley appeared unaware of the more sinister underlying issues of the porn trade. He offered me some non-pornographic books which he had taken against an $80,000 debt for more dubious material. "You can have them for $15,000, I only want to get rid of them." He showed more zest for packing the books into every inch of space than for the deal itself.

I learnt to my cost that handling books was not selling them. There were eight lorry-loads of academic books with trendy titles like

The Bibliography of Memory. Owning 2,000 copies of one book required a new approach to selling and I was unfamiliar with the remainders market. Jim was well suited to exploiting the wealthy academic market. He fed my over-enthusiasm by arguing that any book could be sold if the approach was right. "We should gather together every unsaleable history of England," he suggested, "and sell them as a collection of Comparative Historiography." I began to be lumbered with books which would stay in Hay for the next twelve years and, in some cases, forever.

Jim was becoming a major figure in the business and seemed capable of solving most problems. He moved into the Castle and, after selling my Rolls and keeping a considerable commission for himself, suggested I get a financial backer to help with my worsening situation. I employed Geoffrey Andrews, a Liverpool businessman who looked the business over and concluded that my cash flow was not as good as I believed. I saw two possible ways out of my predicament. The first was to improve my publicity; the second was to make one massive deal that would solve my problems at a stroke. This led me into unwise deals. I bought 1,000 copies of an out-of-date accountancy book and eighty tons of the *Initial Teaching Alphabet*, an anticipated educational breakthrough which ended up as a lorry-load of scrap.

More books arrived from the North of England where an enterprising waste-paper merchant had saved them from destruction by hosing down the top layer of books with water, but covering those underneath with a tarpaulin. I bought 2,000 books on Japanese flower-arranging which the market was unable to absorb, but which, I thought, had vast future potential. In spite of this unprofitable book-buying, I was still regarded as a tycoon and it even reached a stage when an authority on American millionaires intended to write about me. But my financial position was becoming increasingly desperate.

"I won't let you down," said Geoffrey, on agreeing to advance me the money to fly to Australia. During my impending bankrupcy, I would regard this remark as a milestone. On the way I stopped in New York, where Milton Epstein sold me his entire stock of remainders from The Ideal Book Company. But academic titles were no longer a gold-mine. Academics' reputations rested upon publication, and works of yesterday's vanity were pouring onto the second-hand market. Rather than being prestigious, reputation-boosting publications, easily recycled among the scores of universities, they were vastly overproduced and available to those in the trade for a few cents. It was hard for a bookseller who had known the under-supplied market of only ten years earlier. Britain was also beginning to feel the effects of the glut. Visitors to Hay were unimpressed by the relentless stream of academic output. "Oh dear," said a Swedish lady in my shop, "you have everything about Dylan Thomas but nothing *by* him."

While we were in New York, Eggy persuaded the bank to help us purchase a large property in the centre of Hay to solve our eternal problem of lack of space. Once an old workhouse, Cockcroft House was situated in a populous council estate. Nine rooms were knocked through to make an enormous theology department which we christened 'The World's Longest Bookshop'. It was a disastrous buy. Only a trickle of customers made their way to the shop, which was invisible from the main road, and its rambling rooms were hard to organize. But it attracted Ian Paisley, who visited us with two of his bodyguards. He was, like many politicians, an ardent second-hand book buyer. Michael Foot bought the Romantic poets and Denis Healey a copy of Charles Mackay's Victorian bestseller, *Memoirs of Extraordinary Popular Illusions*. Socialists are the more avaricious buyers, whereas Conservative politicians are inclined to pick fastidiously at nice antiquarian sets of Disraeli.

Ken Gjemre from Dallas, Texas, helped my finances momentarily by buying a large number of theological books. Ken pioneered the concept of chain second-hand and remainder bookshops. He had ten in the USA. The idea of such chains, which depend on local trade for both buying and selling, conflicts in principle with that of a Book Town like Hay, which draws customers from afar. Fanatical dealers and collectors are unlikely to travel to a chain bookshop. Like chain restaurants they are efficient, profitable but uninteresting to the genuine gourmet.

I flew to Dallas to see Ken. "I'm afraid I can't take you on the route John took," he said referring to the route followed by John F. Kennedy's car on the day of his assassination. The road now formed part of a one-way system. Dallas has two museums which collect books about Kennedy. One supports the conclusions of the Warren Commission and the other is dedicated to alternative theories alleging the involvement of the Mafia, Lyndon Johnson, Castro and others. The thirteen-volume report of the Warren Commission is the most valuable of all the Kennedy books. Another Kennedy book of great value is *PT101*, written by John's elder brother, who perished in the Pacific war. Ken's main store was impressive, with a vast array of stock which included magazines and records. "People don't read history in Dallas," he remarked while showing me round his large section devoted to the subject.

"Do you think you'll ever have more than ten bookshops?" I asked.

"My son John, who runs the Austin shop, won't be content with just ten. Besides, we really do need a couple more in Houston." Chain second-hand bookselling seemed easy talking to Ken.

When I returned to Hay there was a flickering increase of activity in Cockcroft House. Parts of the building were for rent. The son of a Conservative MP was installed selling shower curtains, and my sister Anne was selling Classical books. Greek and Roman literature was an area where few were publishing and the demand for second-hand books was strong. Elly Parker and her friend Neffie opened a café in one of the far rooms, where I gratefully ate and drank in lieu of rent.

I began to consider whether the answer to my worsening financial situation might be The Wales Tourist Board, whose budget to revive rural areas and stimulate business in Wales was burning a hole in their pocket. Since Frank Lewis had first introduced us, Mervyn Jones had sent an increasing stream of officials to see me. "Other places have hotels, scenery, monuments," he enthused. "Only Wales has a Town of Books." The public relations officer, Glyn Alban Roberts, knew exactly how the powerful bureaucracies in Cardiff operated. His talent for contacting journalists and mine for promoting the idea of a Town of Books seemed an ideal combination. Journalists from all over the world started to publicise Hay-on-Wye. 'Mid Wales town may become Las Vegas of the book world,' ran *The Western Mail*; 'Turning a Welsh valley into a utopia for bookworms,' wrote *The Times*. A piece in *The Philadelphia Inquirer* was headed 'Used Books Reign at Castle'. 'Thousands of visitors a year tour bookstores that were once cinemas or fire stations,' wrote Jason Marks in *The New York Times*. This produced a trickle of distinguished enquiries including one from the US Defence Secretary of State, Caspar Weinberger, which I was embarrassed to find, much later, in a neglected pile of old papers.

In 1976 it became clear that the 'Town of Books' could generate publicity from January, when ITN gave us a three-minute slot, through to December, when Annabel Olivier-Wright of The Central Office of Information spread the gospel of Hay as far as Mexico City. I began to worship the God of publicity, believing it could solve every problem. "There are two people in Wales: there's you, and there's Julie Christie," said a local.

I found myself acquiring a series of famous and eccentric friends. "I want to be Châtelaine of the Castle," announced Marianne Faithful.

When I knew her she was a cocktail-happy, middle-aged blonde with a raucous laugh like a female Master of the Hounds who sees a saboteur fall into a dung-filled ditch. To me she is still the aesthetic ideal I first saw in a glamour photograph, aged sixteen, before her relationship with Mick Jagger. In the bath I would often sing, in my out-of-tune baritone, "I beg your pardon, I never promised you a rose garden". It seemed to fit the story of my life.

In a rash moment I decided to marry for the second time, to a girl with black eyes and curved teeth with whom I had been besotted at Oxford. Her name was Victoria del Rio and she was eager to escape from a quiet life on the Canary Islands. It did not take me long to realize that I had made a terrible mistake. We had been married for twenty-four hours when I crept off, leaving her at Madrid airport.

I had had doubts before the wedding but greatly enjoyed talking to her cousin Pepe about a delicious banana that grows on lava in the Canary Islands. The exoticism was enticing. Although I had been obsessed by the vision of Vicky since my time at Oxford, we were different even in the nature of our rebelliousness. Vicky wanted to flout authority, whereas I did not think authority was worth flouting.

Vicky returned to Britain and tried to entice people to stay at Brynmelin. It became a centre for hippies, cannabis and the condemnation of the conventional world. Although she had been raised in elegant Madrid society, where her mother was a friend of Balenciaga, her closest affinities were now for the hippies' mystical philosophy and their dirty dog-blankets. Like many at this time, she believed the future lay with these people, a view I could never entirely reject. However, I found them an irritating distraction and refused any ideas of reconciliation with her. Dr Anderson was more specific. "It's drugs," he said, and Vicky departed for an expensive health clinic. I made no attempt to resuscitate the marriage and received divorce letters from her solicitors. Vicky was too aristocratic to consider his advice even momentarily, and her blasé admission in court that she liked smoking pot and the company of adulterous hippies prevented her winning a heavy settlement.

My aunt Viva's life was blossoming. At the age of seventy-seven she took a twenty-six year-old Maori lover called Tam. He was a charming boy with a talent for stealing her antiques. Not content with this exotic diversion, she then befriended the transsexual April Ashley, whose sex change had made world headlines. After a miserable early youth as a merchant seaman, April became a glamorous female celebrity. Slim and beautiful, she modelled bras on the sides of Paris buses better than any female. When Viva took me to meet her, April was running a restaurant, AD 8, in South Kensington. "Look at my poached eggs," she announced, proudly baring her beautiful, creamy-white breasts which nature had not given her. Urban life was beginning to bore her and she was tiring of inebriated customers trying to embrace her as they left the restaurant. She was looking for a rural retreat and Hay was perfect.

April's arrival caused a sensation. A coiffured beauty in white denim breezed into The Blue Boar. "Must have a slash," she announced and was followed into the Ladies by half a dozen astonished locals. April fell in love with Hay and decided to stay. I lent her a flat and she took a job caring for an old man, who infuriated his family by bequeathing her his house and money. In the 1970s April helped give Hay its flamboyant reputation, but she could also communicate with the locals with extraordinary sensitivity and built up a large following. She caused a scandal by partially accepting the sexual advances of a sixteen year-old schoolboy, his promise to perform being met by raucous laughter from the friends who were egging him on. The headmaster enlisted me as his chief ally in the rescue mission. It was all harmless fun. From her house in Bear Street, April would spit onto the National Westminster Bank, a Georgian mansion several feet below. But the bank's manager had the final say. She was living off rapidly diminishing capital and eventually moved to San Diego to work for Greenpeace. Later she telephoned me after she had been sacked for allegedly touching a colleague in hot-pants. "I don't do that sort of thing, darling," she said – my last and fondest memory of her.

Hay was becoming a fashionable destination for Londoners. The Wales Tourist Board thought it might become as famous as Portmeirion had been in the thirties, when it was the haunt of Bertrand Russell and other celebrities. Its creator, the architect Clough Williams Ellis, an old man of eighty in yellow socks, came to have lunch with me at Mrs Hudson's café in Castle Street. I felt great respect for one who had so successfully utilised the remote beauty of Wales. He appreciated the idea of a Town of Books and thought I might be able to turn Hay into the country's tourist capital.

Following the eighteenth-century tradition of small-scale operas in private houses, Hugh Vickers staged a production of *La Serva Padrona* at Brynmelin. Amyas Martelli painted a richly-coloured set and we raked the audience up in tiers using old book pallets. Praise was unanimous and the soprano Yvonne Kenny, having resisted a badly-staged seduction by Vicky's brother in the middle of the night, went on to sing lead rôles at the Sydney Opera House. There was a fourth, free performance for my workforce, who consumed barrels of beer instead of champagne and were quite unfazed by the Italian dialogue.

In the eyes of Mrs Dearden and the ladies of the town who prepared the dainty opera food I had an unjustified reputation for artistic sophistication. This was largely thanks to Hugh, but despite being appointed head of Decca Records' classical music department, my old friend was shortly to drown in a sea of alcohol. He staged another opera for the Spanish Ambassador in Belgrave Square, but the event lost enormous sums of money and reduced the audience to shivering misery in an inadequate, rain-soaked marquee. "However stupid a thing one does," he told me afterwards, "there's always someone who will do something even more stupid."

"Get yourself a good accountant," was the advice of the Chairman of The Wales Tourist Board when he heard that one of my cheques had been returned.

"You must marry a girl from central Europe, preferably a Czech," said Frank, who was more anarchic. "Then you can have lots of little bouncers!"

Geoffrey and Jim both believed that I would sooner or later become financially dependent on one of them. Geoffrey had put up money which I had naïvely accepted without checking the attached conditions. When he found an opportune moment to ask for fifty per cent of the equity, he made the mistake of ignoring Jim, whom he saw merely as an altruist intent on creating a truly great bookshop. But Jim's altruism was calculated. "I could kill that man," he said when he heard Geoffrey's proposal. I could no longer afford to hire Geoffrey and did not agree to his terms. "You'll find it terribly hard to run your business yourself," he remarked in my final moments with him.

Jim suggested that I refinance myself by selling him the Castle for a fairly low sum. After that, the relationship between us was less cordial. I had made the mistake of trusting Jim Robson completely. Returning to the Castle from the pub one night, I paused to look up at the stars and heard voices in the courtyard. Jim was loading a van that I had sold to him. I never knew what was in it, but he had access to all the most valuable books in the business, including my father's treasured copy of

Orme's *Oriental Fieldsports*. I tried to stop him but he sped off, leaving me lying in the road with smashed spectacles and a mouthful of dirt. I informed the police but it was a lost cause. Jim fled to Ireland, where he was virtually invulnerable. Several months later, I heard that he had bought a massive house on the west coast, and he would even send me the occasional customer. Initially I felt very bitter about his disappearance but, in retrospect, I think it was fortunate that I did not have a financial or emotional partner in my youth. Had I done so, I might have been urged to take a very different path.

Jim left because he believed I was doomed. After he disappeared my position was indeed desperate. I suffered a mass exodus of staff, including my beloved and indispensable secretary Julia. Eggy resigned his directorship in a fury over Jim's mismanagement of the business and even Norman began to realize he would be far better paid as a lorry driver. Cotters stayed faithful but wanted an essentially isolated existence. However, I was distracted from these bitter events by a scheme looming on the horizon.

"Hay-on-Wye has attracted more publicity than any other place in Wales," Glyn Alban Roberts told me over lunch in Penarth. In 1976 the town would receive £50,000 to celebrate the bicentenary of American Independence. The Tourist Board and I were united behind the project. They wanted camera-carrying American tourists and international publicity, while I saw America as the best source for books. My thoughts went even further. If I could arrange a huge influx of cheap books they might encourage a re-evaluation of American culture. We would do with American books what Japanese prints had done for Oriental culture when they first arrived in Europe as the humble wrapping for china.

My metamorphosis from an eccentric bookdealer with questionable financial and sexual habits into the official Welsh venue for the celebration of American Independence was due to Glyn's talent. In the process, he suffered a lot. "Who is that dreadful little man?" hissed Marianne, who felt anyone involved with the press was an abomination. Glyn could not be diverted; his greatest triumph was enticing the American Ambassador, Anne Armstrong, to visit Hay. She was a rising star in the Republican party and was tipped as a future presidential candidate.

The preparations were fraught. We were to open an American bookshop which would sell 80,000 books either published in America or on American themes. Finding, sorting and shelving the books had to be undertaken in a terrifyingly short space of time. We made a list of the books on offer:

> **The Establishment** – Presidents, Ambassadors, Generals and millionaires: an objective survey in over a thousand books.
>
> **Crime, the Detective Novel and Prohibition**
>
> **Machismo, the American Male** – Tarzan, Ernest Hemingway, Shark Fishing in Florida, Canada Club advertisements and beer mats.
>
> **Junior America** – Little Lord Fauntleroy, Huckleberry Finn and Pollyanna.
>
> **The American at War** – Book Bargain Emporium: 10,000 books at three for a dollar.
>
> **'They called them Yanks, M'lud'** – books written about America by Englishmen.
>
> **Spaniard bashing and other bashing** – a great theme of Anglo-American history: Sir Francis Drake, the Mexican Wars, West Side Story, the Bay of Pigs and Vietnam.

The Wales Tourist Board launched the event with a press conference. The Ambassador arrived in a magnificent pale pink suit surrounded by Secret Service men and followed by her deferential billionaire husband. The entourage drove slowly through Hay in a sleek black line of limousines, into which a few Tourist Board officials had managed to squeeze themselves.

They stopped outside Cockcroft House and I escorted Anne through the winding corridors on a tour of 100,000 American books. I now realize that they were not the sort that would particularly inspire cultural co-operation. Our main display was made from chipboard covered by torn black hessian which had seen better days in a 'Decline of the Country House' exhibition at the Victoria and Albert Museum. But the visit went well and one of the Ambassador's aides even managed to buy a cookery book.

Bill Dutton had sent his daughter Doris and her friend Claudia over from California to help prepare eighteenth-century costumes. They wore them with pride but had a hard job injecting our sleepy rural town with the sophistication which ambassadorial visits require. Yvonne Kenny sang a superb rendition of American songs and the party clambered up the steep stone steps to the Castle for tea and Welsh cakes. Slumped in the kitchen, Frank had been consuming considerable amounts of alcohol in anticipation of the Ambassador's visit. He entered the drawing room and was given a cup of tea which slopped messily around in the saucer. Glyn saw the danger and moved diplomatically between him and Anne Armstrong. "Get out of the way, you little bastard," Frank snarled at Glyn. We drank our tea quickly and hastened on with the afternoon.

The celebrations were a far cry from the ordinary task of bookselling. With the problems of the business pressing in from all directions, it was a form of torture for me to have to spend a whole morning in Llandaff Cathedral while the Chairman of the Wales Tourist Board read a lesson celebrating our common Christian heritage. This was the kind of occupation only the bureaucrats had time for. They said that tourism was an 'industry', but what other industry would have spent thousands on an unnecessary church service? The American celebrations taught me that the priorities of the Wales Tourist Board were very different from my own and my belief in their policies began to wane.

Chapter Ten

I am the King

Nervous preparation for the coronation with moral support from Reg Clarke.

"Hay is an integral part of the United Kingdom."

1975, the four-hundredth anniversary of the English invasion, was a sacred year in the history of Ireland. As a suitable commemorative gesture I considered inviting the IRA to occupy Hay Castle. For obvious reasons I demurred; such an action would have put me directly in the tradition of Sir Roger Casement, who was executed for treason after he tried to enlist the Germans in support of the Easter Rising in 1916. But the idea stayed in my mind and was perhaps responsible for a bold declaration I made to a journalist from *The Sunday Mirror* in The Wheatsheaf:

"Hay is going independent of Britain!"

"Do the people of Hay support you?" he said, his nostrils quivering.

"Yes," I replied, "they're all for it." I had only thought of the idea five minutes before.

"We'll bring down a photographer then."

One duly arrived and suggested that some revolutionaries pose in front of the Castle. A flag was made and twelve of my staff posed in a howling blizzard in the town square. Credibility was established through *The Sunday Mirror*'s prominent article and photograph. Almost immediately newspapers and TV stations started telephoning from all over the British Isles to find out what was happening.

We decided to declare our independence on 1st April 1977. Having reached this momentous decision I gave a dinner party at the Castle to make plans and generate ideas. It was suggested that the boundaries of the new State should be the old Castle territory. Towards the end of the meal, in drunken high spirits, we began filling aluminium cigar tubes with matches in order to fire missiles of wet banana onto the far end of the table. At the precise moment when a splatter of banana finally hit its target, Major Bill Beere rose and exclaimed, "I've got it! If we're going independent, you must be King!" I would be 'Richard Coeur du Livre', the monarch with more pages than most.

A political philosophy was needed but this did not present much of a problem. My Royal Manifesto stated that the highest civilizations the world has ever seen were the small city states of Renaissance Italy and fifth-century Greece, where decisions had been dominated by human knowledge rather than bureaucratic control. Hay-on-Wye was declaring independence from the bureaucratic control of Central Government.

My Cabinet was picked in five minutes in the pub. Most were wearing jeans and there was a high proportion of lorry drivers. The advantage of Hay's small population of 1,500 was that I could give everyone a top government post. Mackendrick, a Scottish stone-mason, was appointed Minister for Scottish Affairs on account of his accent. The Welsh Office was occupied by a vaguely nationalist telephone engineer. There was a unanimous veto on having a Minister of Arts for fear of encouraging ponces. Norman Radcliffe had had so much to drink he could not remember whether he was supposed to be Prime Minister or Minister of Defence. "Just like real government," someone remarked. The Minister for Social Security was well qualified, having been on the dole for six years. My closest remaining minister after twenty years is Gerry Taylor, who sees his own small village of Winforton as a frontier outpost of the Kingdom of Hay. When the bell rang for last orders we had all cheerfully agreed to bear the heavy load of responsibility placed upon us.

Hay-on-Wye had to have a protected economy. Revolutionary theories were eagerly put into practice. Girls with large bosoms were procured. 'Balls to Walls. Eat Hay National Ice Cream' was emblazoned across specially designed tee-shirts in the house style of a famous ice-cream maker. The inevitable wobbles stimulated the kind of pub humour around which Home Rule for Hay was built. 'Get Laid Lyons Maid,' said another. The message was clear: cheap, mass-produced ice-cream was imported to the detriment of local varieties. Boxes of matches were distributed called 'Hay-on-Wye's Glory – Plyant & Gay', provoking a solicitor's letter from Bryant & May Ltd.

I believed I was representing the frustrations and bitterness of people who objected to the destruction of a 1,000 year-old tradition of craft and agriculture by government-backed industrial food. Our bread campaign was waged around the slogan 'Father Died of Mother's Pride'. Factory-produced bread turns to slime in water and allegedly causes colonic cancer: 'There's no dough in the bank and little in the bread, so why not create fifty jobs in a Hay bakery?'

More difficult than a founding political philosophy were the practical measures needed to implement it. I naïvely believed the best advances could be made by writing. I had just completed *The Country Life Book of Book Collecting* and used the royalties to publish a booklet called *Independence for Hay*. On the cover was my rotund gardener, Charlie, holding a broom behind his head, sleeves rolled to the elbow, ready for action. The last page was a full-length photograph of April Ashley captioned 'If I can change, why can't Hay?'

Jokes and puns flowed. The booklet was full of them, some ingenious, some excruciating. Writing it occupied most of the time leading up to Independence Day. Its main points were:

Democracy does not exist; it has been strangled by bureaucracy. I criticised decisions the Council were making locally and discussed the typical problems of a declining rural area. In the last fourteen years the town had seen the closure of grocers, electricians, clothiers, a cobbler and the gas works. The loss of the railway serving the town and the worsening public transport system means that it now takes a Hay resident longer to travel the fifty miles from Hay to Gloucester than the two hundred miles from Gloucester to Scotland.

Everything superior is made locally; everything inferior is imported. The Hay sausage, Clyro Court marmalade and the Reverend Kilvert's chutney must be offered to the visitor instead of industrially produced food. People will not come to Hay for what they can obtain elsewhere. The new kingdom of Hay must be famous for the uniqueness of its products.

The decline of rural areas is not inevitable if we take our destiny into our own hands. The resources of the town and surrounding countryside must be developed for the benefit of local people. Tourists coming from all over the world to buy books should also be able to buy artefacts produced by skilled local craftsmen instead of cheap, factory-made souvenirs.

The booklet was at least one practical manifestation of Home Rule, although its pub humour has not stood the test of time. But should members of the Establishment regard our humour as indefensibly scabrous, in our defence I can point to a list of jokes circulated by the County Council, of which the following is an example:

"What was the Rear-Admiral's vice?"

"The Vice-Admiral's rear."

Because the Council routinely took such bad decisions, we felt random chance would better assist us. We made a giant Decision-Maker, a white, green and black spinning wheel that stopped at the pull of a lever: *Have a Drink – Try Bribery – Spin Again – Appoint a New Committee – Get a Rural Development Grant – Forget It – Do it Yourself – Defer to Next Session.*

Whatever the drunken merriment at the Castle, ahead of me lay reality. I had to arouse the enthusiasm of a largely sober and suspicious populace, few of whom were prepared to participate. "Come on Richard, admit it's a cheap joke," said a Powys County Councillor. I invited the whole town to a reception at the Castle but it proved fruitless; if I wanted to get anything done I would have to behave like a real king and be autocratic.

As it happened, I received the greatest assistance from those who least wished to give it. One day a notice was pinned up outside the Hay Council offices: 'The Hay Town Council unanimously wish to make it clear that they have never, in any way, been associated with Mr Richard Booth's U.D.I. proposals, neither have they any intention of doing so in the future. *M.A. MORGAN, Clerk to the Council.*'

The Chief Executive of Brecknock Borough Council declared indignantly, 'It is perfectly obvious that Hay is an integral part of Brecknock Borough under the Local Government Act of 1972. No changes can be made except through Parliament.'

Such po-faced denunciations were observed with the utmost glee by my small band of supporters. It was the opponents of Home Rule who gave it the greatest credibility. Militants even considered that their loyalty to the United Kingdom required breaking a few of the Castle windows. 'Sir,' wrote Doreen Gibbons to the local newspaper –

> Hats off to the gentlemen from Tredegar House, Hay-on-Wye who had the guts to stand up and be counted against Richard Booth's silly nonsense. Are the people of Hay going to let this come to pass?
>
> Who is going to man the Border Pass and pay the wages? Where is Hay going to grow all its food when the fields are not in his so-called kingdom? Import it, I suppose, like his books.
>
> We were pleased to learn that Hay Town Council has refused to support him. It seems he can't fool it. It seems the April Fool had backfired this time. Hay is part of Wales and always will be. We don't want people who were not born here to come and tell us what to do.

'Storm Clouds of Belfast loom over Hay,' wrote *The Daily Mail*.

Other headlines followed: 'Will Hay fall for King Richard?'; 'Book-shop King plans his own Free State'; 'Welsh Book King Seeks a Real Throne'; 'Freedom Fighters liberate Chutney Town'. All in all it was not difficult to convey that there was a genuine border dispute and that Hay-on-Wye was well on the way to becoming a small independent state between England and Wales. The reaction to Independence showed the high level of media credibility in rural areas. Orson Welles's famous radio broadcast once convinced millions that aliens had actually landed; I think I probably achieved similar credibility in rural Wales. I could see how easy it was for the media and politicians to blind people to both logic and reality.

'Town in Wales May Try to Form Own Kingdom,' reported *The Sunday Star* in Peekskill, New York State. With worldwide publicity, curious, amusing facts began to emerge. We heard that the people of Enkeldoorn, a tiny town near Bulawayo, Rhodesia, had decided to issue a Declaration of Independence when Ian Smith had declared Rhodesia independent of Britain. Immediately we rang the Enkeldoorn Hotel, only to find the barman too drunk to articulate the objectives of his Home Rule movement. Nevertheless it was decided to preserve the telephone on which the call was made for a future National Museum of Hay. (Sadly, the museum never materialized, though I did begin work on the town's historical greatness, from the Battle of Haystings to Haybraham Lincoln, and I still have the library collected, including Huxley's *Antic Hay*, *The Hay System Cook Book* and Noel Coward's *Hay Fever*.)

I was contacted by Christopher Martin of the Micropatrology Society in St. Louis, Missouri. He had tabulated the 287 recorded attempts to establish small nations and introduced some of them in a speech in The Wheatsheaf. The Principality of Sealand is an old concrete and steel fort off Harwich. The Republic of New Atlantis, a marine-biology raft operated by Ernest Hemingway's brother somewhere in the Caribbean, issued its own stamps and coins. Archzibland is a beleaguered holiday camp surrounded by Israel. We received a letter from the Free Independent Republic of Frestonia in London, 'a nation of about eight acres, three rather slummy streets and two communal gardens', which was fighting the Greater London Council's proposed demolition of their homes.

Early on the morning of Independence Day a small motor cavalcade came to collect me from Brynmelin and escort me into Hay. Two moped outriders flanked the car, leathers flapping in the wind. The sky looked thunderous and a breeze caused roadside daffodils to bob their heads in reverence. Overnight, windows had been daubed with anti-Booth slogans but most Hay citizens were quietly shopping and ignoring the impending events. My wonderful girlfriend Annabel Olivia Wright bravely paraded around the town in black tights as my Queen. She faced the fury of a few local inhabitants, who met this affront to the town's dignity with pinched mouths and waving fists. Lord Ivor Windsor gave me a fourteen-inch Mexican cigar for which I was extremely grateful as I needed the nicotine to calm my nerves. Later he suffered the ignominy of a journalist asking how much his title had cost.

We proceeded to the river, where Major Bill Beere (subsequently honoured with the rank of Field Marshal) and Auten Wilkes of the Hay Navy were waiting in a gun boat. This was a twelve-foot rowing dinghy with a long piece of drain-pipe in which gunpowder was ignited in simulation of a six-pounder. As the start of the new era was signalled, they drifted out of control into the middle of the river, which is fortunately only four feet deep. After the slow unfurling of the green and white Hay flag with its red heraldic lion, the Cabinet and Ambassadors lined up in front of the Castle for speeches. Beneath them, in the market square, the local population was outnumbered by scurrying journalists and cameramen. The Cabinet's only role as a body was to be photographed. Every Minister was wearing a grubby sweater and crumpled work clothes apart from Gerry Taylor, whose white whiskers made him look like a Regency gentleman from a BBC drama, and April, dressed in a black fedora and a long skirt.

Drawing heavily on my cigar, I addressed my subjects:

"Hay-on-Wye is the first town in the British Isles which has expressed its intention of declaring independence from the bureaucratic control of Central Government. The extraordinary talents of the people of Hay have enabled them to take steps which no other town in the world has achieved..."

The proclamation of Home Rule was followed by the Hay National Anthem, *Bridge over the River Wye*, a Mike Oldfield remix by Les Penning. "It's a bad version of Colonel Bogey," said a girlfriend. My honoured guest Captain Sean Feehan, appointed Irish Ambassador, gave a rousing speech and persuaded the wife of the local cowherd to appear in a skin-tight fawn suit as Lady Godiva.

After the speeches I happily responded to journalists' questions.

"Are you serious?" I was asked.

"Of course not," I replied defiantly, "but it's more serious than real politics."

From over the Castle wall came thick smoke and the smell of burning. John Napper's valiant but doomed attempt to spit-roast an entire ox made us aware of skills from the past lost in the curriculum of modern education. The wind changed direction and blew the flames about in a fearsome manner, leaving him with singed eyebrows and almost blind. Despite a fourteen hour roasting, the heat had only penetrated a few inches. By the end of the day the half-raw ox was being urinated upon by small boys perched on the Castle wall.

Harry Bryant, a mine-owner in Rhodesia and South Africa, arrived wearing an enormous rawhide colonial hat. He introduced himself as the Enkledoorn Ambassador. In fact he was the owner of a manor near Crickhowell and an active supporter of Home Rule. The Rhodesian Commander in Chief was named Walls, which naturally interrupted the circulation of our 'Balls to Walls' tee-shirts. Members of Dad's Army from New Zealand helped themselves to mugs of cider from a barrel. Prince Leonard of Hutt River, a 12,000 acre independent kingdom in a remote part of Australia, sent his ambassador to assess me and issue me with a passport. He was regarded with the same trepidation by the authorities as I was and a Japanese television crew had once been forbidden to film him. Once power was bestowed by media exposure one was treated with extreme caution by the authorities, who are no doubt concerned that fantasy might become reality.

Somehow I found time to knight two small boys, one being the son of my friend Jeremy Sandford and the other a member of the Heber Percy family. As usual my organization let me down and I did not even have a title scroll to give them. April Ashley was proclaimed Duchess of Offa's Dyke. I once referred to her title during an interview on Canadian radio but was immediately cut off; to Canadians, Offa's Dyke was not a Mercian earthwork on the Welsh-English border but slang meaning an outrageous lesbian. Many years and several hundred titles later, interest was shown in publishing a Hay edition of *Debrett's Peerage*. Sadly, all records are lost. Monarchy, to me, was anarchy, but somehow it was to last twenty years. I am still referred to as 'the King' by a garage owner in the parish of Llanigon. He is an Ayatollah and his chief mechanic a Duke.

In the evening we gave vent to our elation by playing loud music. The distinguished Breton poet Youenn Gwernig played the guitar but failed to compete with the general noise. I tried to give a radio interview in the midst of it all. At the end of the day a ceremonial dinner took place at John's Steak Bar during which time Air Chief Marshal Griffiths looped the loop over Hay and nearly crashed. "Fly Hay State Airlines," announced a pretty girl. "Bring goggles and a scarf." A small Hay airline did seem practical, but the idea was suffocated by the tightening grip of financial problems. The Hay Treasury was painfully empty. I lacked the body of volunteers so vital to any political party; most of those involved in Hay's Independence were on my payroll.

My new manager John Rogers started work in these weird circumstances. He was shepherded into John's Steak Bar to find us all riotously celebrating Home Rule. I think he was baffled as to why the staff of a semi-bankrupt business was enjoying such celebration and international publicity.

Independence attracted thousands of pounds' worth of free publicity, though the news was about the eccentric Book King rather than my heartfelt beliefs. For my ignorance I am now grateful because had I concentrated on the serious issues I could well have seen a collapse in publicity. "You'll never keep it going," people said to me, but I disagreed. Independence for Hay was something I had just begun learning about; soon I would be able to take considerable steps forward.

Independence for HAY

30p inside Hay
35p outside Hay

The first booklet

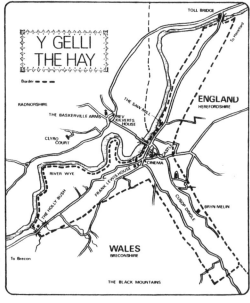

The ancient lands of the Castle were charted as the New Hay Territory.

Declaring Independence –
the press conference

The new King relaxing
in front of his Castle
with two young admirers.

Hay Money: edible rice-paper currency

The Hay international passport

Icons of Independence

Independence car-sticker

Royal notepaper

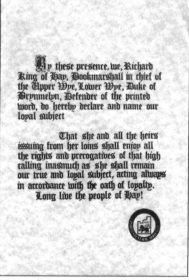

By these presence, we, Richard King of Hay, Bookmarshall in chief of the Upper Wye, Lower Wye, Duke of Brynmelyn, Defender of the printed word, do hereby declare and name our loyal subject

That she and all the heirs issuing from her loins shall enjoy all the rights and prerogatives of that high calling inasmuch as she shall remain our true and loyal subject, acting always in accordance with the oath of loyalty. Long live the people of Hay!

Title scroll

John Napper, Lady Caroline Windsor (left), Gerry Taylor, and the raw ox. The wind changed direction and blew the flames about in a fearsome manner, leaving John with singed eyebrows and almost blind.

We proceeded to the river where Major Bill Beere (subsequently honoured with the rank of Field Marshal) and Austin Wilkes of the Hay Navy were waiting in a gun boat.

Hugh Vickers (left); Reg Clarke (right) was the real genius behind Home Rule.

Home Rule was boosted by a variety of stunts and the genuine anger of the population.

Annabel Olivier-Wright, a brilliant film-producer from the Central Office of Information – she spread my name all over the world.

Glyn Alban Roberts likewise spread my name all over the world via the Wales Tourist Board. I loved and respected them both more than their organizations.

The Bishop of Southwell, Mrs Hudson (the owner of the last traditional café in Hay), Lord Windsor, myself and Patricia Carlton-Scott.

The Hay Herald

Incorporating

(The Independence Times Literary Supplement)

Autumn Issue 1978   5c Pence

HAY QUITS EEC

POWYS COUNCIL BORROWS DECISION MAKER

COMMUNITY THREATENED

THOUSANDS OF HAY CITIZENS WEPT for joy last night when they learnt that for them the oppressive reign of Europe's bureaucracy was finally over. Hay had rejected the Common Market. The official decision to withdraw was made in accordance with the outcome of the Referendum held to mark the third anniversary of the disastrous British Referendum on the European Economic Community.

EXCLUSIVE SECRET DIRECTIVES OF BRITISH GOVERNMENT REVEALED

SCOOP!

Who thinks ducks eggs are more important
Find out in King Richard's (second) exclusive
than the Magna Carta?
with himself: page 8

The decision maker – Vi Jenkins is
always very kind about the stupid
decisions of Richard Booth.

The Hay Herald, *our National Newspaper. Interesting
arguments are not necessarily effective arguments.*

*'Bring back horses.' A protected economy
is the easiest route to creating 500,000
jobs and ultimately one to make me a
friend of Arthur Scargill.*

Mervyn Jones, Chairman of the Wales Tourist Board, the man whose generous hand I bit.

Welsh cartoon by Elwyn Ioan for Lol *magazine. Frustrated hatred of the official was everywhere in Wales.*

The First Hay Independence Anniversary, 1978. Not even the relentless downpour could dampen the fervour of the crowd inspired by twelve months of liberty and several barrels of free ale…

Chapter Eleven

The Worm that Turned

Some beautiful Gujaratis from Leicester celebrating the first Hay Independence Anniversary with myself, Dr Rosenberg and John Napper.

"Mischievous and doomed to failure."

"I have interviewed John Kennedy and the King of Saudi Arabia, but you are the most extraordinary man I have ever interviewed," said Rose Kaneatarka from Yokohama.

Nobody had seen more of the modern world than my friend Rose, who laughingly called herself 'Tokyo Rose' after the Second World War propagandist. She flew all over the world, receiving free tickets from Pan Am Airlines, and presented Japan's longest-running TV programme. I see Japan more as a country where the traditional economy has been protected than as the technological salvation of the world. They have, at least, restricted the importation of American rice. As my father-in-law so wisely pointed out to me, "Britain's problems began with the abolition of the Corn Laws."

As a famous television personality in a shimmering silk dress, Rose was here to make a programme about the Kingdom of Hay-on-Wye. Surrounded by tubby little officials from the Tourist Board, here was a person whose importance justified her existence; every expensive meal and gift bought for her was worth a thousand times more in publicity value.

In the film I walked across the hills, pointing out the boundaries of the Kingdom of Hay-on-Wye. We returned across a field of staring sheep and into the garden which was a forest of pink and white rhododendrons. At Brynmelin's semi-circular kissing gate I stooped to give her a quick kiss on the cheek. Even some book-dealers playing a game of tennis on the lawn were of interest to the camera crew. The short ceremony in which I proclaimed Rose Duchess opened the floodgates to Japanese visitors eager to buy titles in the new Kingdom of Hay. Generally they settled for a knighthood but Dukedoms and Earldoms certainly crept in. When she had finished shooting the film Rose returned to Hay to stay with me. I made the mistake of taking her for a long ride in the hills. A small, delicate lady, she was terrified and miserable on a horse. Although she visited Britain regularly, Rose mostly circulated in other parts of the world, filming, for example, the excavation of a sunken Japanese submarine with twenty-five officers still preserved inside, at Truk naval base. I am sure that being a pioneer of international life was a hard and lonely existence. All I could do was to admire her from a distance.

In 1979 Rose sent me a ticket to Japan for the twenty-fifth anniversary of her programme. I stayed at the New Otani hotel along with thousands of optimistic foreign businessmen. Walking down the street, all I could see were the round, black heads of hundreds of Japanese. I was a clumsy, over-sized European. The universities were impossible to approach directly. Waseda's 450,000 students made it the largest in the world. I walked around Jimbocho, the second-hand book area, and Maruzen, the largest bookshop, but immediately got lost in the Golf Club department. At night, lorries full of shouting youths with white headbands drove through the streets. The followers of Mishima wanted to return to a traditional Japan, as I wanted to return to a traditional Britain. Mishima was a best-selling homosexual author who, as a protest against Japan's changing values, had committed hara-kiri on a balcony in full view of a regiment of Army Cadets by drawing a knife across his stomach.

I went to the same bar in Shinjuku five nights in a row. In the end I broke the ice and had a massage. I lay, face down, on a wooden bench while someone therapeutically walked up and down my back.

On my return April Ashley gave a fashion show, twirling about in some of the fifty kimonos I had brought back with me to sell. But behind the frivolities John Rogers was working on identifying the problems in the business. In short, I was overstocked and overstaffed. "Don't shoot till you see the whites of their eyes," he growled, and urged me to stop buying in order to create some liquidity. This I have always found difficult. New stock stimulates the selling of old; a customer is more likely to visit regularly if he thinks there is a constant flow of books. It is often difficult to assess second-hand books and I was always prepared to take risks, even if it meant adding to my debts. Indeed, the popularity of Hay was largely due to my reputation for constant and irresponsible buying. As the ex-head of the Rhodesian Booksellers Association, John was fairly contemptuous both of the quality of our customers and the quality of our stock. "The unspeakable in search of the unreadable," was his opinion of the crowds searching for bargains in the Cinema. When he joined the company he presented me with a finely-bound reprint in a cardboard box about a classic journey across Rhodesia in an ox cart. This, I suppose, represented the degree of his concession to the second-hand book business.

"John Rogers doesn't understand that he's not still in Rhodesia," complained Alex Williams, a local artist who was making a most successful business out of selling prints. In frustrated misery, Rogers puffed through several packets of cigarettes a day and watched as the last few pounds of liquid capital drained away.

"You should have pretty girls selling books," he advised. Sex was perhaps one method of stimulating an erratic second-hand market to more lavish spending, but I don't think he realized that the experienced dealer and fanatical collector are largely immune to the effects of promotion. "You don't need Tourist Board girls in situations like this," he said referring to my use of Patricia Carlton Scott whose public relations skills were increasing our trade and media exposure. But again I disagree: the relationship between bookselling and tourism is vital.

I also employed a defrocked bishop to give me a wholesome image, hoping that it would lead to good libraries. Gordon Savage was the young and brilliant Bishop of Southwell until he became victim of the tabloids. He was reported basking on the beaches of Spain with a topless dancer who ran a poodle parlour. When he left the clergy, he sold me his magnificent collection of books on the Liturgy and I offered him a job. During his period in office I presented a potted plant to the Lord Mayor of Cardiff and received a wooden shield of the city in return; these were niceties I could never have dreamt up myself. However, all my staff had to undertake the essential manual work of sorting, shelving and loading books. Gordon was a little too old and frail for this and he went to work for a charity.

"You must produce a brochure," stated Emyr Griffiths, the pleasant Marketing Manager of the Wales Tourist Board. "We'll pay half the cost and you can raise the rest from local organizations." As I frequently worked a fourteen-hour day just looking for books it was a lost cause. I neglected to discuss shared advertising costs with suspicious Welsh landladies. I was growing disillusioned with an organization that would commission expensive market research to see whether housewives would choose a Welsh holiday if given the chance to win a free fitted kitchen. The Tourist Board was plainly incapable of handling the responsibility placed on its shoulders. It could not revive rural Wales and did not have the integrity to tell the government. It was increasingly prepared to enjoy the enormous publicity I was generating but increasingly failed to consider the needs of my business in return. The final straw came when the Marquis of Anglesey's house was bought by the National Trust and no-one from the Board even thought to tell me that his library was available.

This was a period of dire financial crisis. I juggled bills and stalled creditors. John Rogers could not match income to expenditure and left the business after a few months. I went through four managers in little over a year. Rogers was followed by Jack Duncan, a hard-drinking television producer who regularly had three pints at lunch time and, more disastrously, subjected my unreceptive staff to a stream of memos. My secretary Margaret replaced him but claimed I was "being bled dry by a load of parasitic women". I had offered accommodation at Brynmelin to three ladies – a witty journalist, a Danish-speaking nurse and a dreamy Buddhist traveller with whom I had a two-year affair. They loved the herbs and vegetables that grew in abundance but Charlie, my gardener, was not susceptible to their charm and saw them as a threat to his fruit and vegetable empire. Cathy, his wife, was my housekeeper. I was part of their world and all intruders were unwelcome. But the ladies were my friends and I was glad to escape from the bachelor society of farm labourers which had been my first experience of Hay.

Most working days now involved 'blood runs' in which either Andy Cooke, or Ron Smart sped to Lloyds Bank in Abergavenny to stop cheques from bouncing. But it never occurred to me to give up. Something would happen.

Because the location of Cockcroft House was so bad I rented a large central building in Lion Street which had been a general merchant's store. There were painted Victorian tiles with sheep, cows and pigs on the front. 'The Limited' was to become my flagship. Opposite was a large building known as 'the triangle block' which had been bought by Paul Minet in 1970 and from where he ran coaches to and from his London bookshop in Piccadilly. This idea had the potential to revolutionize Hay but he did not get enough local support. Suavely dressed in a silk cravat, Paul was the balding son of a distinguished Huguenot family and was the first big and friendly London investor to come to Hay. Although he certainly had the confidence of his customers, running bookshops in two major locations is very difficult. Some time later Hay Paul founded *The Royalty Digest* magazine, which has an interesting dual rôle, containing scholarly articles about central European monarchies and the fall of the Tsars, whilst also serving as his catalogue. His *Royalty Digest* congresses are regularly sold out. I see him as a pioneer in the successful linking of books and tourism.

'King Richard says: "Put your money where your mouth is!" ' Italian TV loved the edible paper currency I invented for my kingdom. It was, in truth, the most buoyant currency in the world. I produced Hay stamps, my head depicted in a pastiche of the Queen's. They could be stuck on an envelope next to those of the Royal Mail. Ralph Spencer, a marine engineer on an oil tanker renowned for drinking bottles of Scotch through the optic, even claimed that he had entered Saudi Arabia on a Hay passport.

I needed some Crown Jewels. I was fortunate enough to have a superb Equerry, Reg Clarke, who looked something between an advertisement for digestive tablets and a prize choir boy. An expert designer, he was set to work on my Crown. Finding a small poodle squashed on the road, he extracted a red jewel from its collar to make a sparkling centrepiece. For the Royal Orb, a lavatory ballcock was studded with gems in the shape of an 'H'. A piece of copper piping from the methane industry was turned into the Royal Sceptre. At one end there is a hand with two fingers extended in a 'V' sign, which also proved useful for holding my cigar. My Royal regalia was perfect for state occasions and appeared on hundreds of television programmes. They even acquired a romantic history after they were stolen by hippies. The Crown was recovered from a muddy ditch nearby; although a little misshapen, it remains a vital symbol of Home Rule.

Reg went on to make me a magnificent patriotic machine. It is a bright green wooden box with a peep-hole cunningly placed at a height which makes respectful kneeling unavoidable. The subject kneels, puts ten pence in a slot and watches an inspiring scene pass before his eyes. While the National Anthem plays, the Hay flag waves and a portrait of me in ceremonial dress is illuminated; my eyes flash red and a troop of soldiers fire. A white flag emblazoned with the words 'Bureaucrats Beware!' shoots out from a revolving turntable.

The winter of 1977 was bitterly cold. One evening I stacked up the Castle's fireplace with a great tree trunk in the hope of finding warm embers there in the morning. In the night, I awoke to hear loud crackling noises. The night sky looked pale and strange. Reflected in the window I saw a glimmer of flame: the Castle was alight. The fire was leaping dramatically from the hearth of the first-floor study and into the second-floor bedroom, where I could see smoke drifting through the floorboards. Had I awoken ten minutes later it would already have filled the narrow back-staircase down which I escaped. The fire was roaring ferociously. I turned the extinguishers on the burning blaze. This was like putting a water pistol to the back burner of a jet engine. I gave up and walked onto the lawn to join a small crowd of interested onlookers. We waited anxiously for the Fire Brigade to arrive. The light from the fire lit up our faces and the sound of slates falling from the roof was like machine-gun fire. "Join the ranks of the homeless," remarked a hippy standing next to me.

In the morning, members of staff did a valiant job clearing up. Many of the books on the ground floor had been destroyed by thick soot. The oak-panelled drawing room on the first floor and the medieval beams were tragic losses. Through scorched rafters I could see the sky.

Frank crossed the market square and blinked up incredulously. The windows were smouldering black eye sockets and the lawn was a mass of debris. He saw an opportunity to impress some tourists. "You see that castle?" he said, his breath reeking of whisky. "I burnt the bugger down!"

A day later my accountant Gareth Jones appeared in great excitement. "You're insured," he announced. The sum would almost certainly avert my impending bankruptcy. As part of his conscientious reorganization of the business, Gareth had increased the Castle's derisory cover. He had helped save the business, though perhaps not in the way he had intended. I received a good settlement for the lost books. My insurance agent in Hereford was not too displeased. Only a week before, the large risks had been transferred out of his area to Worcester.

As always with major disasters, it took several days for the full horror of the fire to sink in. It had swept up to the roof and along the rafters and medieval beams, and large parts of the structure had crashed down. What escaped the ravages of fire had received such a drenching from the firemen that the plaster ceilings and mortar from the walls was washed away, leaving the stones precariously balanced. Four-fifths of the building was severely damaged. Even worse, the fire revealed that the most historic feature of the Castle, the twenty-five ton, oak central partition, was completely rotten after four hundred years of damp.

"Restoration will cost much more than the insurance money," I was told by Roger Capps, who had been restoring a castle in Glamorgan.

"You'll save £40,000 if you replace the partition with steel," an assessor told me. Stubbornly, I insisted it was replaced in oak but then found I did not have enough money to repair the roof.

The history of the Castle's restoration has been a troubled one. In the 1980s, after an argument with Roger Capps, I hired Stansell & Wells who had worked on Wells Cathedral. In spite of a bill for £300,000, the company had a very low standard of work and the architects failed to keep them in order. The first floor was completed at three times the estimated cost for the whole building. Although the roof was finished, the Castle was unheated. In winter a chilling cold rose from the damp flagstones and penetrated the bones of book-browsing visitors.

"One Independence Day is bad enough – two are stupid," complained Cotters.

Repeating the world-wide publicity for Home Rule on its anniversary, in April 1978, was far more difficult than staging the original event, especially as the authorities had begun to fear we might be serious. A National Holiday, 'Hay Day', was declared and we held a large and noisy procession to generate patriotic fervour. Reg Clarke dressed in the uniform of a General from the banana Republic of San Itaria. Gold braid and rows of tin medals swung on his chest as he beat a large drum. "I think Hay's the only sane place in the British Isles," he said. Reg was closely followed by a dexterous dancing majorette with perhaps the most elegant wriggling bottom ever seen in the town. She was a Jewish girl from Brooklyn married to an army education officer from Chepstow. "Darling, it's in our blood," she explained to me.

The local police sergeant was less imbued with the spirit of the occasion: "We will oppose everything you do in the future and are going to charge you on four counts: after-hours music, breach of Lord's Day observance, abusive language and breach of the peace."

Gujerati was made the official second language of Hay and Dr Rosenberg sent bus-loads of very beautiful Gujaratis from Leicester to join the celebrations. He was worried by the implications of Enoch Powell's oratory, which had encouraged racists to put shit through their letterboxes. Powell got things the wrong way round. The trouble with Britain is that there are *too many* white people in government, banking and the bureaucracies, all of them making life duller and deader. A day spent watching the Gujaratis dancing gracefully in their flowing saris had a wonderful effect on Hay.

'Hay Quits EEC' was the headline in *The Hay Herald*, our national newspaper. It made its first appearance on Hay Day 1978, and reported: 'Not even the relentless downpour could dampen the fervour of the crowd inspired by twelve months of liberty and several barrels of free ale.' The newspaper was our chief counter-blast against the bureaucracies. The centre-spread was a photograph of me next to Prince Charles captioned 'Royals hit it off'. The back page contained an exclusive interview I had graciously granted to myself. Georgie Young, a journalist who had moved to the area, produced such witty and amusing *Hay Heralds* that I wished I could have used her talent more commercially. When I look at the thousands of books by journalists, TV announcers and other famous media people, I always think of Georgie's word for them, 'Mediaocracies'.

My Declaration of Independence had contained many of the ingredients of a political philosophy. In January 1978 I wrote another booklet, *Abolish The Wales Tourist Board*, which scrutinised those charged with the revival of rural Wales. I focused on the Board's officials who, with their high salaries, pension schemes and good intentions, were busy meeting the challenge with a series of chaotic and incompetent decisions. I wrote:

> The Wales Tourist Board is one of the largest grant-giving bodies in rural Wales, whose product, tourism, is said to be the single reason for the economic advancement of a depressed rural region... A number of grants have been totally counter-productive, producing no increase in prosperity and simply creating bad will and envy in poor, neglected areas. The fact that a Board consisting of ex-politicians, a trade unionist and a caravan-park owner, amongst others, should have the power to allocate millions of pounds with the abandonment of drunken sailors must be fundamental to the continuing decline of the British Isles.

The pamphlet revealed what I had seen with my own eyes on my travels around Wales. In rural areas, over-subsidized luxury hotels were breeding like stray cats, and were just as unwanted. There were many examples. *The Western Mail* had given the opening of Don Maura-Cooper's hotel a lavish spread promoting 'a unique experience in gourmet dining'. They did not write about its demise just a few months later.

Another was Colin Stone's Claro Court, a former country house which had become a school and was now semi-derelict. It received Tourist Board backing to become a luxury hotel. Each room had a different theme – Arabic, Persian, Russian and so on – and a sunken bath in the middle, presumably for sexual frolics. Colin was a generous host and the personification of a powerful international businessman. He would stroll from room to room carrying a briefcase decorated with a Concorde sticker and inviting everyone to his house in Malibu. But after becoming Claro Court's telephonist, receptionist and hall-porter rolled into one he went bankrupt and creditors rushed in. He later received a short prison sentence for financial misdemeanors.

It was clear that expensive new hotels would not actively attract tourists but, since everyone hoped that grants and publicity would save their businesses, no-one criticised them. Into this bottomless pit the Wales Tourist Board tipped much of its budget. One of their policies was to call everything in Wales a tourist attraction and then claim credit for having increased trade. A local hotelier told me that if I was too drunk to drive a horse and spent the night in his hotel, I was classified as a tourist. Ridiculous statistics were being invented. My demand to abolish the Board met with some local support but was largely ignored. In a rural area where many saw only the advantages of tourism, mine was a dangerous, isolationist point of view and engaged me in a struggle that persists today, twenty years on.

Tourist Board candidates were chosen to promote government policy rather than guide it. Mervyn Jones started to expound a lot of conflicting rubbish. "Tourism is the greatest aid to international understanding," he proclaimed in statesmanlike fashion. When lager louts descended on various parts of Europe, Mervyn quickly embraced the next fashionable policy by proclaiming that ninety-five per cent of tourism was domestic. A domestic focus was vital for the financial interests of the government.

Abolish The Wales Tourist Board led me to a conspiracy theory. Why was such a long series of disasters not being exposed by the press? The overruling aim of a government is to stay in power. They do so by 'paying' their chief supporters. One of these is the media and tourist policies were a source of advertising revenue in exchange for wholesome publicity for the government.

A new Chairman of the Wales Tourist Board was appointed. with the brief to provide the Government with more success stories. In favourable conditions Lord Parry looked like an animated garden gnome. There were photographs of him proudly shaking hands with the Chairman of West Park Developments, a construction company declared bankrupt a few months later owing four and a half million pounds of public money. As a journalist, Parry had nauseating articles published in *The Western Mail* describing to Canadian schoolchildren what it felt like to be an English peer, or what it was like to go necking with a pretty girl a few miles west of Carmarthen.

Prys Edwards succeeded Parry as Chairman. He had good Welsh-speaking ancestry but no relevant expertise, rather like the Duke of Westminster, who headed the English Tourist Board; both had social credentials but no will to question the motives of the Government.

I gave a vicious nip to the hand that was feeding me. The Tourist Board had nurtured in their midst a desperate radical who was now denouncing them as puppets of a media-created system.

"Mischievous and doomed to failure," was Parry's brief assessment of my activities when they were brought to his notice.

Chapter Twelve

Amazing America

The University of Minnesota

"You're a pro with the blade, man!"

I went to the USA five or six times in 1978, although the many problems arising from trading with the States would have halted more sensible dealers in their tracks. Buying in Britain, one could sell books before they were paid for, but America damaged my cash-flow because of the time it took for books to cross the Atlantic. As a British dealer I had less knowledge of American literature; furthermore, issues such as the New Deal, the Civil War and Native American culture were not nearly as popular with British readers as they are now. Lorry-loads of bad Presidential biographies inspired panic among my staff.

On a trip to the States early in 1978 I saw how educational establishments could change sides fairly quickly. Cornell University was selling the Boyce Thompson Institute, the agricultural research body which had given the world DDT. Flicking through their house journal I came across pictures of men in white coats posing proudly with enormous and perfectly formed carrots. I was familiar with books born of scientific and medical optimism. Invariably published before 1940, they portrayed science as the key to solving the world's problems. The 1970s, however, were years of scientific pessimism which reflected fears for the world's ecology and of incurable maladies like cancer. If Rachel Carson had not published *Silent Spring* in 1962, in which she explained that the advantages of DDT were outweighed by the horrendous long-term effects of chemicals on ecosystems, it would probably have remained one of the 'solutions' to the world's nutritional problems. Cornell University had to perform somersaults to protect its reputation. DDT was completely forgotten and they were quickly boasting about their publication of *An Ecological Atlas of the Hudson River*, showing considerable concern for the fate of the sturgeon. This hypocrisy irritated me nearly as much as the enthusiasm for DDT.

By the mid-1970s universities were receiving less funding from a cost-conscious Nixon administration which propounded conservative economic doctrines. "It's either a hundred dollar book or a hundred dollar shell," said Peter Kraus, a young dealer who saw the writing on the wall. Military spending was not going to suffer, if other things were. Servicing the educational market was no longer a licence to print money; besides, too many entrepreneurs had entered the field. I was worried. I employed twenty people and needed as many easy sales as possible. But ultimately the strength of the second-hand economy meant that demand remained healthy. Shopkeeping began to revive. During the university boom many ambitious dealers had despised shops, but now the mass of academic publications on the market made low-priced selling through second-hand bookshops a necessity.

"There's a fortune on the road from Buffalo to Boston," said Jack Joram. "There's not a stop-light for five hundred miles." The large, stone country-houses and Utopian communities along the Finger Lakes contained extraordinary libraries and many treasures survived. In Cooperstown, where Fenimore Cooper's father died after being hit on the back of the head by a political opponent, cheques signed by the famous author had been found in a bank where they had lain forgotten. Each one was worth fifty dollars. "We must make the run," Frank Pollard enthused.

We climbed into an enormous old silver shooting-brake in Toronto and drove the five hundred miles to Albany in New York State. Frank was a Canadian who had come to work in Hay with his Polish wife, whom I once found passionately necking with Gerry Taylor in the shop where I sold leather bindings. Gerry, incidentally, has a stammer that gives him the peculiar ability of managing to seduce a girl between the beginning of a sentence and its end. Frank had useful contacts in Canada. Our first call was at the western end of the Finger Lakes, the largest wine-growing area in the States, where an overweight schoolmaster called Jim Brunner hoped our spending power would be increased by the consumption of steaks the size of briefcases for lunch.

One could argue about the prime geographical location for books in America. Are they best found in the huge Victorian houses in Chicago or in the charitable libraries on the East Coast? My own choice would be western New York State. Everywhere we went there were books. The Interstate Route 90 offered nothing, but the parallel Route 20, an extremely decorative time-capsule dotted with 1940s motels, had twenty or so 'Book Barns'. These are old wooden barns in farming communities adapted for the sale of second-hand books and offering some of the finest nineteenth-century books in America at amazing prices. Remaining close to their agricultural past, I had to crouch under low beams to survey dimly-lit books on makeshift shelves. "We swear by the tomato box," one enthusiast told me.

At a Book Barn in Danesborough the owner made a remark that stuck in my mind. "You know, Richard, I think Upper Mohawk Valley needs an Antiquarian Booksellers' Association." This indicated a bright future.

Many of the Book Barns were owned by Christians who were unable to earn a full salary from their communities. A Baptist minister in Stourbridge was supporting his ministry by dealing in second-hand books.

"Where do you sell your best ones?" I asked him.

"To Matthew Needle," he replied.

Matthew and Cheryl Needle lived in an eighteenth-century house in Chelmsford with their elderly landlady. Two thousand unsold copies of her Spiritualist work, *We are the Ones,* lay about the house. Matthew's long, black beard made him look like a youthful Rasputin. The son of a Jewish-Ukrainian sandwich maker, he was one of the best scouts for rare and interesting books. His beautiful wife looked like an early pioneer and entertained us with home-made cakes. She was perhaps ill-suited to the rough Jewish Americanism of Matthew. The Needles were to become close friends. As a customer I offered Matthew mixed benefits. I was always prepared to buy far more stock than I had money for; wisely, he allowed me little credit. Their house on North Road was a perfect base to hunt for book treasures emerging from the area, the Massachusetts turnpike being a through road to New York.

A valuable source of books were the Peabody libraries, founded by a nineteenth-century idealist. Perhaps anticipating the degradation of future years, each library had a treasure room in which the most precious books were stored, such as a hand-coloured eighteenth century folio on the gardens of Paris. Rather than protect the books, the treasure rooms were an easy target for vandals. At a Peabody library in Newburyport the librarian saw no customer demand for his books and the price I negotiated was a pittance.

Until the British blockade of 1812, Newburyport had been more important than Boston. It had a fine eighteenth-century bowling club where George Washington used to relax and was home to Lord Timothy Dexter, a millionaire eccentric who filled his garden with life-sized statues of the famous because he thought them better company than his neighbours. The present community of retired middle-aged divorcees centred around a bar called The Thirsty Whale.

Matthew and I decided to buy the surplus stock of Portsmouth Public Library. We drove through Maine to New Hampshire, where car licence plates proclaimed 'Live Free Or Die' in support of the State Governor who had just said that the National Guard should have nuclear weapons. Through the car window I saw overweight residents in pink shorts sitting on lawnmowers which moved backwards and forwards over the green squares in front of their houses.

"Gee," said Matthew, "I hate the people of Maine and New Hampshire," and searching for the ultimate expletive, he concluded, "they're almost as bad as the people from Canada."

We collected the books from Portland in a large truck but it broke down on the interstate, at which point I discovered that large American trucks only did nine or ten miles to the gallon. Another time we were driving books from Minneapolis to Long Island when the truck broke down, this time with more serious consequences. When the repair team arrived, the vehicle was so overloaded that the crane ripped the body right off the chassis. My driver, Andy Cooke, deftly managed the situation by asserting the principle that "the customer is always right".

Andy was the son of my old friend Bill Cooke, also a lorry driver. He worked for me for ten years and adjusted to America with a genius few could rival. So much did I admire his survival skills that once, when I was asked the secret of second-hand bookselling, I replied, "Having the ability to make a U-turn at the wheel of a five-ton truck in Atlantic Avenue, Brooklyn, in rush-hour traffic." On one occasion I was buying thousands of pounds' worth of books from a print dealer in Pennsylvania and found that I was unable to pay him. Instinctively, Andy jumped into the truck and accelerated into the sunset.

In May I took a Freddie Laker flight to San Francisco to visit Moe, of Moe's Bookshop in Telegraph Street. He was the only bookseller I knew to be erecting a four-storey, custom-built shop from the profits of second-hand paperbacks. We surveyed the construction site together. "I'm giving a hell of a party when it opens," he said. "I've spoken to the

Police Department and they're going to close off the whole block. I think I'll have myself carried onto the scene in a sedan chair." Moe's success was built on the careful selection of cheap books for which he charged more if they were paid for with exchanged goods rather than cash. "The trade-in system has enabled us to build up the volume," he said.

The West Coast was profitable because of its good quality paperbacks containing texts of value to students – the major philosophers, for example. In Europe at this time there was a limitless demand for books like Jack Kerouac's *On the Road*, the autobiography of Malcolm X, and writers such as Hemingway, Kierkegaard and Aldous Huxley. These books accompanied the hippy movement and student revolts at a time of rebellion against industrial society. My first view of the West Coast hippy movement was a rainbow parade of several hundred of them, and almost as many VISA signs, selling crafts along the pavement of Telegraph Street. "When you've bought one ceramic bull, that's that. You don't want another," commented Mo sardonically.

San Francisco was the spiritual home of Jack London. Of all the literary societies I was to come across this was perhaps the most influential and there were three Jack London bookshops in the area. The San Francisco Society dwarfed all the literary societies I knew at home, although the Dylan Thomas Society lies south-west of Hay-on-Wye, the Arthur Machen Society is to the south-east and the Reverend Kilvert has a large following in Hay itself. Literary societies seem to worship their heroes with the fervent fanaticism more usually seen in minor religious cults.

From San Francisco I flew to Los Angeles, where I met Stanley Slotkin. The multi-millionaire founder of Abbeyrent, a franchised rental company, Stanley was a lithe seventy-eight year-old who intended to enjoy another twenty-five years of vigorous life. Joining him was his thirty-two year-old bride. Two years previously Stanley had mystified me by buying hundreds of eighteenth-century religious folios in poor condition. These items were difficult to handle and unpopular, but, due to their age, I kept them. Aware that the additional cost of postage to the US tripled Stanley's original purchase price, I was even more curious. Why would anyone pay hundreds of dollars for books I would happily have thrown away?

Now he explained that, owing several million dollars in taxes, he had had a page from one of the folios expensively framed and mounted and appraised at several hundred dollars. He then donated several of these to churches throughout America as a tax loss. His friends were as shrewd as he was: one had made millions for Coca Cola simply by instructing staff in outlets to say "A large one?" to each customer who ordered a drink. Stanley took me to his lavish country club. The subscription was $25,000 and membership was restricted to Jews.

I left Stanley for Santa Monica, California, to see David Wallechensky, son of the famous writer Irving Wallace. He and his father had a library of 30,000 books distributed between two large houses furnished throughout with dense shelving. Like the Reverend James Hastings in Aberdeen they had used their library to compile three books, *The Poor People's Almanac*, *The Book of Lists* and *The Class of '65*. Both father and son produced very successful books but reflected the diverse attitudes that comprise America. David believed his generation should emphasise their Russian-Jewish origins whereas his father preferred to be a best-selling author under an impeccably Scottish name. David had also fulfilled a common businessmen's fantasy by marrying a TWA stewardess whose slim figure, complemented by the red uniform, he ascribed to her vegetarianism. This made me feel slightly uncomfortable about my own rather gross form.

He has a very serious manner and an offer to look at his library lasted three hours, during which time we hardly spoke. There were several hundred books about round-the-world travellers, people walking around it backwards, on one leg, leading a donkey and so on. "We've got just about everything," said David, "from Magellan to the guy who arrived back in Los Angeles after a world tour by bicycle. One guy even tried to walk round the world with a big mirror strapped to his back – he got two-thirds of the way round, too!" I liked the shelf of books about curious subjects, with histories of funeral cars and factory chimneys, books about the ecology of stray dogs, telephone evangelism and aquatic art, and a treatise named *How to Kill*. I felt inspired to embark on collecting unusual books myself but ultimately I did not succeed. David's library confirmed my view that the book is far better suited to the hands of an individual than the body of an institution.

In Atlanta I stayed with Faith Brunsen, the head book-buyer for Richies of Atlanta, any of whose eleven department stores would rival Harrods. She introduced me to the world of modern American bookselling. Everything in America depended on selling and I enjoyed the company of a woman who ordered thousands of pounds' worth of books at a time and was pestered by middle-aged Cadillac owners who wanted to take her out to dinner. These men were sales representatives from the major publishing houses in the South. "The best employees in a bookshop are women over fifty, when they've passed the romantic age," she told me. Although she looked like the sort of ordinary American female who goes on package tours up the Nile, Faith was a sophisticated person who through her work for the Antique Booksellers' Association had seen America at its most commercial. I had great respect for her. She took me to see the world's largest Farmer's Mart, where I was amazed to see a stand specialising in double-yolked eggs. We talked about the debasement of food by commercial interests, and Faith remarked with considerable passion, "Oh God alone knows, what *hasn't* big business done to food?" The remark inspired me to continue attacking the insidious activities of supermarkets in rural economies.

Faith introduced me to Mrs Talmadge, widow of the famous politician whose career as Governor of Georgia had taken something of a dive after thousands of dollars were found in his raincoat pocket. They had a beautiful plantation where all the animals were named after Civil War heroes. It included a well-constructed hutch containing 'Rabbit E. Lee'. She also took me to a meeting of the American Booksellers' Association in the Shoreham Hotel in Washington. It was like an Arab bazaar. Gay Talese was distributing heavy gold key-rings to promote his new book, a history of *The New York Times* called *The Kingdom and the Power*. To the alarm of the assembled intellectuals a black policeman started wandering around with a drawn gun. I was so transfixed that I stayed the night and took the early shuttle to New York. "I can see you're one of us!" said Faith.

My next stop was Patchouque, a small town on Long Island and one of many in America made redundant by the out-of-town mall. The owner of Patchouque Books had been sleeping at the back of his shop in a filthy sweat-shirt, surrounded by old tyres which partially fortified him against a group of Puerto Rican youths clustered in his doorway. Car tyres rested against first editions of Aldous Huxley. Small-town America was no longer material for paintings by Norman Rockwell; it now provided better subject-matter for a Holocaust artist.

On my return from the States, Eggy was helping to unload a container when he suffered a heart-attack. He died shortly afterwards in Hereford hospital. Without his enthusiasm in times of trouble, the business would have been barely possible.

When I next visited America the legendary Jim Rizzeck met me at the airport in a light-blue Cadillac with a cocktail cabinet. Jim was a Palestinian bookseller who lived in Brooklyn. In his office on Atlantic Avenue he plied me with Macanudo cigars and apologised for sipping

Freshca, the colourless, fizzy drink which was the only cure for his alcoholism. Thin and elegant in an immaculate blue suit, he hobbled about with a silver-topped cane, looking more like a Spanish Duke at the Savoy than a notorious member of the book trade. Jim was waiting for a precious collection of sixteenth-century books to come onto the market from a Puerto Rico cathedral. He hoped to obtain letters written by Christopher Columbus. Books I could never have dreamed of possessing somehow came his way. I bought a £10,000 Gould from him, a rare-bird book with beautiful plates. It turned out to have been stolen from Harvard University. I had not questioned its provenance, not least because Jim's firm, Scholars Windmill, was prepared to give me almost limitless credit.

We regularly had dinner in sumptuous Lebanese restaurants in Atlantic Avenue. Always full of unusual anecdotes, Jim told me how he had been in an East Coast prison and had watched matchsticks floating down corridors awash with blood. One evening we walked around the historic Brownstone district of Brooklyn, where Gregory Peck, Churchill's mother and a host of other celebrities lived. As we looked across the water at the sparkling lights of Manhattan, Jim remarked, "Gee, Richard, to think this nation has an energy problem!"

Jim was from Bethlehem which, apart from being Christ's birthplace, has another boast. "Twelve hundred of the fourteen hundred residents of Bethlehem are called Rizzeck," he told me. This is the kind of information I have always enjoyed receiving.

Arno Zohn was a slim, charming, ex-airforce aviator with a private jet. His recipe for becoming a millionaire was very simple. He reprinted every book on the reading list of American colleges; the books ran into 16,000 titles. The university boom enabled him to be one of thirty-four publishing millionaires in New York, of which Robert Maxwell was one of the most famous.

When he was in Germany with the British Army, Maxwell found a warehouse full of periodicals from the war years. This was a gold-mine. Americans lacked periodicals from this period and would pay a premium for them. He reprinted them, laying the foundations of a business that subsequently became so devious. Maxwell enhanced the plausability of his empire by persuading academics to sit on the board of the new publications, thus giving gross overcharging and seedy scholarship a veneer of credibility.

Arno had two warehouses in Miami full of unwanted titles from Books for Libraries publications. Wanting to see the product rather than buy from a list, I flew to his warehouse in Hialeah Lakes. Big stacks of chrome fruit-machines were waiting to take over the space now occupied by academic books. I ripped open the boxes and spent several days selecting the books I believed I could sell.

"You're a pro with the blade, man!" said a young Puerto Rican warehouse assistant as I slashed open a box. It was one of the most treasured compliments of my bookselling career.

Arno had invested his fortune in his estate on Long Island, where his wife Naomi Macrae was planting a million wild flowers. The couple avidly studied and published Gertrude Jekyll, William Robinson and other English horticulturists and gardeners of the late nineteenth century. After two years of my failed attempts to pay him, Arno kindly forgave me a debt of $80,000. Perhaps he knew that he would never live to collect it. He was found to have a terminal illness and died before I had a chance to thank him.

While I remained oblivious to the dangers of spending so much time and money in America, the downward spiral of my neglected business was momentarily halted by a piece of luck. Patricia Carlton Scott, who had been extremely conscientious and far-sighted in developing the publicity side of the business, had cultivated a journalist from the Belgian newspaper *La Libre Belgique*. This led to a call from one Comte de Selys Longchamps, who wished to sell his enormous library fifty miles south of Brussels.

I immediately flew over to see it. Chateau Halloy was at the end of a magnificent avenue of lime trees. The family had been beneficiaries of redistribution during the French Revolution. Their most recent exploit of note had been on 20th January 1943, when a cousin in the family, Jean de Selys Longchamps, had single-handedly dive-bombed the Gestapo headquarters on the Avenue Louis in Brussels during the Second World War. The present Comte had been a distinguished diplomat but now lived with his beautiful black Panamanian wife and enjoyed frequent visits to hot mud-baths. His brother Charles was organizing the sale of nearly 30,000 antiquarian books. Sotheby's had selected a few of the better items and left the rest to rot. Prestigious auctioneers rarely have time to examine large antiquarian libraries properly and it is impossible to assess the contents of a book from a quick glance at the spine. We were more thorough, and wedged behind a bookcase in one of the library's twelve rooms we found a hand grenade.

Although the library had suffered from the natural hazards of many fierce Belgian winters, only a very few of the books had suffered the worst effects of damp, such as inseparable pages, crumbling edges and leather lifted from the cardboard covers. All the books were dusty but they were in good condition. The library gave a fascinating picture of the family's main interests, both professional and private. Always active in politics and administration, its members had served as deputies during the French Revolution and as senators from the time of Belgium's creation in 1830. The family's scientific curiosity extended to the collection of everything from pamphlets describing new industrial processes to seventeenth-century works on the practical applications of water divining.

In the Law section I found *Causes Criminelles*, a sixteenth-century work with woodcuts depicting gruesome scenes of torture and execution. There were also early documents and plans relating to the construction of the Belgian railways. One ancestor had such a passion for them that he positively welcomed a line built through his land.

The first books sold from the Halloy library were to Noel Anselot, a pink-faced Belgian entrepreneur who was buying coal in Merthyr Tydfil. A scholar who had written the standard book on Ardennes cookery, he was also interested in the history of Liège, where he had been a student. The Selys Longchamps family had been the hereditary Princes of Liège so he was delighted to find a stock of eighteenth-century books about the city in Hay. We did not yet know that Noel was destined to follow closely in my footsteps and start a Belgian Book Town which, in turn, would herald the beginning of the Book Town movement throughout Europe.

Chapter Thirteen

Rural Revival

I regard this as beautiful scenery; the Development Board for Rural Wales regard it as a suitable building-site.

*"Don't get involved with any women – they're only
after the money!"*

The history of my relationship with women is largely one of immoral curiosity. Some I have admired intensely and perhaps should have married, but a stable relationship was difficult in Hay, where I was isolated by my frequent travelling and social contact mostly limited to book-dealers. Unwittingly I collected a stable of female journalists, TV announcers and film-makers. At least they were mobile.

When the Central Office of Information started to make films about me, I met a pretty, dark-haired producer called Annabel Olivier-Wright. Despite her incompatible love of jazz and London she became an exceptionally close friend. Annabel spread the name of Hay throughout the world and taught me that all government depends upon information. Two thousand people worked at the Central Office of Information; its head Joe Haines would become Harold Wilson's right-hand man. The control of information in a democracy is as important as its distortion in a communist country. Although Annabel's job was to make films about British bulldozers for Mexican television, the story of Richard Booth crept in three times. My ideas were rambling and uninformed but she saw the point of my attack on the rural regeneration policies employed by the Tourist and Development Boards.

Perhaps it was not surprising that much of my early support came from girlfriends. Women were more likely to support this kind of idealism. From their experience of manual work in the home, many women instinctively know that the quality of life is much improved by a good garden and eating well. Lovely, laughing, sophisticated Annabel was far too intelligent to see any future in our relationship but remained a distant friend for the next twenty years. Another girlfriend was the blonde and beautiful Kate Hadley, who rose to be an editor of *The Sun*. She chose the Page Three topless shots for the paper and spent business weekends with the management at expensive hotels in the Cotswolds. Top editors consoled themselves after her rejection of their clumsy, drunken advances by referring to her as "the iron maiden". She wore a red trouser suit as an expression of her socialist principles and knew from personal experience how left-wing people were constantly manipulated by right-wing power, although she was prepared to compromise these ideals for the sake of her job. She taught me to treat the whole system with suspicion. All journalistic skill and writing was subordinate to the commercial interests of large advertisers and media magnates. "Tourist Board lunches are dreaded by all journalists," she remarked to me. "Only the lowest of hacks fill themselves with Tourist Board food; the better ones go out and find their own stories."

In 1981 I wrote a pamphlet called *God Save us from The Development Board for Rural Wales*. As the Tourist Board had invested money in failing hotels, so the Development Board was doing with factories. I wrote about my visits to three industrial estates in Newtown which had received an enormous slice of the Development Board's budget.

The first, on the Vastre Estate, was assembling Japanese imports for the home market. The premises looked prosperous. "We intend to stay," I was told by a salesman who looked like an advertisement for Moss Bros. The policy of subsidizing Japanese products seemed highly suspect to me. The next factory I visited was Hilton Office Equipment, which imported Yugoslavian paper clips. Here the mood was less sanguine. "We'll be bust by February," a gloomy sales manager told me. At Boynes Confectionery they were making sugar mice for all they were worth, but things were not as they seemed. An employee told me the owner had only taken the factory to enable him to buy back the lease on some premises in London.

So far the Development Board had encouraged foreign imports and subsidized London property deals. At Karen Developments there was a great deal of floor space but very few employees. The place was full of plastic bottles of bubble bath and it was impossible to see what the few workers were actually doing. The owner of the factory cleared enough space in his office for us to sit down and eyed me aggressively. He told me that they had also taken the factory next door for storage, although I had been told by the Development Board that this practice was against their policies. I left the Vastre Estate feeling I had merely skimmed the surface of the Development Board's largesse.

Dyrrin on the Welshpool road looked like a slum, a landscape of deserted factory buildings with smashed windows and an overturned, decaying car. A Securicor sign declared that roving Alsatians awaited the trespasser, but before they appeared I was fortunate to meet someone from a local factory who seemed happy to help with enquiries. He told me that the factories were only forty to fifty per cent full. "What you really want to see, mate, are the empty houses, dozens of them. They move the factories, you see, and the people have to move on too. The Development Board's going to run down soon. There's no more money for grants and the balloon will burst." We spoke about Ladywell House, an office block that dominated Newtown. It was, said my friend, "the biggest white elephant ever built". Not a single entrepreneur had been wooed into the vast spaces and the biggest office, covering the whole of the third floor, was used by the Development Board itself.

I wanted to know about a new Development Board scheme for twenty-five selected villages which had been trumpeted in the Welsh press. I was directed to the office of Paul Pennyman. The only light he shed on the scheme was that it had been planned with a pair of compasses on the map adorning his wall. I asked him about the 'Skilled Craftspersons Register'. "If I can get one person a job, I'm happy," he said piously. He told me that he bought books in Hay and, should I want a factory, his colleague would see me straight away. I disregarded this friendly offer and went on with the attack.

"Why don't you re-use old buildings for factories and workshops?"

"I wish I could, but no one has ever asked us." It seemed a particularly fatuous answer.

"Do you think that the Development Board has encouraged businesses to expand beyond their means and has actually increased the risks of bankruptcy?"

"That's an interesting idea," he mused, looking up at the ceiling.

I had heard that the Development Board was having a meeting in Talgarth which would give me the chance of open engagement with the enemy. I telephoned an ally, George Dear of Talgarth Pottery. We met for a drink beforehand and sat contemplating the evening apprehensively. At the meeting was an audio-visual display about local entrepreneurs who had made good.

"This system was made in Mid Wales," said the Development Board officer Granville Jackson cheerily as he assembled the equipment. The programme ranged from Laura Ashley to cottage industries. The final subject was a lady who made Oxford frames at her house in Crickhowell. George whispered to me that she was the wife of a Development Board officer. Finally, Granville Jackson asked if we had any questions.

"What about all the Development Board's disasters?" I asked, rather aggressively.

"You can read about that in the report," he replied.

"That's not true," I declared. Granville Jackson looked dismayed.

"I went to the Development Board for advice on colour-printing," said George, joining the attack. "They suggested a firm who quoted me over £1,000 for the job, so I found someone else to do it for a few hundred."

"You have to be careful about advice," said Granville Jackson, his smile becoming even more forced. We asked him how small shops would survive the abolition of Retail Price Maintenance, which was a sensitive political issue. Up to now the retail price of many goods had been legally safeguarded, thus protecting smaller shops from lowering prices indiscriminately. With two pints inside us, our heckling brought the meeting to a close. We invited Granville for a drink.

"I'm giving another talk in Knighton next week," he said. "For God's sake don't come!"

My friend Robat Gruffudd, a publisher at Tal-y-bont near Aberystwyth, showed me his protest against the Board. He was printing some diaries in Welsh which included Development Board advertisements. Instead of printing 'Development' (*Datblygu*) he had substituted 'Destruction' (*Difetha*).

After two marriages and Queen Annabel, I fell madly in love with a Rhodesian girl. I would have married her but what Annabel did intellectually, she did literally, deciding that the worship of Buddha was far more important than a relationship with a lunatic and relocated to northern India. Although I was briefly attached to a beautiful scholar of Greek vases with musical connections, I did not like her music or scholarly pretensions, or London, where she lived.

My private life at this time was not helped by my being looked after by a fuzzy-haired, stubbly ex-Commando called Paddy. He was fond of reminiscing about his experiences as a seventeen-year old boy during the invasion of Normandy. "This man came across the field jabbering at me in a foreign language, so I shot him," he said. "I thought he was German." At the man's funeral Paddy was shocked to discover that he was a French farmer.

Paddy was a professional in warfare but was unable to adjust to the subtleties of civilian life. His slightest movements betrayed his fighting ability. Once, when the police came to question him about some unimportant matter, he opened the door clutching a carving knife in such a threatening manner that the policemen opted for a speedy retreat down Brynmelin drive. Cooking me simple food as well as he was able, he was a conscientious housekeeper with a simple philosophy. "Don't get involved with any women," he advised, having scattered wives and children throughout the British Isles. "They're only after the money!" I was as unable to follow his advice as he was himself.

"Put a few words in for old Paddy," he said when he saw me writing my diary. Some weeks later, he disappeared. Rumours were of suicide. I did not have the resources to look for him. Although he only stayed in Hay for about a year, he is one of the people I remember most clearly.

In the spring I mentioned to Charlie, my gardener, that I wanted a horse. He found me a magnificent dun Cobb called Goldie. He was a wonderful, gentle animal and, by eating hay, contributed to the local agricultural economy rather than that of the oil companies. Charlie was an experienced horseman; his father had been a timber haulier carrying full loads across the hills by horse and cart.

I escaped from the cares of my business by exploring the beautiful herring-bone of bridleways around Hay on horseback. I would duck from the gentle brushing of low branches in the heavily-wooded Cusop Dingle and canter past farms so remote that they remained undisturbed with trees growing through their roofs. Eventually I would reach the empty moors, where the howling wind and fierce rain made life almost intolerable for a bad rider in an ill-fitting duffle-coat and poorly adjusted spectacles. Despite the bitter weather, Hay farmers used to walk miles into the town where they sought shelter and warmth, even if it was only in a cider house. They were the reason for Hay's plethora of pubs. The hard life made the hills an almost exclusively male society. Often the animals had a better quality of life than human beings.

Riding a horse contradicted the gospel of advancing social progress. There were few concessions made to my chosen form of transport. The old wooden gates, beautifully hung and easy to open with a whip while still mounted, have all been replaced by cheap iron ones which crashed and clattered as my shell-shocked steed and I tried to force a passage down a lane that had been in perfect order until a century ago. The Forestry Commission and the Welsh Water authorities are wealthy organizations that disregard such vital operations as brashing a tree or building a gate. The dead grey interior of the forests reminded me of H. G. Wells's *Island of Dr Moreau*. Trees were suffering from intensive planting and windblow. I was reminded of a book bound in navy leather with grey silk endpapers and a foreword by HRH Prince Phillip: *A History of The Forestry Commission: 45 Years of Service*. It had been produced with public money by officials purely for the purpose of self-congratulation.

I rode Goldie nearly every day. Rising at six, I imagined myself a Welsh farmer. Sometimes, descending a steep slope, he would stumble and we became a rolling mass of human and horse. But on the whole I was a cautious rider. Sometimes I rode with Roger Capps, who was restoring the Castle. His father suggested it would lead to a better working relationship between us. "You should make your horse Prime Minister – Caligula did," Roger said, and he wanted the first floor to be strong enough for horses to be ridden up the stairs.

Horses had a place in my radical philosophy. Charlie's brother Pete had been a wheelwright and we decided to build a cart. I bought a banding plate, a shaft bender and one or two other pieces of equipment. Although we were not very accomplished, I learnt a lost rural skill. I tried delivering books around the town from a horse and cart and appeared in the local paper leading a small Shetland pony with a bookcase strapped to its back. The landlord of The Red Lion of Govilon, Charlie Perry, preserved the last vestiges of the horse-based economy. Whether raising money for the local hospital, going to his daughter's wedding or taking the Labour Party candidate to the polls, he invariably used a horse. Whenever I rode Goldie to his pub at Blaenavon, Charlie would feed me a gigantic dinner. Blaenavon had had a major pit employing 1,400 people. After it was forced to cease production the Tourist Board proudly opened 'The Big Pit Museum', which employed about six. I found Charlie's pub, with its three hundred miners' lamps, far more interesting. A pub regular known as 'Chunky' agreed to attend my 'Garden Party for Disappointed People' to which I invited all the customers who had visited Hay and left empty-handed. Chunky was to mud wrestle and have eggs thrown at him. He did a valiant job but several muscular youths felt it was a matter of local pride to give him a good thumping, so poor Chunky had a very hard time.

At this time most of the local families considered me unworthy of inclusion in their circle. Exceptions to the rule were my dear friends Louisa and Alexis de La Falaise with whom, every month or so, I would have long serious conversations over dinner at their house in the remote Radnorshire hills. "Get the dust off the old books," Alexis would say. Despite being a French marquis, the only work he could find in the locality was as a chef in the local hotel. Nevertheless, they managed to make a life for themselves in a rural area. When they moved to Paris in the early 1990s Alexis became a successful designer, proving that modest success in a rural area is far harder to come by than fame in a metropolis.

He suggested that I visit his mother, Maxime de La Falaise, when I visited New York in 1980. Sophisticated and perceptive, she introduced me to Andy Warhol, perhaps aware that we both had a common interest. His was in the second-hand object and mine in the second-hand book. However, with a studio in the most fashionable and expensive part of New York, he had no time for a second-hand book dealer. "I'm an aerial Jack Kerouac," I told him, but he stared straight past me. New York is a place where a starving man could have thirty-four television sets in his basement, and I feel I have perhaps seen more of this side of America than Andy Warhol ever did, having entered thousands of shops and homes all over his country. I see his Campbell's soup tin as a kind of industrialised hand-grenade hurled at the rural economy, obliterating all local production. After his death in the mid-1980s I was fascinated by the fever of excitement over the auction of his possessions, which occurred during a boom in the second-hand economy.

Enjoying dinner with Louisa and Alexis one night, I expounded my new enthusiasm for horses. "You must meet Hope," Louisa said. "She's one for the horses." Not only did I meet Hope, but I fell in love with her. I confess that many might find the thought of an eccentric castle-owner declaring himself King rather obnoxious and the publicity I generated might be unappealing to those who prefer to conduct their affairs in a less prominent fashion. I was a well-qualified candidate for Margaret Nicholas's *The World's Greatest Cranks and Crackpots* in which there was a full-page photograph of me as the only living eccentric now that Keith Moon, The Who's drummer, was dead. The chapter was headed 'Bees in their Bonnets'; I do not think that this is totally fair as I merely react to situations that occur to me.

Possessing such a peculiar reputation, the woman who was to be my third, final and only successful wife was not particularly anxious to meet me. She was visiting Boots Bantock, a booming-voiced poet and painter.

Dressed in a flowing Victorian coat and bowler hat, he had installed himself on the hillside in order to paint Hay Castle and the surrounding landscape. Hope was beginning to tire of his small gypsy caravan and his attention-seeking sheepdog. She overcame her initial reservations and accepted an invitation to stay at Brynmelin.

Our mutual passion for horses brought us together. Hope had considerable experience and kept a magnificent black Dales stallion for breeding. He was part of her collection of black animals – a black pig, ducks, some chickens and a pet crow that appeared from nowhere, out of the sky, to land on her arm when she called it. She lived alone in an isolated hunting lodge in Northamptonshire while her husband Rob Stuart ran a successful gallery in Chelsea. Hope was losing interest in the venture and detested the accompanying social life. "Everyone kept dropping in for wine," she said. Although she was devoted to her two grown-up children, Lucia and Orlando, whom she educated brilliantly as a superior form of animal, she had little tolerance for human beings. Gypsies, from whom she occasionally bought horses, fared the best in her estimation. My visits to Hope became frequent. I once arrived with two black sheep in canvas sacks. She also collected books, although a local dealer described her houseful of books as 'A Barnardo's Home for Books'.

In the 1970s Hope had been a news photographer and had campaigned passionately for Biafra. She was still accepting freelance work and I suggested that she be the photographer for some of my radical pamphlets. The first one we produced together was *The Rhayader Guide*. Rhayader is a small town in remotest rural Wales between Hay and Aberystwyth. One day I was buying cigars from Mrs Powell, the town's newsagent, and she lamented the absence of a tourist guidebook. "I could sell thousands of them in the summer," she said. I felt that a guide book would be a good vehicle for my thoughts and offered to undertake the project.

The research and exploration was done on horseback. I rode Goldie and Hope was astride a small, pretty grey called Princess. As we trotted down the road I noted that local youths had amended a sign that read 'Passing Place' to 'Pissing Place'. Within weeks *The Rhayader Guide* was completed. There were anecdotes, like Shelley sending a toy boat down the Wye with a five-pound note as a very extravagant sail, and recommendations, like Mr Lloyd's Museum of Rural Artefacts with its salmon spears, pig-bristle scrapers and cheese presses, but we also attacked Development Board activities in the area. As a result Mrs Powell was almost reduced to tears and many of the shops would not stock *The Rhayader Guide*. The Development Board did not want their policies commented upon and they had made this clear.

My mother had christened me Richard George William Pitt, perhaps hoping that the man who became Prime Minister at the age of twenty-four would inspire me in my future career. As Pitt lay dying he said, "Roll up that map; it will not be wanted these ten years." He realized that his efforts to curb Napoleon had come to nothing after the Emperor's great European victories. Echoing Pitt, my last statement will be "Roll up the map of Powys; the Tourist Board and the Development Board have invaded every village within it."

Chapter Fourteen

Sink or Swim

Goldie, my Prime Minister.

"Hippies: Hygienic Itinerant Peace PeopleIn search of Earth Solidarity."

199

1 981-2 was a very cold winter. Charlie had to take me to work on his tractor as Cusop Dingle was a solid mass of icy snow. It destroyed ninety per cent of sales, bounced cheques and led to uncooperative bank managers. Central heating was an unaffordable luxury.

Fortunately a dealer called John Rees was stranded in my shop for several days because of the weather. Like many dealers at this time, he was making collections for Japanese universities, who remained blissfully unaware of the vast quantity of rubbish produced in the West. "I want to spend £2,000 on the American constitution," he said. It was a gift from heaven as every American container had a sizeable amount of literature on the subject. John now worked for a businessman called Leon Morelli who was anxious to invest in the book trade. "Why not sell some of the business to him?" he suggested.

Morelli arrived for the meeting in a smart blazer. Only his laugh, which was like a Japanese soldier advancing into Burma in the Second World War, and his gilded teeth gave the impression that he was not just a grammar-school boy on the way up. He studied my accounts carefully and suggested that my debts could be completely repaid by selling him the Cinema bookshop, the most profitable part of the business. The sale was put into progress but, at the last moment, Morelli unexpectedly knocked another £10,000 off the agreed price. My position was so bad that I had to agree to everything he said. I had also thought I was retaining Derek Addyman, an experienced and much-needed member of staff, but he went to work for Morelli for higher wages. "You can't stop people improving themselves," Morelli said.

He appeared to operate with a different logic. Nobody expected to see much of him. What would a rich London businessman want from a tiny Welsh town? But his move to Hay was marked by a grand firework display for charity. "We want Richard in Hay," his staff said patronisingly, as if my departure was imminent. Morelli held a party to establish whether the town wanted me to be King or him to be President. A very broke April Ashley was asked to be hostess, for which she received £100. She stood in the foyer handing people a free glass of sherry if they threw a dart at a picture of my face. It was fundamental to Morelli's plans that he should have the democratic support of the people of Hay, and the result was the majority he sought. In his election address he stated that the Development Board had a lot of good ideas that he intended to follow. As clear as daylight, I had a sinister new rival in Hay.

Morelli gave the town's institutions new names to increase their authority. The Tourist Information Centre became 'The Tourist Information Bureau' and The Chamber of Trade, of which he was president, became 'The Chamber of Commerce'. From henceforth this was his seat of power and the people with whom he was in contact were like those devoted Japanese employees who, in traditional obedience to their master, will happily say, "Yes, Sir, certainly, the crows are white."

"Morelli will never be satisfied with being anything but top dog," John Rees warned me quietly. But at this time I was uninterested in him.

I stood for Parliament at the 1983 General Election with a poster by Alex Williams which read 'God gave the Rain but the Devil gave the Water Board'. Hope and I campaigned in a horse and cart. Most evenings I went to The Swan Hotel, whose landlord Dai Radcliffe was a successful borough councillor. It was perfectly positioned for the majority of the town's population, which was to be found in the large council estates of

Gypsy Castle and Wyeside Gardens. Dai's wife Mary was much-liked in the town and a passionate horsewoman, her mother having delivered milk in Birmingham by horse and cart. Mrs Thatcher won a sweeping victory and I lost in Hay, but won a local election against the sitting Labour candidate by a few votes and was accepted onto the Borough Council. But it was a false dawn; my political career was to prove hopelessly vulnerable to Morelli's financial power. Only my career as a bookseller saved me.

Morelli was very active in his first few years at Hay. Never before had the second-hand book trade been exposed to such financial power. He was the dominant force at hundreds of book-sales, but his natural arrogance was incompatible with a trade in which knowledge is more important than wealth. "We left them with feathers in their mouths," he announced loudly after outbidding all the dealers. "He's got a deep pocket," said the leader of the ring. Morelli bought bookshops in Bournemouth, Brighton, Cambridge and London, and a large, three-sided shop opposite mine in the centre of Hay. From his office on the top floor he could watch the traffic in and out of my shop, but during the several years he was in occupation, we barely spoke to each other. On one occasion he was invited to Andy Cooke's birthday drinks. Andy, in traditional rural fashion, managed to consume twenty pints, but a small, neat collection of untouched ports were discovered where Leon Morelli had been sitting.

His bookselling abilities were so limited that I believe he seriously damaged Hay's reputation. Morelli's manager regularly made trips to Tokyo, where the taxi ride from the airport cost more than someone in Hay earned in a week. A book priced for the Tokyo market was guaranteed to alienate many visitors to Hay. I think it is far better for a customer, whether dealer or collector, to find bargains because it adds to their enthusiasm.

Morelli decided that, if books were not selling in Hay, he would take them to London. So, utterly ignoring the purpose of the town, books were dispersed in van loads to his other shops. "I asked for books on opera and they told me they had been moved to Bournemouth!" said an irritated professor from the north of England.

"When I was breakfast chef in Cornwall," Frank reminisced, "easily the simplest breakfast to serve was boiled eggs, but nobody wanted them. When I called them 'Cornish boiled eggs' they became enormously popular." Morelli lacked the care and imagination required to sell thousands of pounds worth of stock. But his lack of finesse as a bookseller led me to underestimate the determination he put into establishing a powerful position for himself. Prominence in a small community was as important to him as commercial success. My impending bankruptcy led him to undervalue my abilities as a bookseller. Many locals advised us to co-operate, but for the next fifteen years we were locked in bitter competition.

"You're the bookman in Hay," said Sid Wilding when he came to work for me at The Limited. Sid had started his working life as a porter on the railway thirty years before and had also worked as a delivery man for National Carriers. His great grandfather had been the servant of Reverend Kilvert, the famous Victorian diarist who had lived in the area. The Wildings had been peasants in Radnorshire for hundreds of years and many had migrated to the mining valleys. Sid was proud of the fact that soldiers from the South Wales Borderers had won a record number of Victoria Crosses in the Boer War. His meticulous work revealed that if theology books were the curse of the nineteenth century, military books are the curse of the twentieth. He painstakingly categorised every single book on the subject: 'Early Wars', 'The Crimea', 'Regimental Histories', 'Churchill', 'The Home Front', 'Nazi Germany',

'Russia', 'France', 'Europe', 'Far Eastern Wars', 'The Middle East', 'The Spanish Civil War', 'Guns', 'Armour' and so on. We grew to loathe books with the dark silhouette of a paratrooper advancing against a sunset background, which entered the shop ten times faster than they left it.

At work Sid wore his old National Carriers' uniform, a blue boiler suit. When Spanish television filmed us burning books, Sid was banned from the shoot because he reminded them of the fascists. Aside from the public outcry, book-burning proved an inadequate means of ridding ourselves of the unwanted books that were multiplying in obscure corners of the business. Smartly-suited US evangelists and old television and radio presenters could expect certain death by fire in Hay. But the books would not burn without litres of petroleum and when we destroyed a large pyre the citizens of Hay were covered in black flecks of burnt pages that floated through the sky. At one time I thought there might be a future in barter and offered to exchange books for the wood-burning stoves that were very popular in the area. I did receive some duck eggs from a Sennybridge doctor, but to make books properly combustible we needed a blower, or a log-machine to bind them tightly in wires.

Surplus books present one of the greatest problems in my business. An optimist in Los Angeles even wanted me to deal in ten tons of dust jackets. A sculptor used some pristine remainders to build a life-sized model of a Phantom Five Rolls Royce. When he power-sawed through one of my desks I lost patience with patronising the arts, even if it did help dispose of books. My Honesty Bookshop helped combat the problem. Giant bookcases were built along the Castle wall and in the garden with a padlocked money-box for payment. Even then there were so many books that I suppose I should be grateful to those who pocketed them without paying. The surreal sight of bookshelves at the foot of the rambling Castle has been photographed by visitors from all over the world, and the Honesty Shop is one of my most popular and successful. "Won't your books suffer?" the public would ask. If this happened, it removed the mental anguish of whether or not to dump them. At the end of the summer season the books become like wilting autumn leaves; faded and rain-soaked, they tumble damply from the shelves.

On the Borough Council I was slowly learning about democracy in Breconshire. In the south of the county there were still four coal-mines and a strong group of Labour politicians who stuck together, especially on the issue of council-house rents. Less well organized, but surprisingly powerful, were the Conservatives in the north. They never emulated the Labour group by having secret conferences, but still managed to win many issues. Their articulate leader was a Cambridge-educated hill-farmer called Andrew Leonard. A seventy year-old nationalist would sit in the middle of their meetings proclaiming his love of and devotion to the mother country.

When the Miners' Strike was declared I gave a donation to their local leader, big Tom Jones. This six foot four, bearded giant who looked like the prophet Jeremiah was a magnificent representative. I went to their strike meetings but learnt to my cost that the divide between north and south Breconshire was probably greater than between East and West Berlin. In rural areas farm workers earned half as much as a working miner. Highlighting the miners' wages was one of the Government's most successful tactics and served to make their actions seem disgraceful. Free food distribution by the Borough Council at the expense of the ratepayer was an added outrage reported by the press.

The cheerful, friendly miners were seen as devils by the media. Simple country people based their judgements on the information they received in the press, which was no longer concerned with just representation. I spoke to Eric Davies, a Hay policeman who like many others in Wales had refused a picket training-course and the promise of enormous wages to repress the strike. This was not reported. Whether I was watching well-meaning miners being arrested at Orgreave or giving them one of my home-cured hams, I could see how hopeless their situation was. I grew to regard the strike as a struggle against the power of quangos. Government agencies destroyed the mines more than even Thatcher had wanted. MacGregor, the head of the National Coal Board, was dictating policies which were to close every pit in South Wales.

The Labour Party proved incapable of supporting the working-class view. During the 1984 strike I joined them on the fields where they went rabbiting with their whippets. In a haze of alcoholic celebration after the event one of them said, "I'll never vote against my dog".

I believed that even if rural areas have a low population, and therefore weaker representation in government, it did not stop them being right. This statement therefore made more sense to me than the idealist Labour politicians who were trying to ban blood sports. Animals kill each other viciously; I have no objections to man joining the fray. When I reform the House of Lords – I would far rather reform the House of Commons – I shall insist upon the rural voice, with a low population, having just as much strength as the industrial voice, with its large population.

Subsidies to the nuclear power industry far outweighed those available to coal. In a Wales Tourist Board brochure called *Six of the Best* it was claimed that three out of the country's twelve main tourist attractions were nuclear power stations, which was a typical example of quangos scratching each other's backs.

The Welsh Miners' Library published a book called *Miners Against Fascism*. As I have already mentioned, the miners had more respect for education than people believed. One Scargillite I met was particularly interested in the various editions of Martin Caiden, the great authority on the German Army in the Second World War. Similarly, when I visited the so-called 'Centre for Mad Militants' in Liverpool all I found was a pleasant old man in a corduroy jacket eager for the works of the dockland poets.

In the early 1980s hippies arrived in a large convoy to camp on Hay Bluff. The Bluff is a bare, windswept mountain sweeping down towards Monmouthshire. A single-track pilgrims' road stretches like a pale ribbon across the landscape to Llanthony Priory. Traversing the road it is quite easy to see how the monks at Llanthony were so cut off that they failed to realize the Reformation had happened. The ruins are one of the great beauty-spots of the area. "They deserve the Duke of Edinburgh award," remarked Chris Powell, a print dealer in Hay who had himself arrived as a hippy. Intrigued, I rode to Hay Bluff to see them. The snow was two feet deep and all I could see were little mounds where they were camping in conditions like those of the German army at Stalingrad. The half-starved hippies were implicated when an entire field of potatoes disappeared. The situation in Hay was tense. Signs reading 'No Hippies' appeared in shop windows. There was bitterness on both sides. The manager of the Post Office hoped to become a local hero by refusing to pay out their dole money, so that in icy conditions they had to hitch-hike many extra miles into Brecon and back. "For the future of the young people of Hay, there is no way we can tolerate their presence," announced a Councillor.

Stories abounded of how they would infect the local population with hepatitis and local lay-bys were illegally blocked by the County Council. It was only possible to move them on if they had diesel. "The van is my pride and my life," one explained to me. "Blocking the lay-bys is outrageous!" my friend Jeremy Sandford protested. Jeremy lived locally and was the author of the 1960s bestseller, *Cathy Come Home*. His parents had started The Golden Cockerel, one of the finest private presses. I would describe Jeremy as the last gentleman on the Welsh border. While many educated people left in droves to become directors of banks and insurance companies, he stayed and allowed the hippies to camp on his land. For two years they were a part of local life, victims, perhaps, of the industrialisation of agriculture. "We used to go fruit-picking," one remarked to me bitterly. "Now they just have these horrible machines which suck all the fruit off the tree." For this reason many small orchards in the area had become uneconomic, so I allowed a farmer to sell his produce from the Castle grounds: forty apples cost £1.

" 'Hippies' equals 'Hygienic Itinerant Peace People In search of Earthly Solidarity'," remarked my friend Geoff Newsome. I allowed them to camp in small numbers at Brynmelin and at the Castle until local vigilantes working for the National Parks enforced their removal. Before departing they defied the stereotypical view of them by giving Hope a bunch of roses and a box of chocolates. When I gave a party for the miners in the Castle grounds the hippies came too. I suppose it was a fairly strange combination.

Meanwhile, Morelli was busy buying hotels in Hay. He purchased The Swan, The Crown and Kilvert's Hotel. "Will this help you make up your mind?" he said to one owner, waving a cheque for £350,000. "I've never seen anyone with money like that," remarked my accountant. My own situation was absolutely desperate. I was still borrowing to survive.

Frank advised me to keep two sets of accounts, but even he was in trouble.

"Mr English, you owe us £2,000," said a tax inspector.

Frank telephoned him one day after a drunken binge. "About the

£2,000 I owe you – would you like it in fivers or tenners?"

Of course, they did not receive a penny.

"Who's this week's manager?" Frank would ask me sarcastically. The latest was Michael Bowers, an unsuccessful writer who had retired to the country with his artist wife. "Don't trust anyone with a beard," said Frank. Bowers had a beard which would have graced a Holbein portrait. Perhaps due to his lack of managerial experience, I unexpectedly received a PAYE bill for £20,000. Morelli suggested that I take over The Swan Hotel in exchange for my shop and someone rang up to ask if I was interested in selling the Castle. Two of my best employees, Pat Thornton and Andy Cooke, were offered higher wages to work for Morelli. They refused. "You have remarkable resilience," Morelli told me charitably. I had no choice in the matter.

In 1984 I was declared bankrupt. Morelli sent his accountant to the hearing in Swansea. The receiver was a kind and generous man who listened to my explanations. "This affair stinks," said an ineffectual official, referring to the switching of assets. I claimed that the business stock was at the warehouse but that my shop stock was private and not to be considered. The bank had removed my company cheque-book and so this argument could not be disproved. Becoming bankrupt in a town where I had no peer-group gave me no sense of disgrace. One or two tradesmen worried about their bills but my cash flow was sufficient to cover them. It was only a few months later that it became an issue. 'Borough Councillor does not pay his rates,' wrote *The Brecon and Radnor Times*, who had been alerted to the scandal by Morelli's secretary. This did not help the mounting tension between us.

My financial problems had been so preoccupying that I hardly noticed the efficient and energetic work of my pink-faced Belgian friend Noel Anselot, who was twinning Hay-on-Wye with a new Belgian Book Town called Redu. He was energetically gathering support from the people of Hay. Both the Mayor, an ex-fish-and-chip shop owner called John Thomas, and the ex-Mayor were enthusiastic about the Belgian Book Town. Redu was a rural hamlet with a population in the low hundreds in one of the most beautiful parts of the Ardennes forest. It had no shop but a magnificent church signified its former wealth. Noel attracted traditional book-dealers and his wealthy acquaintances to the village and utterly transformed it. Second-hand bookshops and restaurants opened, and under his guidance it became a successful example of rural regeneration. "Brussels is one of the worst European cities for traffic," Noel told me. "Redu is the perfect refuge for traffic-tormented bibliophiles."

At the opening of the Book Town, Hay citizens drank black Trappist beer together. We had a closer relationship than we ever did in Hay. In spite of a plaque which was erected on the Castle to commemorate the twinning, the Government agencies concerned did not give it much long-term consideration and exchanges between Redu and Hay were few. Yet for Redu, the Book Town formula was a huge success and my contact with Noel stopped me from total non-conformity. He helped me retain credibility in the dark years of Morelli's dominance.

Chapter Fifteen

Look to the Sioux

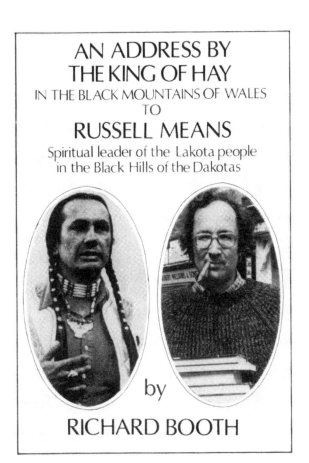

AN ADDRESS BY
THE KING OF HAY
IN THE BLACK MOUNTAINS OF WALES
TO
RUSSELL MEANS
Spiritual leader of the Lakota people
in the Black Hills of the Dakotas

by

RICHARD BOOTH

One morning I went riding in the hills with Joanna Meyer, an American visitor who had been singing with the Welsh National Opera. She talked about her love of horses and her ranch in the Dakota hills. Her father had a summer retreat near Mount Rushmore. I asked her what life in the Dakotas was like.

"Well, there's a real mixture of people there now," she replied. "At first the cowboys resented the hippies and there was sometimes violence, but they soon learned to grow marijuana even better than the newcomers and it's very profitable. It's a pretty peaceful sort of place. Except of course for the Sioux Indians. Some of them are causing trouble right now in the Black Hills."

This remark attracted my attention. "What are they doing?" I asked.

"They've just won some lawsuit or other against the US Government because they're claiming that all the land in those parts belongs to them. They've set up an independent country. They say it's their sacred territory – like Jerusalem."

Joanna obviously disapproved of such goings-on so I said nothing more, but I pondered this piece of information to the clattering of hooves as we rode along Cusop Dingle. Like the Sioux, I felt that my sacred territory, the Black Mountains, was being slowly invaded and ruined by the Tourist Board, the Forestry Commission and the Welsh Water Authority.

The native civilization of small farms and villages was being attacked by countless rules and regulations. In a local slaughterhouse the manager pointed to an official stamp on a sheep's carcass and said to me angrily, "Do you see that circle? That costs me £2000 a month." Mary Morson is a six-foot farmer dressed in shabby brown dungarees whose loud laugh perhaps reflects her lonely existence. "Richard, I cannot sell watercress any more," she said bitterly. During the salmonella scare one old hill farmer smashed two hundred eggs on the ground in an impotent fury. Even the small rural pubs were threatened because of draconian drink-driving laws; many risked their livelihoods to continue socialising in places where their predecessors had done for hundreds of years.

The Gods of the Black Mountains were urging me to go in search of that rebellious Indian camp in the Black Hills of Dakota where a rural people were really protesting.

Knowing Hope would be interested, I plucked up courage and asked her to accompany me there. Rapid City is the capital of the Black Hills, much as Hay-on-Wye is of the Black Mountains. We were greeted by a life-sized plastic dinosaur. It was uncannily similar to a dinosaur erected in Ystradgynlais in south Breconshire. Evidently, Tourist Boards the world over thought that rural areas needed them.

I suddenly realized how naïve and ignorant we were. We knew nothing of the geography or history of the Dakotas, very little about the Sioux Indians and nothing at all about their present problems. Furthermore, we had only given ourselves three days in which to find the Indian rebels. At the Minnesota state line there was a Tourist Information Office. The assistant talked to us patiently for half an hour.

"Have you had any trouble with protesting Sioux?" I asked her.

"Yes, they're very silly. I don't understand it all. Six of them came here to protest about the tourists." I felt elated.

"Hurrah, civilization is not dead!" I enthused to Hope.

We drove to Pipestone, where the traditional peace pipes were quarried. In a souvenir shop two depressed-looking Sioux girls were selling tawdry and offensive little soapstone carvings of Indians saying 'Me drink um firewater!' The Pipestone quarries led to Leaping Rock, a noted Indian site where the first white explorers carved their initials on the rock. The Federal authorities had invested $1m in the site. 'The most sacred sites in the Indian Culture!' stated posters and brochures, but no one said anything about the Sioux themselves or their simmering revolt.

Feeling tired and discouraged, we drove on. Next morning we began to see something of the reality of reservation life for the Native Americans. Circumscribed by government regulations, they had become just another sight for touring motorists. The landscape was dotted with beaten-up American cars, symbols of a culture that could not adapt to its environment. They had been forced to accept the offerings of an alien society. The road ahead stretched as far as the eye could see. Instinctively one scanned the horizon for signs of life. Suddenly, like a mirage, I saw a moving trail of dust which grew larger until we recognised three trucks festooned with flags and banners, with a pack of shouting Sioux running alongside. They were protesting against the fate of Leonard Peltier, the Nelson Mandela of the American Indians, doomed to spend his life in prison for allegedly shooting two FBI agents. This was a spiritual war against capitalist society.

We joined the protesters. Some of the young Native Americans told us that the rebels' Chief was called Russell Means but they could not give us directions to him. We got back into the car and set off blindly, still feeling no nearer to Yellow Thunder Camp.

A little way along the road we picked up a young, drunken hitch-hiker in a checked shirt. His name was Ben Little Moon and he told us proudly how he had taken part in the siege at Wounded Knee in 1973.

Native American people living in the area had taken over the town in protest against white commercial exploitation of the mass grave of Big Foot and three hundred victims massacred by Federal troops in 1890. The siege lasted for ten weeks and people from every corner of America had defied the might of the Federal troops, the FBI and the CIA. Wounded Knee was Ben Little Moon's home town and he offered to show us around. In a small shack he indicated two women collapsed hopelessly drunk on a bed. "My wife and sister," he explained simply. The old School House and the Museum of Local History were derelict buildings which contained a trampled mass of broken glass and old tins. The Sioux had done everything that they could to defile these places, believing them to be a defilement of their own culture. Ben Little Moon knocked a piece of pyrite rock from the chimney-piece in the school room and presented it to us. In spite of his advanced state of drunkenness he behaved with the greatest politeness and kindness.

Outside the village coloured streamers fluttered in the wind. They marked the earth mounds of the graves of Sioux Indians who had fought and died for their tradition. Photographs of the dead were propped against stones. It was a poignant sight, a powerful reminder that the war between the Sioux and the white man was not yet over.

We had been fortunate to spend the day with Ben Little Moon and the protesters on the reservation, but there was still no sign of the Sioux camp, which by now had become almost mythical in our minds. The next morning we drove through Buffalo Park, where a huge statue of Crazy Horse was being carved by a Polish-American sculptor called Korczak Ziolkowski. The unfinished monument looked like the Statue of Liberty riding on a fairground carousel. It was surrounded by huge pieces of rock-moving equipment. Ziolkowski had been labouring on the statue since 1948. He had collected letters from Presidents and Senators congratulating him on his work and even promising the possibility of a future Native American University on the site. The only Native Americans involved in the project were manual labourers of the most menial type.

When I finally met Russell Means he spoke to me about the project. "Crazy Horse lives in the heart of the Sioux. He was never photographed. Korczak Ziolkowski is the ultimate capitalist pig. He will never finish it. After spending tens of millions of dollars all he has achieved is Crazy Horse's armpit." Russell was referring to the original hole in the rock face.

Fortuitously, while wandering about the Plains some hours later we met a broadcasting crew from the local radio station. They told us that Russell Means had settled far beyond, on the other side of Rapid City. At last, trail signs and blazed trees along a dirt track suggested we were on the right route. We rounded a corner to encounter a group of Sioux guards patrolling the entrance to a camp. Their readiness for action suggested that the local rednecks were antagonistic towards their rebellion and I wondered what sort of greeting we would receive. "Is Russell Means in?" I asked rather nervously. He would be back in a couple of hours; if I cared to I could wait. We sat in the dust and peeled oranges while talking to a group of children and a half-Sioux schoolteacher.

The encampment was dwarfed by a massive cliff face. They had been pitched in this beautiful and dramatic scenery for about ten months and were worried about getting permission to erect some essential buildings before the winter. Meanwhile they chopped wood, gathered plants and herbs and gradually established a community life including a sweat-lodge and other traditions of their culture. We had to leave before Russell arrived but we returned next morning at dawn and breakfasted on rice and vegetables beside a smoking fire. Before we began eating, Russell prayed with outstretched arms for protection from the gods of the sacred hills and forests.

Russell had a strong, wide forehead. He wore two long, beaded plaits and a thick bone necklace. His fame had spread as far as Britain. Yellow Thunder Camp was defying 3,000 troops. Hope took a few photographs of children panning for gold in the stream and I talked with Russell and a lawyer called Ned. They told me the Government had offered them a derisory $100m for the Black Hills, less than a dollar an acre or one sixth of the profits that had already been extracted by white men mining gold and uranium from their land. Of course they refused to sell. Their earth was sacred territory.

We became friends for whom speech was unnecessary. Henceforth, I imagined myself as a Welsh American Indian. We shared the same thoughts on every issue. In a rebellion in 1973 the Lakota people gave a moral lead to the Western world by burning down the tourist museum at Wounded Knee. The ethics of a leisure society are an insult to the traditional life of a Native American. Tourism was an offensive smoke-screen behind which powerful commerce could operate effectively. "We live in an age of brochure culture," I said. Russell laughed and agreed. "We like that, man, we like that."

By 1982 the Sioux would have completed their sacred four seasons at Yellow Thunder Camp. They would feel more securely placed and would be able to extend their struggle to the bureaucrats who were destroying their people and culture as surely as the land-hungry pioneers had done before them. Unfortunately, a road ran along the top of the cliff that overlooked Yellow Thunder Camp, making them very vulnerable to attack from above. FBI marshals had surveyed them on more than one occasion although the Governor of Dakota had scornfully dismissed their struggle as "a children's game".

"Education, Christianity and the US Government are the three enemies of the American Indian," Russell told me. He inspired me to write two pamphlets. The first, *Look to the Sioux*, became my best-selling booklet. The second was *An address by The King of Hay in the Black Mountains of Wales to Russell Means, spiritual leader of the Lakota people in the Black Hills of the Dakotas.*

When Russell made a tour of Britain, Hope and I listened to him in Manchester, Bristol and Cambridge. "The government will give you money and then remove it," he warned. Several thousand heard him speak in Bristol, where his welcome was the warmest, but in poorer areas like Moss Side in Manchester, where empathy with his struggle should have been the greatest, there was indifference. Russell attacked zoologists, anthropologists and sociologists. He instinctively knew what I witnessed.

"What can we do to help?" was a recurring question.

"Put your own back-yard in order," answered Russell politely.

The trip was organized by Satish Kumar, who edited *Resurgence* and founded the Schumacher Society. Satish saw the visits to the universities as a triumphant progression. I was more sceptical. University decisions had created such chaos in rural areas that they were hardly likely to benefit from Native American wisdom now. A university graduate is largely someone who has rejected the wisdom of his community.

I visited Russell again in the late 1980s. This time I was shivering in shirt-sleeves, having flown from a warmer part of America. He gave me a heavy woollen cardigan and we shared a taco of dog meat.

Like a mother defending her child, Hope defended the traditional ideals and beliefs of the Native Americans. Our visit to Yellow Thunder Camp brought us together and was the beginning of a relationship that was to last the rest of my life.

Chapter Sixteen

A Successful Wife

My wonderful third wife.

"If we get a puncture, don't stop!"

When I first came to Hay, Jack Like was the big man in town. He was Chairman of the County Council and distributed Land Rovers in Mid Wales. According to local gossip his Council contracts were won after the surreptitious opening of envelopes. As every farmer in the area drove a mud-splattered Land Rover with a lively sheepdog in it, his was a position of enormous power. "Hay will have a university," he pontificated. As local millionaires were limited to Lord Portman, whose generosity had extended no further than a doctor's surgery, we had to forgo the benefits of higher education.

A university is worth many millions to a town. They are part of 'Pork Barrel' politics and much desired by politicians seeking investment in their constituency. I believe that the greatness of the British Empire was in the eighteenth century when we were exploring and defeating the French; the tragedy came in the nineteenth century when the university was taken seriously.

In America, where altruistic millionaires were more common, thousands of small, two-year colleges had been built to civilize areas outside the reaches of the main universities. But the optimism personified by Kennedy was replaced by Reagan's pragmatism. It costs four times as much to train an academic at a small college. Travelling next to an academic from Harvard whose speciality was Chinese, I got the reply I expected when I asked him about the present state of Chinese studies. "There used to be twelve schools in America but we're cutting them down to six so that we can go for a greater degree of intellectual excellence."

The warped logic of academics was that centralization equalled excellence. I was about to reap the benefits of educational centralization. When Tom Loome returned to America in 1979, he did so at an opportune moment. At first he took a job as a schoolmaster in Minnesota but then he saw a unique opportunity for book-buying. By reading out-of-date Catholic directories, he traced all the small monasteries that had become colleges or universities after the Second World War. Now, many of them were closing down. Tom contacted me and I flew to Minneapolis. I looked out of the aeroplane window onto land that the Government had divided into 88-acre lots and given free to the early settlers. The landscape was vast. To tackle distances, cars had a cruise-control button to relieve drivers of cramp in their foot. As a European, I was fascinated by the American sense of distance. "Going to Europe means no more than taking a piss to me," remarked Matthew Needle.

Minneapolis University is the second largest in America with 55,000 students. The Gifts and Acquisitions Department wanted to dispose of hundreds of books which had been donated by alumni. A bland librarian called Don Osier agreed to send me a container every few months for five hundred dollars. Seeing books available like pebbles on a beach must have convinced Don that it was a more worthwhile hobby collecting beer cans. Although he lived two hundred miles away from Milwaukee, the beer capital of America, he was a true connoisseur. He would carefully drain each can by inserting a pin in the bottom as if it was a delicate bird's egg, never dreaming of vandalising it by ripping off the ring pull.

Don became a good reason for regular visits to the Twin Cities. He was shortly replaced by a black politician who did not have the gentle sophistication of his predecessor but with whom I quickly established an emphatic relationship. "Hi, Booth!" he would greet me loudly, as if I were a voter on the fourteenth precinct. He sold me some Catlin first editions very cheaply and I barely blinked. Catlin was a famous traveller who lived among and painted many Indian tribes in the 1830s. University incompetence no longer astonished me.

In spite of its considerable wealth and an efficient security system to hinder unauthorised entry, chaos reigned in the University of Minnesota. Despite a cost to the taxpayer of millions of dollars a year, it was impossible to slow the production of doctoral theses. It was a peculiarity of many universities to store them in the Gifts and Acquisitions Department. When the truck came to collect purchases, the wrong items would inevitably be loaded and I would find myself the owner of unique theses which lay forgotten in Hay for several years. I have one example in my bookcase, *Development of a Front End Stimulation Technique for Decision Making in a Supermarket*. It left me wondering what hope the small shopkeeper has against the millions spent promoting supermarkets. Similarly, the university seemed to approve of the consumption of junk food and the advantages of using technology rather than human beings. In the students' canteen there were nothing but vending machines. A row of six foot high, black robots in concrete corridors, they looked like a publicity shot from a science-fiction film. They gave birth to almost anything that could be sealed in a plastic bag. Universities are the loyal servants of corporate funding and industrial food.

I visited a couple of private dealers in the area. Clark Hansen was almost bald with a few flecks of russet-coloured hair. At the age of forty he still lived at home with his two dominating parents and found therapy in buying books which he assembled in their warm, carpeted house and the multi-car garage outside. Kind and uncommercial, even his better books were only a dollar each. Lelien, an ex-Army lieutenant who sold books in the centre of the Twin Cities, told me, "You can tell if a dealer is a Republican or a Democrat by whether he has a large collection of books about either Custer or Crazy Horse".

In November 1986, Hope and I drove to Waterford College. It was the hunting season and Wisconsin was full of hunters. There was a local government drive to dress tourists in Day-Glo orange to prevent accidental fatalities at the hands of over-zealous stalkers. One month's rifle-shooting season was followed by a three-month crossbow season. It was rare to see a car without a dead deer strapped across the bonnet.

At Waterford College there were 50,000 books in a hall the size of a football pitch. The only inhabitants of the abandoned monastery were two monks we found in a remote kitchen containing a solitary sauce bottle and a packet of Kellogg's cornflakes. There was a loading bay near the library and we packed two canoes and a half-ton barber's chair in addition to the books. Ignoring American geography, I decided that this would be the very chair in which Albert Anastasia was shot by Al Capone. Chicago was two hundred miles to the south but the revelation was sufficient to get me BBC coverage back home.

Cheap books in the USA were like snowflakes in a blizzard. "You switch a button on a modern press and 68,000 books an hour shoot out," I was told. In terms of retailing them second-hand, it seemed that the quantity outperformed the quality. Exposed to so many, I developed a strange neurosis. "The only decent books are those published before the invention of shiny covers," I told customers.

Added to this were the quantities of books imported by non-English-speaking Americans as the most sacred memory of their homeland. As Europeans fled to America during various nineteenth and twentieth-century persecutions, they took their precious books with them above all else. This was the case in many of the small monasteries of the Mid-West. The town of Oconomowoc in a remote part of rural Wisconsin had a beautiful small monastery which, as a past refuge for German monks, contained valuable eighteenth-century folios. They were in an ornate, balconied library and had to be carried down a small, awkward spiral staircase. On East 3rd Street, New York, we purchased another German monastery. Around the corner were the police headquarters where Kojak was supposed to have been sucking his lollipops.

In Delevan, Wisconsin, an old bookseller called Ed Chesco owned an exotic duckpond. A disused boat-house was packed to the ceiling with high quality detective fiction. I left him to cash a cheque in the town, where I found a huge statue of a prancing elephant in the square. Delevan is the circus capital of America. Each winter fifteen circuses shelter there and one of the problems is how to bury dead elephants in the icy ground. We did not stay long in Delevan. Travelling such great distances meant that we were often in a hurry as the next stop could be hundreds of miles away.

In Belleville, Illinois, we cleared a fine library to the smell of Negro soul food. Belleville is a suburb of St Louis. On the sidewalk a queue of destitute people waited to sell their blood. We were advised not to stay in the area after four o'clock when schoolchildren were on the loose. The rough parts of the city were referred to as 'DMZ' – 'the Demilitarised Zone' – by a friendly Jewish dealer. In richer areas of the city palatial white homes with Corinthian columns stood in acres of grounds. The illusion of wealth was slightly tarnished when I learnt that the columns were made of tin.

Hope and I preferred small libraries; they were more spiritual. In Mansfield, Ohio the head monk dressed up for us in eighteenth-century costume and demonstrated how to fire a musket, splitting a post from a hundred yards. Another shaky, eighty-year-old monk helped us load books using an old wheelbarrow.

Perhaps the most remarkable library we visited was Los Gatos on the West Coast. It was the head of the Jesuit Provincial and had three hundred smaller schools under it. The affluent monastery was on a hill overlooking the rapidly industrialising 'Silicon Valley'. Had the monks obtained permission to develop their land they would each have been able to afford a private jet, but to their irritation a group of ecologically-minded millionaires had stood in their way and the land remained green and fertile. The monks I talked to were very fond of television and great admirers of Jane Fonda. They were extremely tanned and fit. Physical health had replaced spiritual health. It was impossible to look out of the window without seeing a jogging Jesuit. They wanted to clear the library of dusty old books so that it could be transformed into a glistening gymnasium with a forest of metal equipment.

The library included 3,000 books on the learning and teaching of Latin. Collectors of modern Latin, often referred to as Barbaric or Renaissance Latin, are quite common. Hope was amused to find a copy of *Winnie the Pooh*; *Winnie Ille Pooh* was the nearest a Latin book was likely to come to a best-seller. Such minority interests may be fading in the modern world but they are never far away in the second-hand book trade. The local bookshop had a window display entirely devoted to glossy new books about artificial intelligence. Even the second-hand bookshop had a proprietor who was convinced that the entire Second World War, and indeed the future of the West, had been decided by Sir William Stephenson and the enigma codes.

Los Gatos was the second oldest winery in California. I obtained a precious eighteenth-century book about wine with an inscription proving its Californian origin. We bought several cases but the Mexican labourers conscientiously packed them on top of the books so that they were immediately seized at customs, who fined us heavily. I also had a hundred-year-old set of steers' horns from Minneapolis confiscated on the grounds that they were from an endangered species.

We moved on to Detroit, which is about half the size of Wales. The vast factories created by Henry Ford were once the pride of America but, rather like Liverpool, the focus of civic pride has now switched to its musical history. Diana Ross and other beautiful black singers were now more often in the news than Detroit's car industry, which was suffering badly from Japanese competition. 'The cops killed Applejack,' said graffiti on a railway bridge. 'Is that special?' a more philosophical member of the black community had scrawled. Art predominated. We met a dealer in film books who had amputated one of his fingers to get compensation from his health insurance. The money enabled him to make a horror film about a bed that ate people.

Millions of dollars had been spent on the Duns Scotus Library in Detroit. Beautifully-crafted little cubby-holes modelled on medieval times held a superb and comprehensive collection of books from History to Botany. Built in the last thirty years, it had been stocked as if for eternity. Certainly the Duns Scotus Library in Merton College, Oxford did not have such a fine collection. Removing the books was the finest achievement of Paul Harris who had to carry every one an enormous distance along the corridors; he was a thin, hard-drinking employee from South Wales. I bought the lot for little more than $2,000, though large numbers had to be consigned to the 'dumpster'. As we drove across the smashed, drug-ridden areas of Detroit I was aware of the thousands of dollars that had been lost by Duns Scotus College in the name of a better future.

John King's Detroit bookshop had been established for twenty-five years and was of a size only ever found in the Mid-West, where I would have at least a dozen competitors if I ever claimed to be the world's largest bookshop. It was very well organized and reminded me of one of the problems of my profession, namely the need for people prepared to spend their life religiously putting books in order on a shelf. Smaller dealers, such as George Barry, Ken Rosenberg and

Mary Beth, all carved out enclaves of human contact and prosperity in the grim and gloomy city.

The sheer size of America made book-buying overwhelming. The country was awash with books. We needed to buy selectively, but simply clearing the libraries quickly and adapting to a strange country drained one of all energy.

As the business recovered during the 1980s I imported over a hundred twenty-foot containers of books from America. A container to be loaded over a period of one or two days is referred to as 'a dead man'. 'A live man' is one which has to be loaded and removed in a couple of hours. One had to work very fast: a twenty-footer amounted to about four hundred boxes of books and could not exceed the thirty-eight ton weight limit. If a forty-foot container was accidentally overloaded it would break every weight law in Britain and America, quite apart from threatening death if a tyre exploded. A forty-footer is always a hazard to Hay-on-Wye's fragile houses, and an eighteenth-century pediment on the corner of Bear Street and Brook Street bears the scars of our international business.

Each time I went to America I became a little more frightened by it. I was only robbed once, in a good hotel in the centre of New York. In the night a thief stole my clothes and my wallet from the bedroom while I slept. Never have I seen a more uninterested man than the sergeant asked to investigate the affair. Paul Harris had his passport stolen four times and got lost in the violent South Shore district of Chicago. "I wouldn't stay around here if I was you, friend," said a kindly black man when he stopped to ask the way. "Whitey," yelled irritated blacks as we inadvertently drove the van down the Martin Luther King Avenue in the same area. Feeling a conspicuous and unwanted European, I shivered in my shoes. "If we get a puncture, don't stop!" muttered Hope.

I was very fortunate that the closure of the monasteries and two-year colleges occurred as my relationship with Hope stabilised. At this time my financial situation was desperate. Using her credit cards, I was able to trade seriously again and began to recover. For three years Hope and I travelled alone to the remotest parts of America buying libraries. From a library of 25,000 books we would have to pick and pack five or six thousand in a very short space of time. Although she was little bigger than a couple of boxes herself, Hope struggled manfully with the fifty-pound cartons. Whatever I did she was a tremendous help, following me through blizzards in a hired car as I drove a twenty-foot truck along icy roads. As our affair deepened, her husband Rob issued an ultimatum.

When Hope decided to live with me it soon became clear that she was the perfect partner. At our wedding in Hereford Registry Office I was an irredeemably dishevelled bachelor dressed in such torn and dirty clothes that the Registrar tried to marry our witnesses, Vera and Gerry Taylor.

The Limited, Lion Street. Moving into this old agricultural hall, my business also became the largest employer in the town.

The cinema was densely shelved but the open spaces in The Limited made it more customer-friendly.

Myself with Mr Travis, a small Welsh farmer. Their economy, like the miners', I regarded as undemocratically torpedoed by quango organizations.

1984. A Miners Support Group in the Dulais Valley.

The National Parks – proficient at paying the bureaucrat but not the labourer.

Rosebud, South Dakota. An Englishman just beginning to suffer from middle-aged plumpness. The Run was to Free Leonard Peltier. We had a 'Free Leonard' sticker in the window of our shop in the south of France for ten years.

Sid Wilding – if we had men in suits in the business, we would not be able to drink tea.

Hope Stuart. Her credit cards saved the business.

1987: Hope's efficient organization enabled us to begin rebuilding the Castle, but it cost nearly half a million without getting much further than the first floor.

--------♦--------

Chapter Seventeen

Sleaze

Dr Simon Nothman, at his bookshop in Long Island.

"It's the Antiquers who are in the front line against the Malls."

By the mid-1980s my affairs were improving rapidly. This was almost entirely due to Hope. Our relationship began in 1981, at the time of my bankruptcy. She stopped the business being buried under an avalanche of disasters. By buying half of Brynmelin she gave me much-needed capital and as a newcomer to the business she could see its flaws. I was capable of making large deals but Hope could see their faults and, importantly, she had the meticulous organization necessary to get the books requested by specific customers. When I am buying books my energy is used in approximately the same way as a prostitute's: I form an intense personal relationship with those selling the books for a very short time. A few minutes are vital and afterwards I do not much care what happens to them.

Hope is different. To improve the quality of her collection she will check the dates of editions and search for an earlier or finer copy. Although a tiresome occupation for an ambitious entrepreneur, it is a vital operation if selling to private collectors. She took great pride in having been to the Scottish College of Commerce and was far shrewder over the handling of money than I.

When Hope moved into Brynmelin the first problem she identified was that everything, from the family silver to bottles of duty-free whisky, disappeared with regularity from the house. Charlie, despite having been a wonderful servant to me and having introduced me to rural life and the horse, had managed to buy a large new car and live in considerable luxury by stealing from me. His steadfast loyalty combined with cold-blooded thieving made him rather like a larger-than-life character out of a Russian novel. His son-in-law was likewise inclined; whether it was wandering geese or an abandoned screwdriver, he too was an incurable kleptomaniac. Assisting them in their domestic imperialism was my accounts clerk Gary, who apart from giving himself an unauthorised wage rise, had been giving Charlie two weekly wage-packets. It was very fortunate that Angela Wheaton, who was running the History department, emerged as a talented financial organizer. She and Hope positioned my business in such a way that, for the first time, it could operate efficiently.

My relationship with the Manchester and Liverpool book trade was always vital. "Will your cheques bounce?" asked a suspicious Manchester book-dealer called Eddie Hopkinson. Eddie had started life as a postman and must be one of very few human beings to have grown a thirty-penny-weight gooseberry. His stall was outside the Arndale shopping centre, where paperbacks by Barbara Taylor Bradford and Danielle Steele were like gold dust. He advertised in the Yellow Pages as 'Manchester Bookbuyers' and was prepared to sell me all his unwanted purchases. Manchester has some notoriously deprived areas. "If the vendor is sweating slightly and wants to sell me brand new books, I never buy them – he's into drugs," remarked Eddie.

I was partially helped by jealousy between the Manchester dealers. Little Pete, who had inherited a fine bookshop from Tony Hattersley in Stockport and gave an extremely generous discount to dealers, was Eddie's chief enemy. "Little rat," he would growl. Hattersley had been one of the hardest men in the book trade, going to prison rather than apologise to a judge for handling stolen books. "How did I know they were stolen?" he had argued defiantly. Several of the other dealers had committed the same offence but had apologised. "Richard," he said to me, "I've never stolen a book in my life: I've always paid the porter to do it." Hatty got several months inside whilst the others escaped with a reprimand. On his release he went to live in Whitby, from where Captain Cook had explored the Pacific. A beautiful narwhal's horn decorated his house, which was filled with antique weapons and books. He was far too sophisticated a dealer from whom to buy many books, but I occasionally used to enjoy a glass of Bailey's Irish Cream with him.

In Manchester supermarket expansion had greatly exceeded the capacity of the city to support them. My bitterness was extreme. I wrote a pamphlet called *Why Woolworth's will destroy Brecon*. The store's manager told me that in the interests of economy they did not buy locally. I urged 'a last ditch attempt to save the culture of rural areas by exporting agricultural produce, never importing it'. Supermarkets began by offering a better and more efficient service but they have ended up by destroying the competition and creating a monopoly. At a Hay Community Council meeting one evening, I heard that a Lo-Cost Supermarket was going to open outside Hay. "We must stop this any way we can!" I shouted. They all sat there like puddings. There was no opposition. I left the meeting with a feeling of embittered futility. The following morning I plastered the town with posters: 'The Plague of the-Lo Cost! – the only plague by which the people of Israel were seriously threatened'. Several weeks later I had a communication from the police. Acting on instructions from the Borough Council, they were prosecuting me for criminal damage. At Brecon Courthouse I sensed sympathy from the magistrates but my appeal that the police would not have prosecuted unless they had been urged to do so was turned down. I was convinced that Morelli had used his position as a Borough Councillor to secure victory in what appeared to be another vindictive campaign. I was fined £1,000 and bound over for six months. Any more remonstrations and I would be locked in jail.

In the following years supermarket development exceeded all my worst expectations. In Britain today, seventy per cent of food is bought from supermarkets and most rural parishes are without a shop.

"Are you a supermarket?" said a small, red-faced man standing in my shop. On closer inspection, what looked like a fifty year-old Australian pimp turned out to be the Home Secretary, Kenneth Clarke. "What has happened to your butcher, your baker and your candlestick maker?" he added jovially. "This is a town where the small trader cannot buy a shop because you have bought them all!" Had I been an anarchist, at this point I would have considered assassination a justifiable action. As it was, his pink face merely reminded me of an after-dinner speaker whose drinking and eating was marring his thinking.

I did not explain to him that the supermarket had emptied Hay's shops and that the book trade was the one activity that was filling them. In the public mind, supermarkets are equated with convenience and cheapness, never with the destruction of jobs and businesses. When the supermarket advertises 'Farm Fresh Country Products' you can be sure it is in fact destroying them.

After the Lo-Cost prosecution I flew to America. There, almost by accident, I bought myself a bookshop. After we had cleared a large theological library near Bradley International Airport in Connecticut, we went west into New York State to Duchess county, famous for its early Dutch colonies and the only Dutch President of the United States, Martin Van Buren. He was supposedly responsible for the phrase 'OK', derived from his nickname 'Oude Kinderhoek'. Hudson is a beautiful eighteenth-century town with an opera house and a derelict hotel called The Charles. It was once the centre of the American whaling trade and valuable carcasses were pulled 150 miles up-river to save them from the hands of English pirates.

At 439 Warren Street we found an old dealer called Oscar Sorge who was playing chess with some delinquent children. He had an enormous stock of baseball cards and did not seem to mind that most of them were being stolen. In less than a few minutes I bought the entire shop and its contents for $3,000. It was a spontaneous buy that nearly had disastrous financial consequences. Although one end of Warren Street was a reasonably elegant part of town with some interesting antique shops, the other end was a dangerous area with mostly black inhabitants housing the infamous State Penitentiary. Hudson was the home town of the boxer Mike Tyson. Becoming a world champion boxer was probably a less hazardous occupation than living in Lower Warren Street, where teenage youths clutching knives and fistfuls of dollar bills would exchange drugs in the doorway of our shop. One of my employees, Mark Williams, made a valiant effort to manage it, gallantly sleeping on the premises to save money. Armed with videos and a computer and reluctant to go out, he was joined by his girlfriend. Not unnaturally, he decided to leave his post and set up on his own, having discovered an international market for boxing books.

There were opportunities for trading in Hudson but it was impossible without sufficient capital. After three years the shop closed. I regret losing the acquaintance of George Thompson, a Hartland antique dealer whom we grew to know intimately. "It's the antiquers who are in the front line against the malls," he declared. In America there was secret and bitter, if fairly ineffectual, opposition to historic small towns being destroyed by chain businesses. Hope expressed sympathy for struggling family motels. She tried to book us into one run-down place and was only convinced that it was closed when we saw the half-empty swimming pool full of black water. Later, we read in a newspaper that the dismembered corpse of a prostitute had been found on the property. On one occasion the sixty-five year-old proprietor of a small motel near Madison offered to drive us the thirty miles to a motel that was not part of a chain.

Although my owning a shop in America was not financially successful, it did influence my thinking. War would occur through the collapse of social structure brought about by the out-of-town mall. With more small shops destroyed by supermarkets than by the entire Allied bombing offensive of the Second World War, the stability of the Western world is threatened. General Sir John Hackett, who wrote a book predicting the causes of a Third World War, knew very little about living in inner-city America. A street full of small shopkeepers, based upon the tradition of a thousand years, is far better for social stability than one supermarket patrolled by armed police.

Americans were reluctant to blame supermarkets. "We thought it was drugs," a customer said to me when I spoke about the causes of inner-city decline in the States. She did not see that if the food economy is destroyed the remaining economy will revolve around drugs. Western civilization has gone from reality in the Middle Ages, when humans merely stroked a dog, to the Renaissance, when we drew dogs, to modern times, when, under the influence of a drug, we see a fourteen-foot purple dog.

As an aerial Jack Kerouac, I have spent much of my career travelling. The most technologically-advanced forms of transport are often the most boring. Flying the Atlantic in a modern jet is like sitting in a large cigar tube for several hours next to someone whose only thought is to complete the journey with the minimum mental or physical exertion. There are honourable exceptions. I once flew to America next to an Irishman who was going to the St Patrick's Day Parade through downtown Manhattan. He drank a bottle of whiskey on the way over, went straight to the Parade and planned to fly back again immediately afterwards, fuelled by a second bottle. Concorde is different. Free champagne, cigars and telephones enable one to smoke oneself silly, belch and make idiotic calls all over the world before taking off.

Having flown across the Atlantic many times, Hope and I decided to opt for a more diverting method of transportation. This took the elegant form of the *Queen Elizabeth II* cruise-ship. A fierce storm broke during the voyage to New York, leaving us tilted at an angle for several days. Eighty per cent of the passengers and crew were incapacitated. The portholes were glazed with ice and we were forbidden on deck. This was not the oasis of calm and luxury we had hoped for. The only person unaffected by the storm was a burly fellow in red braces with the distinct look of a Radnorshire farmer about him. He was betting chips worth $1,000 on the roulette table. One evening a chef swayed across the dining room balancing a dish high above his head. With a flourish he presented it to Hope, accompanied by weak applause from around the half-empty room. On the silver platter was a birthday cake. As it was not her birthday, we concluded that she must have been part of a programme to lift passengers' spirits.

Back on dry land, in the 1989 Hay Borough Council elections I suffered the humiliation of gaining fewer than a hundred votes, the same as a young Conservative candidate gaining political experience. In the 1992 General Election the local Conservative Parliamentary candidate, Jonathan Evans, was returned to Westminster. Morelli guessed correctly that power would transfer from the Liberal Democrats to the Conservatives. He changed parties and urged his staff to vote Conservative. Driving Jonathan Evans around in his Rolls Royce and donating fifteen hundred pounds to the party, Morelli prepared the ground for a bonanza of bureaucratic squandermania. Or else he watched television. Morelli loved television. His house in Broad Street had front windows that jutted onto the pavement. Day and night, passing pedestrians would see the blue flicker of a television screen and the back of his head. "Perhaps he's got his accounts on his lap," suggested one mystified local.

The Hay Tourist Information Bureau was reorganized as an independent company. It published pamphlets copied verbatim from Morelli's publicity, saying that 'twelve major bookshops made Hay the largest second-hand bookselling centre in the world'. Previous brochures about the town had said I was the founder. 'It is apt that something of Hay Castle should be left,' it stated dismissively.

"I suppose it's a campaign to mislead tourists," one of my friends said sadly.

In fact Hope was selling some fine books in the Castle. Having trained as a photographer she decided to specialise in that field. Nineteenth-century photographs are becoming as valuable as seventeenth-century Dutch tulips and command enormous prices for fine specimens. Photographic books are the only genre that require artistic judgement. An immediate aesthetic assessment has to be made concerning the photographer's abilities and the artistic merit of an image. The works of famous photographers sometimes slipped unnoticed into other departments. Maeterlinck's *The Intelligence of Flowers*, with photographs by Alvin Langdon Coburn, was for sale in the Natural History department, and a book about the French game of *boules* with photographs by Robert Doineau, famous for his picture of a couple embracing on a Paris boulevard, was in Sport. A first edition of Robert Franks's book *The Americans* is worth eight hundred pounds. In our Americana department it could unwittingly be sold for ten pounds by staff unfamiliar with his work.

Hope also discovered a vast market for the ecological philosophy of the American Indians. Everyone wanted a copy of Dee Brown's *Bury My Heart at Wounded Knee* or *Black Elk Speaks*. I was extremely excited by this; paperbacks that had previously cluttered bookshelves could now be sold for a fiver. By the mid-1990s her private collection of 4,000 books about the North American Indians was one of the best in Europe.

Later we decided to try and sell the entire collection. A small colony of Pequet Indians, once thought to have been massacred in the seventeenth century, had comfortably established themselves near the border between Connecticut and Rhode Island. Aided by state laws regarding tax exemption and Native American sovereignty, they had become wealthy casino-owners in a position to purchase the collection.

When we went to Foxwoods Casino to meet them, their wealth was evident. Flashing golden lights were reflected in a neatly parked line of new Cadillacs. The entrance was indicated by a fourteen-foot alabaster fountain featuring an Indian in a hunting position. Inside, middle-aged ladies in pale pink dresses and diamanté spectacles were working several machines at one pull. Wisely the American Indians appeared to have taken the professional advice of those best qualified to run gambling enterprises. The acres of deep mauve carpet, brass rails and black marble deserved our whispered words, "It's a Mafia joint".

The sale did not go ahead as the plump, white librarian wanted a list of the stock. We did not have one as it would have required months of uninterrupted work but we did supply one of their special requests, *The American Indians as Seafarers*, about New England's Native Americans who were excellent sailors. A more sympathetic Native American who worked in the library suggested a personal visit to Hay-on-Wye to evaluate the collection but she was discouraged. Perhaps we did not convey the fact that Hope's love and passion for her subject made it a unique and wonderful collection. Furthermore the subject is under-supplied, even in America. A New York bookshop specialising in books about Native Americans could not match our stock because he did not cover all areas of the United States and had a bias for Mayan and Spanish-speaking Indians.

Despite successful trading at the Castle, my fight back from bankruptcy was long and slow. Convinced that the Tourist Information Centre was run for the benefit of Morelli rather than the community, I decided to open 'The Official Tourist Information Centre' at the foot of the Castle drive. Some months after its opening solicitors' letters started to arrive. Morelli was alleging that I had libelled him and threatened to sue. The case dragged on for two years and cost £14,000. Hope, who comes from a long line of Scottish lawyers and judges, was defiant. Excellently defended, we won. When the satirical magazine *Private Eye* tried to expose Morelli in an article headed 'Morelli Bankrupt', they were less fortunate. They lost £68,000 in the resultant libel case because the judge did not accept their argument that it was legitimate to link his enormous wealth with his various sexual relationships. Although I am anti-Morelli, I objected to *Private Eye*'s lofty attitude. Were they themselves Morelli perfect?

After a few years both on the Town and Borough Councils, from which he resigned on matters of principle, Morelli cemented his alliance with the Development Board for Rural Wales. Bureaucracies present far less opposition than democracies. In Hay, Morelli's sweet-shop, off-licence, auction house and a couple of bookshops had all opened and closed within months. Nevertheless, the Development Board believed in the divine right of the wealthy. Morelli appeared to wield a power no-one else possessed and raised millions for the town's redevelopment. I could rave with fury at the lack of democracy, but when Morelli claimed the support of Hay Town Council nothing could be done.

In 1992 he received grants – the largest ever given in Wales apart from Laura Ashley – to create jobs in Llanwrtyd Wells woollen mill and for a rock-crystal factory in Rhayader. Teddy Bear Wonderland, one of his shops in Hay, sold six-foot teddies dressed as policemen. That he thought Hay was a place where people could appreciate oversized dolls, jig-saw puzzles and pseudo-Irish rock crystal I find nauseating. There was a tour of his four funded factories called 'Magical Moments in Wales'. It was only in the eyes of Morelli and the Development Board that these moments were magical. At Christmas 1997 the woollen mill closed and all the employees were made redundant.

In the late 1980s the Development Board continued to brush aside Hay's unique book trade. A craft centre was built in the town car park at a cost of £600,000. "They're having an opening party attended by the Under-Secretary of State for Wales, Wyn Roberts; I'll see you there," said my friend Leo Macho. But I was not invited. Six years later the craft centre was sold to Morelli for twenty per cent of its construction cost. There was not a murmur of opposition from the Town Council, nor was this negotiation made known to the community.

The worldwide collapse of the academic dream had been even more profitable for me than the boom which had preceded it, but by 1990 there were almost no more libraries left to buy. Our shop in Hudson had lost money and the recession was beginning. When the University of Miami wished to sell a collection of books from the Venezuelan Academy of Sciences, Hope, Paul Harris and I decided to go to Miami, the front line of American inner-city decay. Our van was almost rammed in Miami Beach. The tiny road between the beach and Route 95 was a leading killing-field, particularly of tourists looking for a short cut. Yet Miami Beach had magnificent art deco architecture and was the largest conservation area in the world. We spent a day there, sitting on white sand under fluttering palm trees which provided some relaxation, but a constant sense of fear made it impossible to feel at home.

The trip was also a disappointment for Paul. After a few large vodkas in the airport bar at New York, he had decided that his marriage to a female truck-driver from South Wales was a mistake and that he wanted to establish himself with the attractive girl next to him. Throughout our trip she fielded telephone calls from all over America, perhaps thinking he was a mobile sex-murderer who specialised in airport bars. Paul continued his pursuit and went to look for her in New York, only to discover that she was not prepared to honour the invitation she had extended in the exotic surroundings of the JFK bar. Paul wasted the succeeding days and his hard-earned wages in expensive New York hotels. Not too dispirited, he arrived back in Hay wearing a cowboy hat.

As well as the University's Venezuelan collection we were offered the stock of John Edwards, a Miami book dealer. The books were packed in three small garages and the heat was intolerable even before we started work. Jet-lagged, we did not check them properly and there were many duplicates. We had the expense of transporting two containers back to Hay, where the books remain unsold. Despite several Venezuelan islands being owned by Sir Macgregor Macgregor, the Scots were not interested in exploring their cultural heritage through the medium of Spanish.

John Edwards was HIV positive, and our debt to him grew so large that he contacted a firm of Hay-on-Wye solicitors called William Beales & Company. They suggested that John petition to wind up my company, demanding a large sum of money in advance to do this. John Edwards was horrified and thankfully refused. We did pay him in full before his death and he insisted in his dying will that all remaining books should be offered to me. However, the callous ambition of a petty solicitor had intruded upon the dying world of a pleasant second-hand bookseller. Like many men nearing old age, I regretted the changing standards of my youth. William Beale's senior partner had at one time been John

Williams, a pleasant World War Two veteran who fought in the navy in the Mediterranean. Refusing to take fees for unsuccessful initiatives and introducing me to my friend John Davies of Lloyds Bank, he did everything possible to help me.

In an anti-solicitor mood I published a postcard and wrote on the back, *The Hay-on-Wye home of Herbert Rowse Armstrong. Armstrong was the last solicitor in the British Isles to be hanged, in 1923. To critics of the legal profession his demise is as famous as that of John Cenci, the last Mafia chieftain to be electrocuted in Connecticut. On being asked if he had a final request Cenci stated, 'Would you please put my lawyer on my lap'.*

Chapter Eighteen

International
Booktowns

Le Village du Livre, Montolieu.

"I am a Huguenot in reverse."

I had never felt the conviction to join a political party. All three main parties seemed to believe too much in education. A romance with the Conservative Party lasted several months in the early 1980s, when Tom Hooson was trying to get into government. He was a young hopeful recently returned from New York, where he had trained with Benton and Bowles, the public relations firm which had represented Nixon. He listened to my ideas and gave me a chance by asking me to present evidence on tourism to the Welsh Select Committee. Reg Clarke suggested I wear a blue silk tie and pose as a party faithful. My criticisms of the brand new hotels wasting thousands of pounds were quickly brushed aside. I was no match for the Tourism Department of Surrey University, who produced a wealth of statistical evidence. When a civil servant called Leo Pliatsky's *Report on Non-Departmental Government Bodies* concluded that the Wales Tourist Board was 'effective and cost-effective' and that the Development Agency proved up to its task, I realized I loved another world than the Establishment.

Nursing a slightly wounded ego, I was glad to receive a telephone call from Noel Anselot. A village in the South of France wanted to become a Book Town and he and I were invited there to give our advice. He suggested that Hope and I join him on the overnight train from Brussels. Gleefully I agreed. "I am a Huguenot in reverse," I claimed, "driven out of Britain by its oppressive policies and forced to bring my ideas to France."

As a bon viveur, I had assumed that Noel would have found us a train with a lavish dining carriage, but we were lucky to grab a greasy hot dog at Brussels railway station. The train was bustling with Lourdes pilgrims. We found our carriage and settled for the night on hard couchettes. Hope lay down weakly saying that she felt ill. In the morning she was in so much pain that she could barely communicate. At first Noel and I did not take it seriously and thought that she had been torpedoed by the Brussels hot dog. Half an hour later it was obvious that her complaint was life-threatening. Noel pulled the emergency cord and the train screeched to a halt. At Montauban station pilgrims in starched habits pressed their faces to the carriage window to see the victim, crossing themselves piously, hoping to influence her fate. She was rushed on a stretcher to Montauban Hospital, where the surgeon told me that her kidney condition was too serious for them to treat. She would have to go to Toulouse, half an hour away, which had the biggest kidney unit in Europe. Its proximity undoubtedly saved her life. The deplorable state of her kidneys, which were found to contain hundreds of minute calcium stones, became a case history in a French medical book.

After several days her condition was stable enough for me to proceed alone to Montolieu, where I met Michel Braibant, the driving force behind the 'Village du Livre'. A thin, bent man with a grey beard reaching to his chest, he looked like a pixie from the Pyrenees. His appearance belied his dynamism, for he had succeeded in persuading the Mayor, Madame Courrière, to turn Montolieu into a Book Town. As we sat beside a trickling fountain next to the bar, the men of the village filed past to rinse the dust off their hands after a game of *petanque*. Michel and I drank thirstily and tried to communicate our respective ideas for the town.

In his life Michel had collected everything to do with the printed word, from a map showing the introduction of paper into the South of France from China, to several handsome antique printing presses. He wanted to establish a 'Musée du Livre' as the centre-piece of the medieval village, whose population had more than halved to eight hundred since the turn of the century. A museum would not have been one of my first priorities. It would need outside funding and I felt that France had lots of museums already. However I was in favour of considering all approaches in Book Towns. Near Montolieu is a little village called Carla Bayle from where the Huguenots originated. Their motto is: 'Tolerance is the cause of all understanding; intolerance is the cause of all evil.' What could be a better motto for a Book Town?

While waiting for Hope to recuperate I visited Montolieu often. In the narrow streets the aromas of *cassoulet*, a local dish of beans, garlic, sausage and fatty pork, mingled with the hot air. The scraping of knives and forks were the only sounds of life in the quiet village, its shutters drawn against the Mediterranean sun. Jan Haas, a devoted helper at the Book Town inauguration, crossed the village on an old, grey moped to show me a magnificent, empty shop opposite a medieval bridge. It was for sale and inexpensive, so I decided to buy it. Underneath the bridge was a deep ravine with the sound of churning water far below. I could see bay trees, olive trees and fig trees from the deepest black-green to sunlit shades of lime. In between the trees were small allotments, rose bushes and stone paths leading to the river which surrounded the village. Expansion or new development was impossible. Montolieu was effectively clustered on an island.

In my new shop I found some bullets underneath an attic floorboard; the window looked directly across the bridge. Evidence of the war was still prevalent. Some men had the blue bruise of concentration-camp numbers on their arms and a girl found a Nazi button on the river bed beside a ruined mill which had been a popular swimming spot for German soldiers. Picnicking there, I imagined the ghostly presence of the enemy stripping off their heavy grey uniforms and plunging into the dark water.

When I first entered France I emerged blinking, as if into a brighter light. No longer was it necessary to tolerate the backward prejudice of a Wales ruled by incompetent officials. From learning that the great philosopher of the area was the Huguenot Pierre Bayle, to visiting the Chateau d'Eau in Toulouse, the oldest photographic museum in Europe, my education had to begin again.

Steve Sage, a wiry dealer in an old army shirt, was appointed to help set up the shop in Montolieu. When he arrived in Carcassonne with a vanload of books, he rolled down the window of his van and shouted to a pedestrian, "Où est la guerre?" The man looked alarmed. He had meant to ask, "Où est la gare?" Half an hour later he drove into Montolieu and parked in the shade of some trees by the church. In front of him was a sign which said *Parking de l'Eglise*. When, to his surprise, he was asked to move the car, he said, "I thought it meant 'Parking for the English' ".

In November 1989 Librairie Booth was opened. The whole village turned out for the occasion. The coiffured young Mayor, Claude Courrière, cut a ribbon and made an optimistic speech about the future of the Book Village. I was impatient to define the real reason for their existence: Book Towns were a reaction to the increasing redundancy of small villages all over Europe, largely due to supermarkets. "There is a new definition of the second-hand book," I said in a short address. "It is an object *not* sold in the supermarket and therefore offering hope to the small town!" My remark was lost like a penny thrown into the middle of the Atlantic Ocean.

We drank sweet, yellow Muscat, the popular aperitif of the area, and listened to squealing bagpipes made out of goats' bladders. I found the French establishment extremely welcoming and hospitable. Claude Courrière gave the most enjoyable dinner parties and, as a close friend of the book-loving President Mitterand, supported the scheme passionately. In retrospect, undoubtedly hampered by my schoolboy French, I regret that I was unable to give her better advice about Montolieu. The development officials in France had not the slightest idea of how matters should proceed. All thought and discussion was subordinate to the acquisition of government grants. The Book Town started with a healthy budget and considerable media attention but few considered the reality behind all the publicity. It would have been valuable to have had a dialogue with the development authorities in the area but they remained mysterious figures in the background. Their wisdom dominated but could not be discussed.

During the winter of 1989 we remained the only bookshop open in Montolieu. We employed a Dutch girl who sat conscientiously at the desk but did not know how to sell books. Eventually she brought her loom into the shop and sat weaving goat's hair. Hope, blessed with a consuming love of her native country, impulsively employed an inept Scottish accountant who so mishandled our initial registration that we received a 50,000 franc bill for unpaid taxes. The high point of our first year was when a farmer gave us a plate of fresh figs from his garden.

In the spring Noel opened his shop in a pretty cobbled street leading up to the church and other bookshops began to establish themselves. Noel and I bought shops in Montolieu more through enthusiasm than for commercial reasons. They provided a perfect platform from which to discuss our different philosophies for Book Towns. Noel was not especially sympathetic to many of my ideas. He saw wealthy, middle-aged people investing in property as the key to reviving a town, whereas I saw the future in young 'bouquinistes' exploiting international connections for the benefit of local trade. Hope and I, from our experience of Hay-on-Wye, recognised the danger signs and protested that the Conseil Municipal was developing Montolieu in the wrong way.

Noel Anselot was surprisingly weak. "We must let people in different parts of the world do it in their own way," he said. As his previous theory had been that we should open our shops in order to give a lead, I found this attitude highly Jesuitical. The Booksellers Association motto, *Amor Librorum Nos Unit* ('The love of the book unites us') represented a fundamental divide between Anselot and others, and myself. Their priority was the love of the book but my overriding belief was in the love of a rural community uniting us.

Government support was misdirected. The Conseil Municipal gave a large grant for the building of a new bookshop nicknamed 'the fish tank' by the locals because of its large, plate-glass windows. Its modern automatic doors were an insult to the medieval beauty of the town and the butt of jokes because they slid open expectantly every time the lightest car passed along the narrow street. The shop contained fashionable, glossy books in French and new books could be ordered from Paris. It would have made a good city bookshop but it was a mistake not to differentiate between the rural economy and the urban. Two years later the shop went bankrupt and the owner, despite pompous talk of building a new hotel, disappeared. He owed the town thousands of francs and was eventually sent to jail for unpaid debts. Even the enthusiastic publicity did not ultimately help Montolieu because it raised expectations that could not be justified so early on.

At one end of the village was the Manufacturie Royale. During the reign of Louis XIV fine textiles had been produced here, then wrapped in paper from the local mills and distributed via the Canal du Midi. The premises looked like a Jean Cocteau film, with crumbling stone balustrades and abundant, creeping ivy. "The future of Montolieu rests on the Manufacturie Royale," I said. It had the capacity to hold several million books in all languages and to draw people from all over the world as the major international book centre, the Eiffel Tower of the second-hand book trade. I felt the rural revival of Montolieu needed the resources of the non-French speaking world in the form of visitors from Japan, Australia and America. A new form of international bookselling had to be developed. However, Noel Anselot and Claude Courrière thought it more important to revive the small, empty shops than the magnificent old factory. I offered to supply the necessary books if shelving could be arranged in the Manufacturie. My offer was rejected and my dreams of an international dimension to the world of second-hand bookselling were ignored. Five years later, thanks to the relentless efforts of the Manufacturie's owners, Sheilah and Marc Guillet, the magnificent old mill finally shuddered to life. Marc runs paper- and book-making classes for students and a Dutch bookseller, Laurens Van Baardewijk, has established a Galerie des Bouquinistes with indoor book-stands rented by different booksellers. The battle for an effective rural economy is being fought over the counter, book by book.

As a young Book Village, Montolieu drifted into new bookselling. Seven of the twelve shops declared their intention of retailing books about Cathar culture. Catharism was one of the chief heresies of the Middle Ages. It differed from the monotheistic Christian religion in its belief in the dualism of a spiritual world which was good and pure, and a terrestrial world which was carnal, physical and corrupt. The Cathars and their high, windswept fortresses were part of Languedoc's history and the feature most heavily promoted to tourists.

Given this, I strongly disagreed that Montolieu's shops should sell books about a subject already exhaustively covered by city bookshops. We would no longer be able to claim that the Book Town was giving a unique service. I suggested that the town should commemorate the golden age of Paris, the period between 1880 and 1940 when Picasso and thousands of foreigners regarded the city as their natural cultural capital, or the centenary of French rule in Mexico, which might attract the Spanish, only two hours away. Initially, Montolieu should have thought how to attract visitors from cities within 200km, such as Bordeaux, Montpellier, Barcelona and Toulouse – which had an academic tradition older than Paris. National sophistication would lead to international sophistication. Visitors travelling from afar will contribute more money to the regeneration of the town than local visitors on day trips. The point was illustrated when Claude Courrière visited Hay. "What a lot of bed and breakfasts there are," she said. There are one hundred and thirty-five, and one even has its own swimming pool.

The French Book Town became a manifestation of French culture.

"Vive le Village du Livre!" I said to a bearded calligrapher in the village.

"Et des arts graphiques!" he responded gruffly.

My French was not good enough to explain that the chances of Montolieu making an impact on the graphic arts world sufficient to revive the economy was slim. French opinion was that culture could revive the economy. My belief was that culture should come after the economy.

Noel employed a very fat, very professional Belgian bookseller called Monsieur Louvard, who traded as if he was in the centre of Brussels and suffered the rural life of Montolieu for two years until, one evening, the executive car that had enabled him to commute rapidly to and from Brussels was stolen from outside the village bar. It was the final straw. Another Belgian in Montolieu was Daniel Olivier, a scowling ex-fighter-pilot who had participated in the student revolts thirty years previously. He loved political minorities and dealt in books about Gaullisme and Jean-Marie Le Pen. There was barely a tree trunk in the area without Le Pen's name carved on the trunk. He offended the Mayor by writing a broadsheet ridiculing her, and the local nuns by sticking a large pile of religious books on a skewer outside his shop.

Although my opinions do not carry weight in the village, I am extremely glad that Hope and I have kept our shop in Montolieu. We also bought a café there for her daughter Lucia. The Café du Livre was a great success in the village. Two years later, Lucia and her friend Poppy transformed the Café into The International Inkwell, a hotel for writers which is still flourishing – for reservations telephone +33 (0) 468 248 117.

In conclusion, I feel that Montolieu's predicament should have been simply and honestly appraised, and upon such an appraisal future action should have been taken. Anselot and myself suggested quite different courses of development. Perhaps because he was a fluent French speaker his wishes predominated. When he withdrew from Montolieu, and the heavily-funded new shop failed, there should have been a democratic review of the situation; it was too complicated an issue for the Conseil Municipal, which was composed largely of farmers. As the seeds for other Book Towns germinated, failure to learn from these mistakes was to damage the Book Town movement as a whole.

As far as I know, no hundred year-old working second-hand bookseller has yet received a telegram from the Queen, but in Guildford, Surrey and Preston, Lancashire, two ninety year-olds still work assiduously with their stock. On Long Island in America Dr Simon Nothman showed me his small pale-blue shorts above a pair of bony knees. "I am entering my second childhood," he said on his eightieth birthday. Many of my friends experienced the Second World War.

For none, perhaps, was it more important than George Whitman of Shakespeare & Co. in Paris. The grandson of Walt Whitman, he arrived in Paris in 1945 as a young GI and became entranced by the beautiful bookshop started by Sylvia Beach opposite Notre Dame. He bought it and has been trading there ever since. His best-sellers are, of course, the

Americans and Irish in Paris: Hemingway, Scott Fitzgerald, James Joyce, Beckett and so on. He buys books from me which are forgotten elsewhere, like Elliot Paul's *Springtime in Paris*, a beautiful description of the city in its heyday before the Nazi occupation. Should there ever be a training course for young Book Town enthusiasts putting their toe in the water of the fast-flowing international stream, I would recommend sitting at the feet of the great George Whitman. Teenage girls beware, though. Recently, the second-hand book trade received a circular asking for support because he had just had a child by one and, due to his age, might not be able to fulfil his parental obligations. For generations young girls have been staying at his flat. I sometimes wonder what contribution this has made to the population of Paris.

In 1992 Frank English died. For a year or so he had been in and out of London hospitals. When cancer of the throat was diagnosed he went to North Wales to be near his brother and I visited him every few weeks in a hospice, desperately hoping the diagnosis was wrong. Violet Jenkins had no such doubts; she had seen Frank smoke packet after packet of Woodbines. "He's going to die," she said and took him a big bottle of Scotch. Throughout Hay he is remembered with respect and affection as 'a good 'un'. Death he approached in the same way as he had life, as something to prompt witty response. The last time I saw him he took a bunch of flowers from Hope and, clutching them closely to him, perfectly mimicked a knight on a medieval tomb.

"I shouldn't bother too much about the Festival," were some of his last words to me.

Since 1988 the Hay-on-Wye Literature Festival, sponsored by *The Sunday Times*, had been using the fame of Hay to satisfy the egos and marketing strategies of various intellectuals. Despite billing Hay as 'The Town of Books', *The Sunday Times* in no way understood the priorities of second-hand bookselling. Why should the town promote new books that it does not stock? The second-hand book trade has a natural integrity. Inexpensive, high-quality literature will always sell. Shakespeare, Molière and Tolstoy are immortal compared to low-quality literature which may achieve a quarter of a million sales. Discrimination and knowledge make the market. I know, for example, that Elizabeth David is the greatest cookery writer of the last few decades because my shelves are empty of her work. In the second-hand trade there is no traffic-jam of authors wishing to write and talk about themselves.

"Each Festival injects four million pounds into the area," announced the organizer Peter Florence. My hackles rose in defence of Hay. I wanted more for the rural economy than the crumbs from a rich man's table. Festival income came in a single week each year and did not create any full-time jobs. Nevertheless, a horde of socialist intellectuals arrived in Hay to talk about themselves, from Wedgwood Benn, Roy Hattersley, Melvyn Bragg and Arnold Wesker to Margaret Drabble. The only person I was a fan of was Vi Jenkins who used to run The Wheatsheaf, where I had been drinking for twenty-five years. "He's a chopster," said Vi of one festival visitor, meaning a talker.

"Chopster" was quite an insult. Hundreds of chopsters were being paid large sums to come to Hay and talk about their books while claiming to revive the area. My final vestiges of respect for the Labour Party vanished when left-wingers swarmed to the Hay Literature Festival, which was primarily a platform for Rupert Murdoch, the pillar supporting Thatcherism in Britain.

Politicians write autobiographies to establish their reputations. Rather than to stimulate thought, they are often used to repress it. In his vanity biography, *The Ascent of Britain,* Peter Walker overreached himself by saying that the future of Britain depended on the Shah of Persia. This error of judgement, I feel, was excusable but when he deliberately omitted any reference to the millions of pounds he made for Slater Walker by skilful and corrupt use of journalism, he should have been disqualified from high rank even in a Conservative government.

John Carey, the Oxford Professor of English Literature, was to be one of the Festival's patrons. A humble Radnorshire schoolmistress could have told the learned professor that Jeffrey Archer, Barbara Erskine and Craig Thomas had nothing to do with literature. I wrote to him along those lines but, as an Establishment mandarin, he did not have to reply and naturally did not. I was left staring rather sadly at a cutting from *The Sunday Times* referring to his 'witty and incisive mind'. I consoled myself with the American Indian belief that the ordinary human being thinks with his genitals and stomach rather than his brain. I concluded that arts people were farts who were only performing for the money, and were therefore also tarts. Our campaign slogan was 'Arts! Farts! Tarts!' My minister Gerry Taylor pointed out that the Festival happened around Ascension, for which the German is 'Himmelfahrt'. He suggested we stage something simultaneously for the local people – a Topless Chainsaw Contest, perhaps? The noise would drown the babble of all the literary lectures. Unfortunately the shortage of willing young females and expensive insurance policies vetoed this.

Most regarded my protest against the Festival as a rather petty vanity. This culminated in a journalist referring to Hay as a place where people were 'nightmarishly provincial'. I saw myself as idealistic rather than egoistic. The end of the Roman empire was marked by festivals; now festivals were marking the end of the European empire. The Development Board for Rural Wales was funding hundreds in Wales alone, just as many centuries ago the Romans ignored economic logic for a few hours of festivity.

My opposition was also motivated by my mistrust of the activities of the Development Board for Rural Wales. The antipathy was mutual. In

1989 the Board promised £5,000 to one of the organizers as long as the enterprise "had nothing to do with Richard Booth". Their personal opinions about me may have been justified but the abuse of democracy was not.

Visitors to Hay-on-Wye are very fortunate that one of the most beautiful and historic routes in Wales must be the Hay to Aberystwyth road. Beginning by threading the middle reaches of the River Wye and ending with the spectacular mountain approach to Aberystwyth, it is a string of glory. At one end William Williams of Pantycelyn composed *Guide me O Thou Great Redeemer,* at the other Handel composed the *Alleluja* chorus in his bath. (An old bookseller friend of mine once tried to buy the taps.) Carving through the landscape in my car, the fields were a smudged palette and a rainbow arched over the valley, reflecting its colours. There was no need for a pot of gold; my cup was full. The history of nineteenth-century English literature would have to be rewritten if the regular guests to the country houses along the route were omitted: Swinburne, Shelley, Dorothy Wordsworth are just a few. At one end of the road is the grave of Prince Llewelyn, the last ruler of an independent Wales; at the other is that of Taliesin, the greatest Welsh poet. Until only recently, when I noticed a Little Chef restaurant sitting by the road like a cancerous crab, I was certain that my journey was a unique privilege which none other on earth could surpass. Sitting in a hot marquee in Hay-on-Wye it was easy to forget what lay beyond.

My opposition to the Festival received considerable publicity. 'King leads shopkeepers' revolt in the Town of Books,' wrote Peter Dunn of *The Independent*, coining the phrase 'Renta Literati'. When *The Independent* took over the Festival from *The Sunday Times*, this weakened opposition still further. Unwavering, Hope and I decided we would be buried in our 'Arts! Farts! Tarts!' tee-shirts. In May 1997 we broke our habit of ignoring the Festival and went to see Lady Brenda Maddox interview the journalist Keith Waterhouse. Our decision was influenced by our friendship with Brenda and her husband John. Everyone seemed keen that I should make a reconciliation with the Festival and I realized that Peter Florence was an honest man. Only an honest man would have driven ahead in his desire to promote it with so little tact.

In 1998 I had lunch with Peter Florence. He has generously forgiven me for my 'Arts! Farts! Tarts!' campaign. I can see the dynamic potential of uniting the Festival's success with that of the Book Towns and I look forward to a happy future together. The Hay-on-Wye Literature Festival has given people an additional reason to visit Hay and I cannot deny that mountains of dusty second-hand books can sometimes be overwhelming and boring.

"Do you know that there are nine-hundred books written about Princess Diana?" a Canadian said to me. I had grown up in a world where Jesus Christ, Napoleon and Hitler had been the most written-about figures; now all three were swamped by publications about Princess Diana. One starts life by thinking that civilization is turning trees into books and finishes it by thinking that a tree is better as a tree.

Chapter Nineteen

Book Town Fever

Henk Ruessink, myself and Noel Anselot, the three Founding Fathers of the European Booktown Movement, at Bredevoort.

"I am driving two megalomaniacs around this city."

The Breton town of Becherel is situated a few miles from Rennes and has an ancient market square which no longer sells agricultural produce but is home to a few second-hand bookshops. The town had more booksellers than any of the other new Book Towns and was eager to become a 'Village du Livre'. The old-fashioned Hôtel du Commerce promoted the local football team and made excellent galettes, a form of Breton pancake. The Mayor, the Marquis de Keunière, suggested twinning with Hay-on-Wye. I was keen on a connection but Noel was less interested. "People do not buy books near the sea," he said. One of Becherel's citizens, Anthare de Schuyter, was an ambitious man from Normandy whom an unhappy marriage had driven to Brittany. Like many provincial dealers, much of his income came from the Paris bookfairs, but he was very enthusiastic about the new Book Town. In honour of Hay's Declaration of Independence one of his shops in Becherel sold English books and he called it 'His Majesty's Bookshop'. It traded with some difficulty and was boycotted by the British Consul, who pointed out that a Queen was on the throne of England.

In Holland, Henk Ruessink, a retired educationalist, was the initiator of the Dutch Book Town, Bredevoort, which was officially opened on 27th August 1993 by the Royal Commissioner of Guelderland. Six booksellers relocated there, alerted by a prospectus distributed throughout Europe. Henk was the first to argue that such an enterprise deserved European funding, successfully canvassing support from both the Dutch and German governments.

"A man from Bredevoort would not sell his house on Broadway; that's why the most famous street in New York has a kink in it," Henk told me. One of the advantages of a life in second-hand bookselling is that it has altered the one-track views a British education had given me. For example, bookselling taught me the importance of the Dutch in America, from Roosevelt to Rip Van Winkle, and to the fact that early documents relating to New York were written in Dutch. I had bought a library in Detroit which contained a register of 123 local history societies in Michigan, many of which showed strong Dutch influence. I remembered my days studying English History at Rugby: "The dotage of the Nation, Lord, is such to fawn on those that ruin them: the Dutch," declared Dryden as a seventeenth-century Royalist.

I was enthusiastic about the Dutch Book Town, though Noel Anselot believed that New York had been founded by the Belgians and that a Dutchman was, in any case, just an inferior kind of Belgian. To him, 'the yellow peril' did not refer to the Japanese invasion of the Pacific or even to the emergence of the Liberal Democrats as a political force in Britain, but to the proliferation of Dutch cars with yellow number plates driving through the Ardennes.

Bredevoort is a garrison town with a population of 1600 in the municipality of Aalten. When Noel and I arrived we found it a surprisingly vital and alive community with several restaurants and cyclists weaving quickly through the streets. This was strange to see after the dusty, boarded-up villages of the South of France. A wooden windmill rotated slowly at the edge of the town, inhabited by a ghostly miller dusted in white flour. Curiosity drove me inside, where I breathed in the smell of malt and listened to the creak of the blades rotating in the wind outside. Through a small window I could see the Book Town, about the size of a book and just as flat.

Throughout the visit we were treated as celebrities and were put up in a comfortable hotel. Breakfast consisted of twenty varieties of cheese and dozens of different hams. The whole of Dutch regionalism and regional pride seemed to be represented in that meal. Ruessink was more realistic.

"What is your national food?" I asked him.

"Schmack Brot," he said, which is a dreary bacon and egg sandwich.

Henk was passionately interested in everything to do with Bredevoort. The town was the birthplace of Rembrandt's second wife and had been the Principality of King William of Orange. Nine miles from the German border, it has a strong tradition of speaking Friesian and had offered a strongly Protestant opposition to Hitler. Amsterdam, 151 miles away, is an important European book capital, not least because of the number of Jewish booksellers who fled there during the Nazi persecution, making it a centre for German émigré literature and subversive anti-Nazi publishing. However, such a dynamic book trade made Amsterdam a threat to Bredevoort's existence. The new Book Town would have to compete in order to establish itself.

"Bredevoort must have a Holocaust Bookshop for Holland, Europe and even the world," I suggested. I thought it should have a direct connection with the Anne Frank Museum, which I had been told was the greatest tourist attraction in Holland. But the idea of a bookshop that was not immediately viable was too extreme for Bredevoort as it struggled into life. It is not generally realized that the glut of second-hand books increases every year and therefore makes revolutionary long-term tactics for selling them vital.

Noel was no help. "If a book doesn't sell, it's not economic," he pronounced. But I believe Book Towns do not always have to be commercially based in order to succeed. Non-commercial activity has its own virtues. Making myself a king has definitely been a loss-making activity. Nevertheless, looking back on the time when I was not a king, I feel it is justified.

My strongest regret about Bredevoort is that the potential of the women's movement bookshop was not fully explored. A narrow side-street shop, 'Vrouwen in Druk' had shelves staggered to great heights with both antiquarian and modern women's literature. I certainly had stock to contribute, ranging in subject matter from the liberated joy of a wobbling breast under a tee-shirt in a book about feminism to biographies about the first female Mayor of Chicago or women boxers.

Along with gay and lesbian literature, huge numbers of American books were about the female sexual dynamic. Internationally, it is one of the fastest-growing subjects in the second-hand trade. Cotters had first introduced the subject in Hay in the 1970s, when he issued a list of books under the title *Hades! The Ladies!* after a 1920s periodical. We offered 'saints and harpies, intrepid travellers and earnest bluestockings, missionaries, mothers and murderesses'. There were characters such as Madame Loreta Janeta Velazquez, otherwise known as Harry T. Burford of the Confederate States Army, who fought in many battles, acted as a spy and blockade runner, went prospecting for gold and travelled widely in Europe and South America. Also included was Dorothy Beale, founder of Cheltenham Ladies College who taught her girls independence and industry, and said of youthful emotions: "Try earnestly to brace them, my dears." Unfortunately the women's bookshop in Bredevoort closed. It would have had to hold about 100,000 books to be competitive worldwide and to exceed the stock of major bookselling cities like Amsterdam.

Exploiting the very narrow specialisations which emerged in post-Second World War publishing is a way of linking European, American and Far Eastern Book Towns.

"What do you mean by 'narrow specialisation'?" a journalist once asked me.

"Specialists in the photography of the bee," I replied.

Indeed, very small subjects could become surprisingly large if every country in the world contributed, but I had no confidence in the ability of small dealers to develop an international specialist market. They appeared to do little trade between themselves or to communicate sufficiently.

In the 1980s a Book Town enthusiast called Heske Kannetiter organized an annual coach trip from Amsterdam to Hay. She introduced me to the Town Clerk of Arnhem, who came on every trip. In him I saw the specialist collector of the future.He had a monumental collection in four languages about the Battle of Arnhem. He possessed everything that had been published about the great glider battle; leaflets dropped by the Germans telling the Tommy to surrender because GIs were fornicating with his wife; British accounts as immortalised in the films I had seen at Rugby; and theses about the emergence of wider strategic issues during the race for Berlin. It was a collection whose sheer physical volume and expense made it an impossible feat for an institution, whereas an individual can make it his life work.

During the Dutch trip I received a cold splash of reality when I found a postcard in my car. Turning it over, I saw that it had been written by my driver, who was escorting Noel Anselot and myself on a tour of Bredevoort.

"I am driving two megalomaniacs around this city," he reported back to his haven of domestic bliss.

"St-Pierre-de-Clages is the Book Town of the future," proclaimed Noel about the pretty village in the Swiss Valais which opened for business in the same year as Bredevoort. Two hundred years ago Rousseau and Voltaire had wandered among the spectacular snow-capped mountains. Now its main product was wine from local vineyards. On the edge of town was a hotel with outdoor thermal baths. As I luxuriated in the steaming water I looked out on the bourgeois day-dream of small, clean chalets dotting the mountains. The town was wealthy but dependent upon a few vineyard owners and affluent tourists. "The buildings in the town are too expensive," said Noel. Certainly, they were not as cheap as the empty properties in small French villages. It was becoming more and more evident that Noel's priority was to invest in property. To the full approval of the Swiss, he explained that this was the entrepreneur's way of reviving a small town. As a shopkeeper I saw the problem as a daily one: would we generate enough money across the counter to pay the wages?

A number of sincere and dedicated citizens formed a voluntary organization to launch the Book Town. Motivated by a love of her small, diminished community, Marie-José Gaist worked hard and enthusiastically. A keen apple-grafter, in her garden were four different types of apple growing on a single tree. The husband of another, Monsieur du Pont, took me to some local *caves* to taste wine accompanied by delicious pieces of brown bread. The polished steel wine tanks looked as if they belonged in an aerospace laboratory. It was a little different from the South of France, where I met an eccentric mayor who boasted that his town was famous for making the little wooden taps on the bottom of the wine casques.

The Swiss Book Town started under Noel's advice that small dealers would provide investment and expertise. He wanted to establish book-fairs but I was more dubious, feeling that they would erode the town's profits as dealers come from outside the town with their books, and take their earnings away with them. Book fairs were a phenomenon which had begun in the early 1970s and flourished in the 1980s, but now there are too many of them. Increasing specialisation means that they can be a very boring experience. For those uninterested in cricket, for example, imagine seeing a stand selling nothing but *Wisden* cricket annuals. Noel often repeated my words that ninety-five per cent of the world's books were published after 1961, but he never took this fact to its logical conclusion. The bookfair and the small shop are out-of-date; the volume of books they are capable of holding is too small. St-Pierre-de-Clages needed the stimulus of a mega-shop. Overheads are cheaper and fewer staff are needed during the winter. I felt that the purchase of a disused railway station to convert into one big shop could have been a vital move forward. The Orient Express used to thunder past on its way from Geneva to Venice. I returned a year later to visit the St-Pierre-de-Clages bookfair, which attracted lots of outside dealers and certainly enlivened the main street.

In 1993, Fontenoy la Joute, with a population of less than 300, opened as a Book Town. It was situated in Lorraine in eastern France, so it was far easier to colonise by the French-speaking Anselot empire than my own. At the opening I received lavish hospitality from Monsieur Cordier, whose two beautiful daughters were studying at the Sorbonne. Their subject was Chrétien de Troyes, a knightly follower of King Arthur, who, despite having established a strong presence in Wales, was a phenomenon that was essentially French: 80% of Arthurian literature is written in French. But, despite this, Wales looked upon Arthur as her own son. Arthur's sister was buried near Hay and another obscure relation was unearthed in Glamorgan.

In the resourceful tradition of Book Towns a cowshed was converted into a dining room and we sat down to a magnificent ceremonial lunch of truffles, salmon and steak. The deputy Mayor left the table three times to perform for the television crew. After lunch I walked around the town, which dated back to the twelfth century. The eighteenth-century houses had narrow fronts but their interiors extended far back from the street. The café and several of the shops still had signs dating from the First World War, and no new shops had opened since then. In

1996 a general bookshop opened under the direction of a Monsieur Daniel Mengotti. He was 'directeur' of the book village, and became our friend. A Second World War bookshop also opened, displaying a green Army jeep from the advance of Général Le Clerc's army in 1945. Because Baccarat, the town world-famous for its crystal, was nearby, I gave Monsieur Mengotti a book about international glassmaking. But being French and xenophobic, he was not very interested in the peasant glass-makers of Afghanistan or western New York State.

That evening in the café a local bought me a drink. The men in the bar stared at me silently as I poured water into the Ricard and watched it turn milky yellow. I was a loner, or I was to them: I think they saw me as a victim of the French Establishment.

Returning to Calais we passed the beautiful Gothic cathedral towns of Laon and Reims. We needed to divert their visitors along the tree-lined roads to buy architecture books and regional guides from the young Book Town. Fontenoy la Joute promoted a book trail. *La Tour de France en Livres* said the poster, a cartoon of a perspiring student on his bicycle with a satchel full of books.

The surprising thing about the international Book Town movement was that American Book Towns took so long to come about. With such vast numbers of books, why did the Americans not create Book Towns themselves? Perhaps because the distances are greater, and the market weakened by an over-abundance of material. I know that attempts were made in the 1960s in Catskill, New York State, and Philadelphia. On reflection, perhaps it is because in Europe we feel embittered losing a small town of medieval tradition, whereas in America the town is generally less than a hundred years old.

Stillwater in the state of Minnesota was the first US Book Town to open, in 1992. It is on the River St Croix, whose wide banks and deep, blue water make the River Wye look like a trickle from a small poodle. The town was popular with tourists, so its economic situation was not as desperate as the other Book Towns. Its history was documented in a book of old photographs which showed the great river jammed with logs. An old man of the town spent his lifetime hooking dead bodies from the riverbed; presumably some of these were over-confident, macho lumberjacks prancing from log to log.

Tom Loome bought a Swedish chapel in Stillwater and filled it with theology books, from pre-Christian to Modernist, which he sold to libraries worldwide. "There's no way a modern church can survive in the USA without a car park," its owners had remarked. They almost gave Tom the magnificent Lutheran place of worship with its gleaming, stained-glass windows. Cheap property was much more prevalent in the USA than in Europe. Two cooperative bookstores opened on either side of Stillwater's main street. At the inauguration ceremony I wore my crown jewels and was photographed with the Mayor. Much to my embarrassment, a speech was given in the Welsh language by a member of the Welsh-speaking community of Minnesota, which published its own journal, *Y Drych*. Many of the buildings in Stillwater had flaking, hundred-year-old advertisements with the names of businesses indicating the population's Norwegian and Welsh ancestry.

In 1995 the famous author Larry MacMurtie invested large sums to turn Archer City, Texas, into a Book Town. It soon achieved a high profile, but Tom Loome felt that as they did not recognise me as King, they should not be regarded as a Book Town. I am still musing over this difficult question.

'People once flocked here for gold, now it's books!' was the proud boast of the Gold Cities Book Town in California, established when the book dealers of two small communities, Grass Valley and Nevada City, formed The Gold Cities Book Town Association. I first heard about them through correspondence with their President, Gary Stollery of Brigadoon Books, who was deeply impressed by the concept of Hay. In December 1997, a few months after his visit to Wales, I received an invitation: the King and his wife were to be Guests of Honour at a banquet in the old Nevada City Brewery. Hope packed my travelling crown (a padded tea-cosy in the form of a crown) and my red velvet cloak (held together by safety pins), and we flew to California.

Driving from Sacramento to Nevada City was a journey through heaven and hell. It began with the very cheapest form of publicity. Huge, gaudy signs lined every stretch of road, advertising cheap chain motels, fast-food restaurants and strip-bars. In the latter part of the journey beautiful pine forests and snow-topped mountains looked more idyllic than the prettiest parts of Switzerland.

Our destination lay 150 miles east of San Francisco in the foothills of the Sierra Nevada. The Gold Cities are similar to those seen in Wild West films, with white wooden buildings and covered walkways. I was fascinated by the perfectly-bored, circular ore samples, weighing as much as half a ton, that were lying in front yards. The Cornish had been considered the best gold-miners and in Nevada City there were four shops selling Cornish pasties. Potato, onion and steak wrapped in pastry, they were the perfect food for taking down the mines.

The banquet was a magnificent affair. We were escorted to our seats by two bagpipers from The Gold Country Celtic Association wearing kilts, sporrans and silver daggers. They were about double the size of the average Scotsman and looked as impressive as the bearskinned Guards outside Buckingham Palace. Hope was elegantly dressed in a black velvet suit and black necklace, but I shambled in wearing a spruced-up sports jacket, which is the most formal attire a second-hand bookseller ever wears. From the long side of an E-shaped table I looked across a room full of journalists, lawyers and booksellers, and one Mark Twain impersonator in a white linen suit.

Feeling considerable trepidation at the prospect of making a speech, I tucked into a vast, juicy prime ribbed steak and tried to exercise puritanical self-discipline over the Napa Valley red wine. I sat next to the guest speaker, State Attorney-General Harold Berliner, who looked like a white-haired lawyer from a West Coast TV series. Apparently, the Nevada City Book Town was the only new development to receive his blessing in a state where he enforced strict conservation policies, forbidding new development in order to protect the exquisite late nineteenth-century architecture. He was also an old friend of Eric Gill and a collector of the fine presses, for which the Italian quarter in San Francisco is famous. He was right to see the Gold Cities Book Towns as a means of positive ecological development. There was more to the Wild West than sadistic paperbacks.

The great advantage of an English-language Book Town is that I am better able to articulate my ideas of co-operation. The dinner was a perfect platform. As the Gold Cities lie halfway between the borders of Canada and Mexico, I hailed them as "the first Book Towns on the Pacific rim". It is hard to give an exact definition of a Book Town because they are all so different, so I focused on one essential ingredient and argued that "what we are really doing is getting trade from an international world because we can not get it from the local world". I finished the speech on a rather more raunchy note. While sightseeing with Gary Stollery I had seen the tiny, wooden shack which had been the birthplace of Lola Montez, the courtesan of King Ludwig of Bavaria. "With modern technology," I concluded, "I could easily fill a room this size with books about ladies who went to bed with Kings." The speech ended to thunderous applause.

During the dinner a bearded man approached me. "I want a cannibal bookshop," he said. It was not such a far-fetched idea. In the nineteenth century, during the drive West, an event made its mark on American history. In 1846, eighty-seven settlers led by George Donner attempted to walk across America. They chose a little-known trail and lost their way. Cattle and the weaker members of the expedition died of thirst in the barren deserts. Wagons and possessions were abandoned. Some of the party reached the crest of the Sierra Nevada, 'hills whose heads touched heaven', as a child in the party wrote. Here they were trapped in a pass by a blizzard. Those who did not perish turned to cannibalism, spit-roasting fellow members of the expedition.

Drinking a can of lager in the back room of a bookshop in Grass Valley, I was shown the original government document relating how the US Congress had discussed the awful atrocities and decided which members of the party were to be hanged.

When I returned to Hay-on-Wye I faxed my international bibliography of Cannibalism to Gary:

> **Kenneth Roberts's** *Boone Island*: a shipwreck off the coast of Maine; starving survivors take desperate measures to prolong their existence.
>
> **Elfred Packer** ate five of the seven surviving Democrats in Colorado.
>
> **Michael Rockerfella** was eaten while making a documentary in Papua New Guinea.
>
> **Thor Heyerdahl's** *The Kontiki Expedition*: a voyage across the Pacific Ocean to visit ancient Polynesian cannibal sites.
>
> **Siege of Leningrad** in 1943: pink and well-fed cannibal butchers demonstrate the healthy nature of their activity.
>
> **Sawney Bean** in Scotland lived in an enormous black cave suitable for storing the pickled remains of travellers, which he fed to his wife and children.
>
> *Alive* **by Piers Paul Reid**: aeroplane crash in the Andes and the moral dilemma of eating a frozen fiancée.

I would not include books about the hot, bubbling Rotaroua springs in Auckland, New Zealand, because the tourists that fell into them were left there, uneaten, to flavour the water. Also, I do not want to offend the moral majority so I exclude Jeffrey Dahmer, who ate the heads of young boys in Milwaukee.

Gary replied that he was going to open 'The Original Cannibal Bookshop' in his back room and, with Hollywood up the road, he hoped to generate considerable publicity.

Driving to the airport wearing my latest gift, a baseball cap with 3D breasts, I felt optimistic. Goodwill would ensure that the sapling American Book Towns would take root as successfully as they had in Europe.

Fjærland, the Norwegian Book Town, opened in 1995. Drilling for oil had made Norway rather like a piece of Gruyère cheese. The Norwegians used the huge revenue to drill tunnels through the mountains, the tolls for which proved expensive on our way to Fjærland. The town is situated 375 kilometres north-west of Oslo. It nestles on an arm of Sognefjord, once a favourite holiday destination of German Kaisers and Russian Tsars. The landscape is spectacular and almost monochrome with miles of beautifully-spaced pine trees reflected in the deep, black water of the fjord. Surrounding me was cold, clean air, the sound of softly-hudding snow and the echoes of cracking glaciers. I felt very insignificant.

The first thing I noticed in the town were the goats standing on the tops of houses. They looked down at me, chewing mechanically. Turf is traditionally put on roofs as a form of insulation. It makes delectable grazing for the tiny animals, who jump up there from the side of the mountain.

The Book Town was the inspiration of Marit Orheim Maritzen, the wife of the Norwegian Ambassador to the European Union. A practical woman in flat shoes and a hooded anorak, she was very proud of the Norwegian tradition of self-sufficiency. We were taken to the house of Astrup, a Norwegian painter who left his life's work to the local community council. Rather than pay exorbitant insurance fees, the councillors took it in turns to guard the paintings themselves.

The Book Town was officially opened by the Minister of Arts, a retired jazz singer who looked like Elizabeth Taylor. Marit asked us to stay at the Hotel Mundal, which had been in her family since the nineteenth century. It looked magnificent standing on the banks of the fjord, rather like a Charles Addams drawing, with round wooden turrets, creaking verandas and crooked balconies. For breakfast there were enormous bowls of fish and prawns with which to make sandwiches before undertaking the local sport of glacier-walking. Previously, Marit's energy had been devoted to creating a popular Glacier Museum. The modern, glass-fronted building contained the history of ice formation, and full-scale models of nineteenth-century glacier walkers.

On the subject of glaciers, I remember a short story in *Wide World Magazine* in which a woman of eighty attended the funeral of her twenty year-old boyfriend. Sixty years earlier they had been on an ill-fated glacier walk together. His body had only just been recovered. The same magazine published the only short story by Winston Churchill, *Man Overboard!*, about a man watching and waiting for his terrible destiny as he heard the sound of his cruise-liner departing into the distance.

On the day Fjærland was officially declared a Book Town there was a lecture at the Glacier Centre. "Antarctica is for women," began the guest speaker. She had crossed it alone on a longer route than Captain Scott, and looked like a female version of the god Thor; the Viking ideal certainly seemed to survive in its ladies. We watched a film in which she dragged six rubber car tyres through a wood in a blizzard to get into condition, and arrived in Antarctica weighed down with all her survival gear. On her blue anorak she had a badge saying 'Antarctica is for Women'. "My God, how specialised the world is becoming!" I thought.

Registering Fjærland as the only Book Town in Norway, Marit was determined to make the small village an international book centre. I searched my mind for what was available for Norway and could only bring to mind some beautiful editions of Ibsen. Marit tried to get European Union support for all the Book Towns. Because her husband had been Norwegian Ambassador to the EU she had excellent contacts, and was the one initiator who seemed to realize that a strong element of idealism had to balance commercial realities.

She and her husband came to stay with me in Hay. As I stood up after dinner, the room spun round and I crashed to the floor, splintering my chair like a felled Norwegian pine. Marit and her husband were very sympathetic. It was either drunkenness or something more serious.

When Noel, Henk and I started the book town movement, it was like setting fire to dry timber. The blaze started because rural economies were desperate, but time revealed that it had no more direction than a forest fire.

In 1996 I heard that an East German town called Waldstadt-Wünsdorf wished to become a Book Town. I began to dream of the Book Town economy crossing the old East-West divide.

"It's only an old army base," said Noel Anselot. His views once again differed from my own. Noel tuned in to the BBC as if the Second World War was still being fought and was an irritating believer in 'The Iron Lady'. In fact, the town reflected one hundred years of German history: the military base was used by the Kaiser, the Weimar Republic and the Third Reich. During the War, Waldstadt-Wünsdorf had been a proud, if secret, monument to German technological superiority and a vital military communications centre. In 1945 30,000 Soviet troops took over from the cream of the German Army's technicians and attempted to use it as a base from which to control Berlin. In August

1994 they left in their wake an extraordinary environment, finally destined for peace. It was certainly the largest prospective venue for a Book Town.

I remembered my first visit to Germany when, as a teenager, I stayed with a man who had been taken prisoner at Stalingrad. I still see his yellow, emaciated face in my dreams. The family took me to see the Berlin Wall. Spiked with barbed wire it wound across the city like a concrete snake, though I was distracted by the psychological and physical torment of being too shy to ask my hosts if I could go to the Gents.

Had I not married Hope I should probably have married an alluring German bookseller called Catherine Clement. Small, dark and slightly oriental due to her Mongolian background, my nickname for her was 'Ulan Bator' after her home town. She was very successful commercially, providing a book-search service for the cluster of diplomats then living in Bonn. She told me how she had bought the library of a German dentist who still remembered Hitler affectionately. "Mein Führer lebt jetzt noch in meinem Herz," he would say: 'My Führer still lives in my heart.'

The German Book Town's administrator was Wolfgang Metz. Although he wore a black leather jacket entitling him to the leadership of a gang of Los Angeles Hell's Angels, he was in fact a rather prim ex-banker from West Germany. When he visited me in Hay I instinctively promised him wholehearted support. Book Towns promoted themselves as a credit to the capitalist economy and yet, paradoxically, they had grown out of some of its least creditable activities, namely the destruction of the agricultural and traditional economy in and around small towns, and the blight of property development. Therefore the idea of a Book Town in the ex-communist state of East Germany seemed especially appealing. I agreed to fly to Waldstadt immediately with my friend Tony Seaton.

I had first met Tony many years ago as a lanky-legged book dealer with the blond-haired, blue-eyed looks of a Hollywood idol. We had been slight friends and business acquaintances for twenty years. The man who met me at Gatwick Airport was by now a rather more haggard Dorian Gray-type idol.

"I've been appointed to head the Tourism Department of the University of Strathclyde," he said jubilantly. "It's the oldest hotel school in the country." I was more cynical, having just purchased the library of a broken-hearted old professor of Theology at Aberystwyth University where the Music, Classics and Philosophy departments had been closed down and replaced with a faculty for Business and Tourism.

On the flight to Berlin's Templehof Airport, Tony was full of enthusiasm for Book Towns. He told me that he had a direct line to the Scottish Minister for Tourism who had told him, "my door is always open for new ideas". This combination of the academic, political and financial could have been the perfect combination for the advancement of Book Towns, yet on our first trip to Waldstadt I felt myself slowly growing more distant from Tony. "I can give you a feasibility study for four thousand pounds," he said to the East Germans, but they were too broke to afford him.

At the airport we were met by a young chauffeur who took us to Wolfgang's flat in a block of slick former US Army flats in Berlin. I was shown to a small, red bedroom overlooking another American Army block. In the afternoon we settled into a discreet German bar in the vicinity. All problems disappeared as we chewed on a large sausage spread with mustard and drank 'Pepper'. This spirit could claim to be, and certainly tasted like, Europe's leading intoxicant. Through the windows the daylight turned to dusk and Wolfgang left us to return to his children and his young Serbian wife, Hannah.

Tony and I decided to enjoy a few more hours of Berlin nightlife but after some more glasses of pepper Tony announced that he was feeling very ill. I telephoned Wolfgang who summonsed a doctor and then an ambulance that carried Tony to hospital. I, more fortunately, returned safely to the flat, where I slept soundly for the next fourteen hours. Tony was discharged the next day with nothing serious to report, though to protect his precious position at the University of Strathclyde we agreed to call his affliction asthma. We had been contemporaries at Oxford but were now nearing sixty; the episode showed that our age was catching up with us. Looking back on the evening, I now know that I spent it blithely unaware that I had a serious illness which could have killed me at any moment.

The following afternoon Wolfgang drove us south to explore Waldstadt-Wünsdorf. Only when we left the Berlin ring road was there any evidence that we were in a country that had been under communist rule five years previously. Hundreds of petit-bourgeois houses stood in a pre-1945 time capsule. It seemed that their gardens had not been cared for, nor their walls painted since the time when mowing one's lawn was seen as an invitation to the Red Army to ransack the property and commit rape and robbery. The 80,000 people killed in the fall of Berlin seemed never to have been forgotten. I felt the dislike of the Soviet army was more due to xenophobia than ideology. After all, as Solzhenitsyn wrote in *The Gulag Archipelago*, the Red Army was composed mostly of sex-starved youths who had been in the field for two years chasing the German army across Europe. Their only interest was in murder and rape.

As we approached Waldstadt-Wünsdorf, I saw, on the left, a magnificent pine forest which presumably provided cover for the military base. On the right there was a picturesque little town where the first Panzer division had been raised. I noticed that it still had a railway which led to both Berlin, twenty miles away, and Moscow, eight hundred miles further down the line. Strategically, Berlin is very well placed for northern and eastern Europe and access to Scandinavia. Geographically, Waldstadt-Wünsdorf could be the most important Book Town in the world.

We started our tour of the town from a smartly refurbished office in the town square where we were offered prawns on German bread, and coffee in thin, white china cups. It did not take me long to realize that only a fraction of the town, namely the municipal headquarters, had achieved this veneer of successful capitalism.

The problems which followed Waldstadt-Wünsdorf's military occupation were a hundred times greater than I had ever imagined for a prospective Book Town. In 1935, it was developed to become one of Europe's largest barracks complex: 150 buildings were constructed to prepare Hitler's war plans. I could see thousands of rotting flats. A few had been bought by a property company but the multi-millionaire Australian behind the scheme seemed to have lost heart. There was no sense of civic or community identity.

Twenty-five empty supermarkets, the Russians' clumsy imitation of Western culture, were still scrawled with graffiti reminding the Germans of their escape from 'the Mongolian hordes'. Some had been ripped down but the impact was minimal. After the end of the War any military buildings of significance were dynamited. A dozen or so had been dutifully blown up, but nobody had seen any reason to remove the rubble, which had simply been left there as a testament to the acrobatics and resilience of East German dandelions. Like a cardboard box in a rainstorm, their walls were bent and nearly collapsed but no one was interested. Beautiful towers sixty feet high that looked like vast lipstick holders remained stuck in the ground. They were built so that Allied bombs would find no flat surfaces on which to explode. The whole area was surrounded by a high wire fence, once useful perhaps for deterring would-be James Bonds but now protecting nothing of value.

The ghosts of the town told me it could not be revived under capitalist society. Waldstadt-Wünsdorf had previously been dependent on Russian or German rulers but it would now have to begin at the beginning. Commercial life would have to be reinvented. As a typical West German banker, Wolfgang disliked the communist regime and pointed disdainfully to the rotting buildings with which East Berlin was replete, but, to his credit, he realized that there had to be an alternative to billions of marks of capitalist investment. "Mercedes Benz gave us a golf course," he said rather lamely. This was not going to revive Waldstadt.

In silence we shuffled through the camp behind Wolfgang. He pointed out the cinema, which had a false entrance concealing several hundred yards of underground tunnels, once the German Army's biggest communication centre. Calls could be made from North Africa and transferred through Waldstadt-Wünsdorf to Paris. The less sophisticated Russian troops had obviously found the passages served them better as a rifle range. I had a sexual fantasy of thousands of beautiful German girls in white blouses wearing headphones.

In its heyday the town cannot have been a bad place to live. Some of the buildings now serving as supermarkets had large gardens. At the end of an avenue of trees was a small museum where the curator told us he received a trickle of Russian visitors who had once been stationed there. Inside were twentieth-century relics from Waldstadt's Russian past. My footsteps echoed on the wooden floors as I peered at statues of MIG fighters soaring into action, battered helmets, identification cards, a prison bed. Here were the last forlorn representatives of the might with which the Soviets had once hoped to rule the world.

There were some decomposing photographs of Yuri Gagarin, the first man in space. I remember Gagarin mostly for being the passion of a homosexual friend who lived in Venice. He collected hundreds of silver photograph frames in which to place portraits of the handsome astronaut. The Italian police did not approve of his activities and persecuted him to such an extent that he jumped out of the window to his death.

The museum was in the house of the General von Paulus, whom Hitler made a Field Marshal in 1943 in a vain attempt to prevent him from surrendering at Stalingrad. He was the only high-ranking officer to have suffered with the troops. In Soviet commentaries about his surrender there are photographs of him, gaunt and exhausted, being led into captivity. Even Russian commentators had noticed the contrast between his personal devastation and the pink-cheeked, well-fed German staff officers surrounding him. Later he converted to communism.

In 1936 the athletic fields and gymnasia of Waldstadt-Wünsdorf were filled with sportsmen and women training for the Olympic games. I saw the open-air swimming pool where Leni Riefenstahl shot one of her pioneering films of muscular Aryan athletes jumping vigorously against a stark sky. We passed long lines of riding stables with stalls and hitching rings for a full regiment of cavalry from the Kaiser's time. Waldstadt means 'city in the wood' and I was offered a horse to ride in the magnificent forests which surround the town. As I looked into the miles of dense, misty woods I felt disappointed that I was due to return to Hay and could not take up the offer.

At the airport I saw that the Berlin Wall had been reduced to tiny pieces of broken concrete, sealed under transparent plastic bubbles which were made into tourist postcards. I sent one to my old friend Lennox, who had just had to sell his collection of Persian pottery after the collapse of Lloyd's. He said he was glad to receive it because it got him into a lower-priced area of contemporary ceramics.

On the flight home I thought perhaps Waldstadt-Wünsdorf could become a centre for exile literature. From Scott Fitzgerald, who lived in Paris in the 1920s, to all the Chilean, Hungarian, Polish and German authors who wrote literature outside their country of birth: some of the most important writers of the twentieth century had been exiles. In 1996 Princess Jean Galitzine and her daughter came to Hay-on-Wye because they were establishing a library in St Petersburg of Russian literature that was forbidden during the communist rule. Much of it had been written in exile by those fleeing Soviet rule, just as many talented German writers had fled Nazi rule. Relying on charitable support, the unique collection is in memory of Prince Galitzine, whose life spanned Soviet Russia. I hope Book Towns will communicate between them to establish specialist libraries like this one.

Other books I dreamt of for Waldstadt-Wünsdorf were those from eastern Europe, in all languages, which were gathering dust in American cities. Millions of books, often unique recollections of the Holocaust and other periods of persecution, are being destroyed in America. The heir to a Polish refugee, for example, finding no market for his grandfather's books in Chicago, either has to throw them on the dumpster or sell the lot for ten dollars.

Although I visited Waldstadt-Wünsdorf again, this time alone, my convictions were clearly not shared. It was not chosen as an official German Book Town. It was much bigger than previous Book Towns and would have had to use books to trigger a wider economy. In terms of property development, the old Eastern zone contained copious, decrepit and unserviced properties several lifetimes away from profitable completion. I wrote to Wolfgang congratulating him on his non-selection: 'An official Book Town is one chosen by officials and will have far less chance of succeeding.' He suggested that I start an English-language bookshop in Waldstadt-Wünsdorf, but I was adamant that nothing should be established there that was not superior to the services already on offer in Berlin.

I enjoyed my friendship with Herr Wolfgang Metz. I saw him as a man genuinely trying to modify the rigid capitalist beliefs of the West and apply them to the problems of eastern Europe. This made him more interesting to me than Noel Anselot, who was a staunch capitalist. Wolfgang tells me that in 1998 Waldstadt-Wünsdorf had fourteen booksellers. Despite this, I believe that they will struggle against great odds. To succeed, you need more than a capitalist philosophy.

"Do you know what has been the most important event in the history of the world since the birth of Christ?" Frank Lewis had said to me twenty years earlier. As keen historians we often had quite lively discussions. "The battle of Stalingrad," was his answer.

The vast battle was commanded by an inhabitant of Waldstadt-Wünsdorf, Field Marshal von Paulus. Nowhere better symbolises to me the German military tradition which ended at Stalingrad. Two vast armies fought each other with an intense, bitter ferocity and an unceasing determination that made history. From this point onwards, Europe ceased to be the shining star around which countries orbited; we became intercontinental. This change was certainly reflected in the second-hand book trade. The romance of travel disappeared and books implied the political system of their country. Travels in South America, for example, would no longer be discussed, as Charles Waterton had done, in terms of how to retain the colour in the beak of a stuffed Toucan. Instead I would open a book about South America to see American monks giving milk to starving children. Books about China were more likely to feature Chairman Mao than the landscape of Imperial Palace Gardens.

The book was used to fight the Cold War. The inhabitant of the West genuinely believed he was facing a bureaucratic and unworkable state in the communist world. I am not sure whether the exotic adventures of James Bond gave a more realistic picture of Western life.

The insidious propaganda which had created the business reality of the West was only marginally dented by portrayals of beautiful Russian spies and uncontrollable villains. Billions of subsequently unsaleable words were written about the difference between the East and the West. The printed word gave little credibility to Russians in books such as *The Russians: are they Human?* and *I married a Russian*.

The standard view that the poor state of East Germany was due to its being non-capitalist is one I reject. Living in a declining rural community, I was seeing the bad effects of capitalism as shops closed and an agriculture practised for a thousand years vanished. This did not draw me to communism but to a kind of post-capitalist philosophy. The capitalist ideal is for a young man to be both a millionaire and Prime Minister by the time he is forty. Book Towns are not the creation of hungry young capitalists but of people in their late middle-age who are worried about the state of their small town and who can find fulfilment working in a small-scale rural economy where people still care for their neighbours. I refer to them as the 'grey economy'.

A man came to me who wanted to start a Book Town in Hollern in northern Germany. "It must be amusing, Richard," he said. "When you have reached the age of fifty and made some money, you need some amusement." I agreed with him. I am sure the grey economy is getting bored by the conformity and standardisation of the capitalist world. Every student wears the same jeans and every car is the same shape. I suppose my proudest achievement has been in separating the identity of Hay-on-Wye from other small Welsh towns. I have wondered whether this could be extended to include fashion and costume. As Hollern had been very famous for its millinery, I responded enthusiastically and suggested a Book Town hat which would be unique in the world. Modelled on the academic mortar-board, it would be an upturned Kleenex box, thus enabling a middle-aged man to enjoy the three greatest pleasures in life, consecutively. He can stagger up to bed with a full glass of whisky in his right hand, a girl on his left arm and some books balanced on the flat surface of his new hat.

His Majesty King Baudouin I of Belgium (left) with Noel Anselot, founder of the second Book Town in the world, Redu.

With the Mayor of Stillwater at the opening of the Minnesota Book Town, two years before the Seaton Report: an absolute refutation of Professor Seaton's theory that American Book Towns did not exist.

The international recognition was embarrassing for the Welsh officials

1992: President Mitterand on a tour of the village du livre with the Mayor of Montolieu, Madame Courièrre.

My shop in Montolieu. I was a little too deaf to adapt to the Southern French accent.

Books arrive at Dalmellington.

Expanding to Scotland I became a passionate believer in the de-institutionalized book.

My driver George, and my nurse Denise, at their wedding in 1992. As you can see he is much better husband material than me.

My friend Harout Gudelekian of Beirut, one of the many Middle Eastern enthusiasts for old photographs and picture postcards, sporting Book Town hats.

April 1998. At the Emperor's Banquet with my wife and step-son, Orlando. With seven MPs in marginal constituencies, the Quangos are the real rulers of Wales. But here, the population are beginning to rally around the Emperor.

Lucia Stuart. Keeping a café in Montolieu, she, like myself, has experience of living in a rural area. This has made her an especially valued co-author.

The Honesty Bookshop outside the castle. If I am not remembered as the founding father of Book Towns, I shall be remembered as the inventor of the Honesty Bookshop which has been copied all over the world.

Chapter Twenty

A Brush
with Death

I slowly recuperated, but it took two years supported mainly by my mother bookshop – a vital fact in Book Town development.

"What day is it? What year is it?"

" Con's wife was a fine girl. The doctors gave her an injection and she was dead in the morning." Discussing how many people the local doctors had killed was a popular pastime in Hay. They were known as 'the butchers'. Like solicitors, their profession protected them from criticism but did not ensure their efficiency. My own doctor was obsessed with the idea that I was overweight. Picking up two heavy medical dictionaries, he once said, "How would you feel carrying these around in your tummy?" Another doctor spent a few minutes poking around at my groin and announced that I had a hernia. After a little more poking around he declared that it was a double hernia and a friend of his could operate within the week. That evening, by chance, I met an old acquaintance who worked in the local hospital. Between forkfuls of pasta in an Italian restaurant he advised me not to have an operation if I was not in pain. I cancelled my appointment and during a medical examination, one year later, I found that I was hernia-free.

Experience of second-hand books had given me an additional axe to grind against the medical profession. Why do doctors think that meeting lots of people gives them some kind of esoteric literary qualification? Opening a promising-looking book only to discover it is the memoirs of a general practitioner with literary aspirations is one of my job's hazards. These books are as digestible as a stone in a sack of wheat.

In 1995 I began losing my balance. The doctor suggested I give up drinking which I did, assiduously, for several months. But I was still unable to balance on one leg and was stone deaf in one ear. The doctor assured me there was nothing amiss. Once again I was saved by a casual dinner-date. Hope's niece, a medical student, invited us to dinner and in the course of the evening suggested that I see a neurologist as soon as possible. Several days later I was informed that I had a brain tumour the size of a cooking apple buried behind my left ear. Though benign, it had been growing for many years.

"I have never seen an acoustic neuroma of this size in Britain," remarked Professor Bell, a leading world expert. I was in mortal danger and he would have to operate immediately. That night I wrote my will in green biro as I waited at the Atkinson Morley hospital in Wimbledon. I needed two seven-hour operations under two surgeons. For the first time in my life I was uninterested in the business. As Hope wheeled me to the operating theatre, I knew from her pallid smile that she was wondering in what state she would see me again. The odds were fifty-fifty.

"What day is it? Who is the Prime Minister?" asked a nurse loudly as I awoke from the operation. I was vaguely aware of having lost all sense of orientation; I was a speck suspended in space. An operation so near to the brain could easily have damaged it, but I had suffered comparatively little harm. The left side of my face is paralysed but this may improve over time following a nerve graft from my ankle.

Professor Bell saved my life by performing an operation that would have been impossible a few years previously. Despite a reputation that took him from Canada to Ceylon, he stayed loyal to a tiny hospital which was threatened with closure. Only occasionally did this highly professional surgeon let his feelings show. "That is the health service of the future," he snapped, after a routine meeting had taken two hours.

Many with life-threatening ailments have to spend hours reading out-of-date *Woman's Own* magazines in stifling wards smelling of disinfectant.

My stay in hospital was lengthened because I contracted the MRSA virus which is immune to antibiotics and is the scourge of hospitals throughout the country. I shared the Isolation Unit with a terminally ill woman plugged into a machine that sucked and pulsated throughout the day. Bland-faced relatives came and sat hopelessly by her bedside. My own visitors had to wear plastic aprons, draw on white rubber gloves and pass through transparent plastic doors to enter the room. My stepson Orlando bought me a soapstone scarab from Egypt. Poppy, who manages the café in Montolieu, sent me a fine carving of a Masai medicine man with an orange skull. They both occupy a prominent place on my mantelpiece and helped considerably in my recovery.

From the Atkinson Morley I went to Unsted Park Rehabilitation Centre in a Regency country-house off the main road into Guildford.

"You have a fine baritone voice," said my musical therapist, one of five charged with stimulating the patients' mental and physical well-being. This statement amazed me: at prep school, my only recollection of the music master was that his head was joined to his shoulders in a lopsided way. In an Art Therapy class I started to design a new Hay Flag but did not finish it out of respect for a Mr Whitley Smith of Winchester, Massachusetts, whose *Journal of Flag Research* has, for twenty years, documented the original flag used in Home Rule for Hay. The physiotherapist was a young girl from Amsterdam whose striking beauty and antics with large blue and yellow beach balls could easily have graced the pages of *Playboy*. The same standard of female beauty was maintained in the five-star restaurant, where the waitresses looked as if they had stepped out of *Vogue*. Their short black dresses must surely have inspired many a normal male to live another twenty years. "The waitresses are for patients with the right insurance policies," I said with a dribbling, lopsided grin to a man on my right, who conveyed his empathy with a dribbling, lopsided grin of his own. Eventually I realized that both of us were in such sordid disarray that any conversation was impossible.

I slowly built up a relationship with Doctor Jenkins, under whose stewardship Unsted Park was prospering and expanding.

"Are you related to Jenkins the National Library or Jenkins the Coracle?" I asked, referring to the author of a book about Welsh folk craft. The first Jenkins was part of the world of Welsh academics with which I was very familiar.

"I only go back for the rugby internationals," he said. Somehow, this man had raised the millions needed to maintain Unsted Park. In Wales such places simply rotted.

My days at Unsted Park were reduced to screaming agony when it was discovered that my prostate gland had collapsed. I was immediately transferred back to the NHS at the Royal Surrey Hospital in Guildford where the operation was performed by Dr Schweitzer, grandson of the famous African leprosy doctor. It was successful but I was clearly suffering from what is euphemistically called accelerated old age. I became dependent on my old blackthorn walking stick to hobble along the hospital corridors.

After two weeks I saw the staff energetically clearing the wards for Christmas and reflected that my first operation had been back in early October. I thought about my first two hospitals, the Atkinson Morley and Unsted Park. The former, run by the NHS, was underfunded and, although one of the best places in Europe for the treatment of brain surgery, it was due to be amalgamated. The latter, financed by expensive private insurance policies, was far too rich. Despite treatment costing hundreds of pounds a day, the benefits were not commensurate. I was offered a room at Unsted Park for a further two weeks on leaving the Royal Surrey but I was desperate to return to Wales.

MY KINGDOM OF BOOKS

While I was in hospital my business had begun to make better profits without me. Local buying is the most important aspect of a second-hand book business and Sid had been buying with expertise in the Welsh valleys, injecting life-giving stock into the company. While working for National Carriers he had learnt the whereabouts of the smallest farms and now he put this knowledge to good use. My efficient manager, David Head, a calm man in a green country-raincoat, telephoned Hope regularly in the various hospitals. In the Natural History department I had the best specialist in Hay, Mary Rose Brooks, the daughter of a colonel whose friendly smiles showed that my reputation in the gentrified circles of the town had recovered.

Before I went into hospital I had been studying six management surveys and one video-proposal for a Scottish Book Town. As I recovered so did my enthusiasm for the project. Tony Seaton had been commissioned by the Scottish Enterprise Board to research the Book Towns of Europe. He came to Hay and stayed at the castle with seven students of Tourism from Strathclyde University. Their report stated:

> Major Welsh tourist organizations give Hay little or no publicity in their guides, despite mentioning just about every ex-coalmine, cycle shop and gliding school in the country. And no government agency has attempted to monitor Hay's economic importance to Wales.

He concluded that Hay-on-Wye is as important to Wales as Stratford-on-Avon is to England, attracting half a million visitors a year, one fifth of whom come from overseas. After several months of research, it was decided that a Book Town in the Lowlands would be an ideal venture for Scotland. The panel to select the town included the Scottish Tourist Board, the Scottish Enterprise Board, Strathclyde University, the founders of the Dutch and Belgian Book Towns, and myself.

The Scottish Lowlands are similar to Mid Wales. Small towns, poor farms and a low population make it a politically unimportant region. In the sixth century it was inhabited by the Gododdin, a Welsh-speaking tribe. In an epic poem which makes *The Iliad* look like a schoolboy outing, three hundred of them thundered south to invade England. All died heroic deaths at Catterick, North Yorkshire. So interested did I become in the Gododdin that, for almost the first time in my life, I bought a brand-new book all about them. I love mythology, as does my friend, the painter John Napper. Very tall, stooping and white-haired, he closely resembles Merlin. His extraordinary collection of mythological epics are the basis for many of his paintings. In his library are 'The Ocean of Story', myths from every country in the world, *The Kalevala*, *The Mabinogion*, tales of early Wales and much more. Inspired by mythology, I dreamt of calling my first bookshop in Scotland 'The Revenge of the Gododdin'.

I had completely forgotten the contest for the Scottish Book Town while I fought for my life, but as soon as I began to recuperate I became eager to visit Scotland. Serious illness does not always equal intense pain, and I was more ill than I realized. Unlike other parts of the body, if the brain is injured it is quite difficult to assess the damage; one receives few warning signals. Although Hope tried to make me rest, I insisted on being driven to Scotland. On the motorway, half way to our destination, I became feverish. My head was still bandaged and the stitched wound began to seep. Trying to remain calm, Hope turned the car around and drove me two hundred miles to a fourth hospital, Bronllys, near Hay.

The consultant, Dr Alisa Dunn, whose plump beauty reminded me of the lovelies who had landed King Farouk in such trouble in the early fifties, seemed more serious than other doctors. Two weeks later I was given the all-clear again. I spoke enthusiastically about Bronllys to everyone I met. "It's what you would expect from a cottage hospital. You were very lucky to have Dr Dunn," I was told firmly. Dr Dunn suggested that I watch television and I was introduced to a world of snooker, motor-racing and game-shows. I agree with Solzhenitsyn that 'Western television is like sewage seeping under the door'. I reread Jerry Mander's book, *Four Arguments for the Elimination of Television,* but did not like his defeatism. Surely the human race is not destined to perish before a battalion of stupid quiz-show hosts?

At home my convalescence was blessed. I had a wonderful nurse, Denise Greenway. Her well-fitting jeans were perfectly designed for the occasional energetic gymnastics that her job involved. She was married to George, whose father had swept up the leaves from the Castle lawn thirty years previously, and now George became my chauffeur. Unable to travel, I remained in the garden at Brynmelin. Wobbling and trying to protect my left eye, in which I had no feeling, I struggled with the Herculean task of seeing that the rhododendron bushes were not being throttled by brambles and nettles.

As she gave me my early morning bath, Denise told me that she was an avid reader of romantic books. Romance falls into two very different groups. Byron, Shelley and Delacroix represent the highest in literature and art, as exemplified by Wordsworth's classic poem about 'A host of golden daffodils'. At the other end of the spectrum is romantic fiction: books with flowing, gold-embossed letters announcing *An Affair of Honour* with a swarthy man, naked from the belt upwards, embracing a lady dressed in a gown which was fashionable in high society *circa* 1850. Of the latter Denise was an avid reader and I suggested she open a Romantic Bookshop. She appeared enthusiastic as she continued lathering my hairy stomach but then said, "As long as it's not the bloody daffodils!" This inspired me to create a more popular market for second-hand books, which are all too often academically orientated.

After a couple of months I was able to go to the warehouse in the afternoon and sort books. George drove me and there I began sifting through the two feet of books strewn across the cavernous factory.

"How is Richard?" Hope telephoned George.

"He's as happy as a pig in shit," he replied.

As the deadline for announcing the Scottish Book Town drew closer, I was lobbied to choose Wigtown, but my preference was for the town of Dalmellington at the foot of the Galloway mountains, which I visited on a field trip in March 1997. Beside my hotel was a small, brick pen covered in crumbling cement which had once been a medieval pigsty. I imagined myself leaning against it like the main character in P.G. Woodhouse's *Blanding's Castle* and having conversations with the locals every morning. Dalmellington means 'place on the mill in the town'. Its past prosperity had been based upon weaving and then coal-mining. Since the closure of all the deep pits, the town was in economic difficulties. In the main street there were several factories in which I saw great potential. The town presented me with a bottle of whisky and a brass band struck up. Dalmellington's community spirit was as strong as the liquor. This is of great importance; over the years I have witnessed the damage wrought by the breakdown of communication in Book Towns.

Finally, in the spring of 1997 and after the expenditure of £40,000 on feasibility studies, two pages on the Internet announced the new Scottish Book Town. Wigtown, the victor, had won strong support because several good book-dealers were already established in the town. But shortly after the announcement the thin ice started to crack. Radio Scotland invited me to comment on the judges' selection. I started to explain my reservations about Wigtown but when they heard a voice of dissent they immediately cut me off. When I was appointed as a judge, Tony Seaton had warned me sternly not to criticise the officials. But I knew exactly what a Book Town needs.

My reasons for rejecting Wigtown were inexplicable to the other judges, for their experience was very different from mine. The Scottish Tourist Board, Scottish Enterprise and the University of Strathclyde had no experience of making a living in a remote, rural town, and to Noel and Henk, Book Towns were merely a worthy occupation for their twilight years. My opinions were taken with a pinch of salt and together they disregarded my thirty-five years of practical experience. The Wigtown report said that half of Book Town trade comes from festivals and that they intended to have six festivals a year. They had not listened to me. I was equally angered by Tony writing in a major trade-journal that American Book Towns were non-operational. In fact we were doing thousands of pounds' worth of business in Stillwater.

Although Wigtown is a picturesque little town overlooking the Solway Firth, its remoteness is a problem. Book Towns have a highly mobile economy and need to bring in a million books and thousands of tourists from all over the world. The nearest large town, Carlisle, is a bad place for books. Edinburgh and Glasgow are a few hours away by road. Dealers would incur extra mileage and expense when supplying books. Tony said driving from Carlisle to Wigtown took half an hour, which earned him the nickname 'Jet Pilot Seaton'.

The Scottish Tourist Board raised £400,000 to develop Wigtown and a Book Liaison Officer was appointed at £20,000 a year, but Government funding is a relatively minor factor compared to the difficulty of supplying books on obscure subjects which are impossible to find elsewhere.

As well as Dalmellington's strong community spirit, for the purposes of a Book Town its geography was designed in heaven. The main street ran past three enormous ruined factories and warehouses. Everything was within easy access of Glasgow and Edinburgh, and just an hour from Prestwick Airport. In these buildings I could form my revolutionary theories. These factories could provide the perfect life-raft for a rural economy. There would be one for wholesale, one for retail and one for the Internet. They could become one 'mother bookshop'. I still had dreams for a book town that was not based on the concept of small shops. However, I was peering through rose-tinted spectacles as the judges poured thousands of pounds into Wigtown.

I tried to persuade the people of Dalmellington to ignore the bureaucrats and declare itself a Book Town anyway. I would support them in every way I could. "What we need is a gold-mine, not gold-miners," I told them. A Book Town is dependent upon the availability of books. We must import lorry loads of books to sift for the precious nuggets. These cannot be found without the right ore. But because the town had one and a quarter million pounds in a Miners' Trust and I had been promised a consultancy fee, I was accused of being mercenary. "You have fired an Exocet missile on Wigtown," said Tony on the telephone. But I did not see why both Wigtown and Dalmellington should not succeed as Book Towns. I wrote a pamphlet, *Why Scotland should have four Book Towns*. The growth of Wigtown would depend on Dalmellington, as there were very few books on the south-west coast of Scotland.

My increasing frustration was soothed by Kate and Mike Adamson, who had me to stay, and the generosity of Dalmellington's garage owner, Kennedy Ferguson, and the local chemist Gordon McCracken, a small dark man who could have played a Scottish sergeant-major in a television comedy.

Gordon took me for trips along the beautiful Ayr coast. He pointed out Ailsa Craig, a superb female breast rising from the sea which produced the only acceptable granite for top-quality curling stones. I told the people of Dalmellington that I had about 10,000 surplus volumes of horror and advised the town to open a horror bookshop. Horror is one of several branches of science-fiction, or science-fiction can be one of several branches of horror, depending how you look at it. It comprises a huge number of books, from the world's best-selling living author, Stephen King, to stories that inspired the blockbuster disaster movies of the 1970s. Even great classic authors such as H.G. Wells and Oscar Wilde have written horror, including *The Picture of Dorian Grey* and *Dr Moreau*. Edgar Allan Poe had enormous influence in France and Europe.

My trips to Scotland brought me into contact with my old friend Peter Dance. He is a book-dealing conchologist with inscrutable academic origins and a strong streak of rebellion against its disciplines. "I do not want to spend my life writing learned treatises which only six other people will read," he said when he had come to work for me after a distinguished career at the National Museum of Wales. As one of the world's top conchologists he was responsible for naming the Shell oil tankers and regularly flew to Florida to judge shell-collecting competitions. At four o'clock in the morning, there are two thousand people on the beach who appear to be fascinated by their own shoes – but who are, in fact, scanning the sand for shells.

I had not seen Peter for several years when we met again in 1998. He looked like Henry VIII in National Health spectacles. His semi-manorial house on the Duke of Devonshire's estate belonged to the grandfather of President Wilson. "Woodrow Wilson is the only US president of Scottish origin," Peter said. "We would not have had a Second World War if we had followed his policies." He collected all his writings.

On our first meeting, at the Cinema Bookshop, Peter invited me to his lecture at the National Museum of Wales about trout in Ontario who grow white furry coats due to the cold. It was entitled 'Mermaids and Monsters', but he found their romantic existence scientifically impossible because mermaids would have needed a warm-blooded top half and a cold-blooded bottom half. I told him I was going to open a shop in Dalmellington dealing in Cryptozoology, a passion we both shared. 'Krypto' is Greek for 'hidden, secret or occult' and the genre deals with mythical creatures such as mermaids, twelve-foot Texan rabbits, unicorns and abominable snowmen. One of Scotland's most famous symbols is 'Nessie', the Loch Ness monster, an aquatic dinosaur who has been photographed by tourists with her head and coils just visible above the misty loch. Lake Tahoe, near the Gold Cities Book Town, has its monster, too. She's called Tahoe Tessie.

Returning to Wales, we usually stopped at Moffat, one of the unsuccessful candidates in the Scottish Book Town Contest. The Haggis and Whisky at the Annandale Arms is unsurpassable. I ate spoonfuls of the pungent offal and spiced oatmeal steamed in a tight, round sheep's bladder and served with mashed potatoes and swedes. Whisky is sprinkled over it liberally. I had supper with a Moffat maths master who was interested in the Wild West, so I gave him a book I found called *Triggernomitary*.

I made twelve trips to Dalmellington. Despite the reservations of my financial advisers, I agreed to accept three large factories on the main street rent-free from East Ayrshire Council. I would stock and staff them myself. But negotiations had taken three years and I felt worn out. I did not receive consultancy fees, but never having been prosperous at any time in my life, I have evolved the philosophy that grit makes pearls.

Much inspired by a small, furry skunk which had been given to me in Nookoomis, in the American Mid-West, I placed it in the new premises at Dalmellington where visitors could see it clearly. Underneath I wrote that, contrary to popular opinion, this was not an official from Scottish Enterprise but a small furry animal from northern Minnesota.

Chapter Twenty One

Conclusions

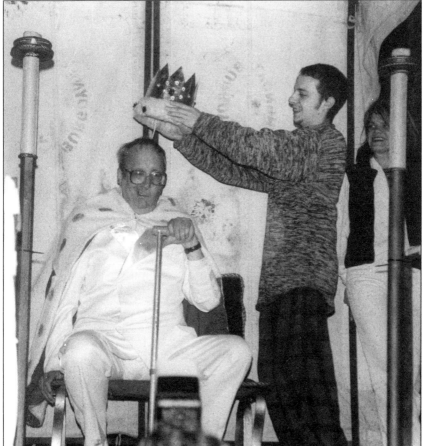

A shy youth placed the Imperial Crown on my rain-splattered forehead.

Photograph by Chris Bradshaw

"Novel Monarch turns a page in history."

I voted Labour for the first time in my life at the 1997 General Election, draping the Castle in a gigantic yellow cloth with a rose emblem in the centre. My minister Gerry gave his full approval, believing that politics and bookselling are complementary professions. "You can knock on the door and say, 'Will you please vote Labour?' If they decline, you can ask, 'Well, have you any books for sale?'"

Labour had promised to investigate the quangos ('Quasi Autonomous Non-Governmental Organizations'). They are experts at manipulating community councils. In Hay the result was corrupt property development and, contrary to their claims, no job creation. But when they came to power, Labour remained attached to Thatcher's stale notion that true jobs could be adequately replaced by ones in the tourist industry. Such hopes rested on false dreams. Nothing had improved for dying Welsh towns. Talgarth, for instance, had very few shops left at all. When I wrote *Abolish The Wales Tourist Board* back in 1978, I had been absolutely right.

Anxious that the Castle should live up to its potential, and to give my attractive, red-haired secretary, Clare Lloyd, something interesting to do, I threw a party at the Castle in support of the Welsh Assembly. It was well attended, with two Liberal Democrats, Richard Livesey and Lembit Opik, and the Euro MP, Eluned Morgan. Over a sausage roll I spoke to her about corrupt property developments in Hay, but she neatly shelved responsibility. It became obvious that we were all there to rubber-stamp the political ambitions of the left wing rather than to confront the issue. Somehow, Mid Wales must repel these quangos just as it had once been one of the few parts of Europe to repel the Romans.

John Elfed Jones headed the committee to create a Welsh Assembly. He was a supreme quango man, having obtained a six-figure salary for deciding how many noughts to put on our water bills. He was the proud owner of a Series 6 Mercedes with a personalised number plate, which made Princess Diana's look like a Chinese rickshaw. The Labour government forgot their promises. The proposed Assembly would ignore democracy, and was based on the theory rather than the reality of Wales.

Afterwards I issued a press release:

HOW WELSH ASSES MAKE A WELSH ASSEMBLY
STOP BLARING BLAIR
STOP VAGUE HAGUE
PUT DOWN ASHDOWN
ARTHUR SCARGILL OUR NATIONAL LEADER

Scargill was the only prominent politician who had had the integrity to risk his career and reputation in an anti-quango battle with the National Coal Board. Because the Welsh Secretary of State was ignoring our problems, assistance from outside seemed essential. I invited Arthur to stay.

Like a small fish swimming into the belly of a whale, he entered Brynmelin hall at six o'clock on a dark winter's evening. He was accompanied by Liz Screen, an idealist socialist with whom I shared an interest in Aneurin Bevan, whose life, like Arthur's, had been dominated by the interests of the miners.

"I'll give you a quiz," Arthur said before we went into dinner. "I have met every single Prime Minister since 1940, apart from one. Guess who." There was a pause, and he looked around the room theatrically. No one guessed the answer: Margaret Thatcher.

At dinner Arthur declined the home-killed pork but devoured potatoes au gratin and talked heartily. He was a practised orator and had already attended nearly ninety meetings that year. He told me that, after the Berlin Wall had come down, 300,000 East German miners who were producing brown coal were sacked; in capitalist terms they were uneconomic. I recalled that I had been told that it was uneconomic to sell books in Hay. I was as immune as Arthur to this rubbish. Both of us believed in political simplicity. If you subsidize an economy you create an official. If you protect it and stop importing foreign coal, overnight there would be thousands in work.

Arthur was very different from the character portrayed in press reports. His gentle, scholarly face was that of an eighteenth-century dandy too fond of port. I was reminded of a remark by Wedgwood Benn whom I had grilled on the corruption of the press. "I think they're too pro-leadership," he said. True or not, something had prevented them from assessing Arthur properly.

If Arthur is less successful than other politicians, he will live longer in the memory. The dip in his fortunes today – inevitably linked to the declining power of the National Union of Mineworkers – will be seen by history as a minor setback in the career of a brilliant and talented man. He had not lowered himself to becoming an MP and was one of the first to raise the banner of defiance against the insidious phoney capitalism of Thatcher, the Labour Party and the Liberal Democrats. "We are not like the other three," he said proudly of the Socialist Labour Party.

The following morning we had a Socialist Labour Party meeting in the State Room of the Castle. Arthur produced his manifesto and a delegate from Pembrokeshire seemed particularly bitter about the issue of nuclear power. Arthur told him about a nuclear cloud drifting in from France. Liz Screen decided to stand for the Welsh Assembly and I came away from the meeting more or less convinced that I would do the same.

At The Limited we were being asked to help re-create libraries. I first came across this concept in the early 1970s when a Yale professor was searching for books with fine, heraldic bookplates of his hero, Horace Walpole. Reassembling Walpole's exact library was his passion.

Ancestor-worship, rather than the minutiae of scholarship, seems to be the usual motive in the re-creation of a library. A rich stockbroker landed his helicopter outside Hay and explained that a family house had come into his possession, and he wanted to re-create the library of his grandfather's first cousin. He produced an old library catalogue written in faded manuscript. Reconstructing the aesthetic appearance of a bygone library is impossible even if all the titles are found. Books age differently; those of a pipe-smoker are tobacco-stained, or the spines may be bleached by the sun. When random books are reassembled the collection usually looks patchy.

The most ambitious project I have encountered was established by the town of Freiburg in Germany, which wanted to re-create the library of the German Army during the Second World War. It incorporated 6,000 instruction manuals with titles like *How to erect a Field Latrine on Frozen Ground* and *How to oil a Machine Gun*. In the 1980s we put together a classical English country-house library for a facsimile English village being created in Japan. Despite my reservations about whether neat sets of Jane Austen and Walter Scott were relevant to the tradition of the English squirearchy, the order was satisfactory and the book assumed a new rôle as an unread tourist attraction. On another occasion we reconstructed Lytton Strachey's library for a film. The author apparently had a large collection of his own work, but all in foreign editions.

The reconstructed library is, I suppose, the last flickering light of Carnegieism, the desire to revert to a time when every rural area was proud of its own inheritance. In the nineteenth century the millionaire philanthropist Andrew Carnegie built no less than 2,059 libraries in the United States, Canada and Britain, believing a community library to be more valuable than a church or a hospital. Although ultimately his libraries failed and most have been sold, he had a clear vision of decentralized culture which makes me better disposed towards his creations than the monstrous, concrete city libraries that were built after the Second World War.

Professor Hywel Francis, who came from a distinguished family of strike leaders, tried to reassemble one of the Mine Workers' libraries and, by doing so, hoped to reconstruct a strong pride in a close-knit community. Regrettably, the project failed. Not only had the most valuable volumes been bought up by wealthy collectors, but titles were no longer in their old context. A religious man would place a book on Africa in the religion section, because his main preoccupation was how to convert the heathen. Today the same book would be a first edition placed in 'Africana'. The miners' libraries were built by a people whose interests were motivated by physical work, by the lumps of coal they held in their hands. They were, for example, fascinated by palaeontology, the grasses, shells, stars and other fossils embedded within the rock-face. For Professor Francis it was impossible to turn back the clock.

I am often asked what I read, and which are my favourite books. This is a question which has always flummoxed me. If I had a disposable income to spend on second-hand books I would use a specialist dealer who has knowledge and discrimination from a lifetime spent handling books.

"What books are selling the best?" I asked Clifford Elmer, the famous criminology dealer in Cheshire.

"Serial murders," he replied.

Although Clifford was a highly serious dealer in criminology classics like the 68-volume series *Notable British Trials*, he found that the modern

phenomenon of serial murder was the subject of his best-sellers. I would
have been one of his better customers. Books on serial murders are a
specialist form of criminology which only came into being after 1980:
homosexuals who kept their boyfriends' heads in the fridge, men obsessed
with raping and murdering waitresses who worked in doughnut chain-
restaurants throughout America, and so on. A more mobile society has
led to identical murders being committed in different locations.
Sometimes they cross state boundaries, which led to the FBI 'profiling'
killers. These have shown that a murderer reads *Master Detective*, a real-
life crime magazine. He imagines his are the hands and cuffs clutching
the throat of the screaming victim on the cover. I wonder what I would
do if I was buying a library and found a pile of them under the bed?

I have great admiration for Edna Buchanan, a crime reporter on *The
Miami Herald* for seventeen years. Believing that every murder must be
reported, for the sake of the victim, her lightning pen reported more
than 5,000 violent deaths. "Harvey had it all, but somebody with a gun
had just taken it away."

The horrors of inner-city America are depicted in what are known
in the trade as 'police procedure novels'. I can read two in a day. Ed
McBain is my hero. Other twentieth-century phenomena like the
suicide of nine hundred followers of James Jones in Guyana, or the
appalling massacre of five hundred women and children by eighteen-
year-old Oklahoma farm boys at My Lai in Vietnam, also justify my
reading a 300-page book in one day.

As my close family knows, I also have a passion for books about the
Mafia. Should, by some fluke, a university offer me a research fellowship,
I would write the standard work on the literary landscape of Chicago.
My proudest possessions are a pair of two-tone, brown and white leather
shoes which Hope found in the Mafia stronghold of North Clark Street,
where the best second-hand bookshops are also found.

I do much of my reading while waiting at airports, though I feel a natural revulsion towards the copious literature celebrating entrepreneurial brilliance. I have seen them in airport bookshops all over the world and no lower form of literature exists. If you wanted to condemn me to hell, you could do so with twenty copies of Donald Trump's *The Art of The Deal*.

As a result of living in Hay for the past forty years, time seems like the interval at a cinema. E-mail, allied to my frequent publicity, means that old friends often contact me.

"I hope you now stock my work on forensic medicine," said one e-mail from Charles Lewis, my Surrey tennis partner from years ago.

"Everybody is immortal in Hay," I replied. "If we don't have your work now, at some time we will."

I suppose, like many small businesses, I found myself with several completely useless computers and a series of frustrated secretaries. "Why don't you use them to compile a list of all your customers who have a squint or a stammer and invite them all to a party?" said Reg Clarke. I have not come up with a better use for computers since.

When I began bookselling, most academics were of the opinion that 'the library is the heart of our institution'. Thirty years later they are putting books onto rapidly-dating technology for the Internet and claiming that the book is out of date. This would appear to shatter their earlier conviction, but events in my life have made me cynical in my expectations of educated people. When customers ask me what I think of the Internet, I say that I think that the *Encyclopedia Britannica* may disappear; they have always had a fairly low second-hand value anyway, as they date very quickly. But the threat posed to the book by the Internet and modern technology has not been reflected by book sales, which continue to grow. I believe that the book as an information system cannot be rivalled by the Internet and the computer. The digestion rather than the mere reception of information is a major task of our lives. Standing in the middle of a library, the ordinary human being is aware of his inability to benefit from all the information within an arm's reach. Multiplying this a million times over on a computer seems one of the follies of mankind. As the millennium approaches, the human race is having to subsist on another form of communication. Five hundred years of non-electrical information is challenged by fifty years of electronic technology. It is left to the second-hand bookseller to fight for what, until recently, was the main platform for the traditional and spiritual culture of the world.

I believe books will not be defeated by technology but rather by their sheer physical size. National Libraries are bursting at the seams trying to contain the books published in their respective countries. They are dinosaurs of the nineteenth century and can no more represent the culture of the book than a horse can do the work of a forty-foot lorry.

The twenty-first anniversary of Hay's Home Rule in 1998 took me by surprise. There was a spontaneous cry from the town to appoint me Emperor. At first I was dubious but, since I was advising Book Towns all over the world, it seemed that if anyone had a right to become an Emperor, I did. I still believe, as I did twenty-one years ago, that rural towns need human not bureaucratic control, which is merely a smokescreen for vicious and dishonest men. It is necessary to keep the cannon blazing from the battlements.

The restoration of the State Room, sweeping the length of the first floor, was almost finished. It had oak window-seats and stone fireplaces at either end. A red and white silk parachute was draped to obscure the crumbling wall. "You must have a banquet in here," urged Jessica, the daughter of my racing-driver cousin, David Gill. We made arrangements for an Emperor's supper. A suckling pig was to be roasted by Alfie Jones in the bakery and I chose slabs of Welsh cheese from the market. To reinforce my feelings about corruption in Mid Wales I asked Rowena Gill, Jessica's sister and a fashion designer, to make two beautiful Anti-Sleaze suits for the occasion.

On Saturday 4th April, the day I was to be crowned 'Emperor of all the World's Second-hand Book Towns', *The Independent* ran an article with the headline 'Novel Monarch turns a Page in History'. That evening fifty people had dinner in the Castle. Hope was beautifully dressed in her white anti-sleaze dress, its back a cobweb of glistening diamonds and transparent beads. My white suit had stiff, satin lapels and on my feet were enormous white trainers which gleamed like the scrubbed side of an expensive yacht.

Dinner parties are not my favourite occupation because the brain tumour has left me deaf in one ear and my speech remains slurred. Between mouthfuls of soft pork I struggled to talk to the two ladies opposite me, one of whom I had adored passionately in my youth. For the first time I think the people of Hay were really looking for leadership. I was supported by some traditional members of the town: the manager of the television shop, his uncle, whom I made an Ambassador, and Lucy from The Three Tuns. All were concerned by the threat of property development.

Protests by the Hay Conservation Society had fallen on deaf ears. In 1998, council land previously allocated for a town football pitch became a construction site for a private property company. Half a mile of ancient hedgerow had been bulldozed. I wrote to the Council asking what had happened to the £13,000 that had been raised to buy the football pitch. I requested audited accounts but the question was simply ignored. When we had all finished eating I stood up and gave an impassioned speech about the property development issue. I said that the town was being threatened by a million-pound development scheme inspired by the Development Board for Rural Wales. A proper democratic discussion was vital. Democracy was best protected by royalty. There was loud cheering.

Castles are used to defend a town from its enemies. As a symbol of this I have a twenty-foot, carved totem pole lying on the edge of the lawn. It represents a Development Board officer who has been shot in the foot. That evening, rain lashed down on top of him, soaking and staining the wood. The bitter weather presented difficulties for the hundreds of patient townspeople who had gathered below the Castle to watch my crowning. Looking like a tropical bird in his red and gold coat, Ken Smith the Town Crier escorted me from the State Room and through the deep mud outside. Stooped against the rain, I climbed slowly onto a high, wooden platform like a condemned man onto the gallows. To the onlookers I was a non-musical Liberace, an inexplicable eccentric who waged illogical battles. I looked towards the market square but could see nothing but pitch black beyond the floodlights. The wind carried away all human noise. I was suspended in the darkness and drenched in bright light.

"Oyez, Oyez, Oyez," called the Town Crier, bellowing through the wind and the rain. He went on to proclaim:

> 'To all here assembled, let it be known that I have been commanded by the goodly town folk of our ancient medieval market town of Hay-on-Wye to bring greetings to King Richard on this most auspicious day.
>
> Twenty-one years ago, Mr Richard Booth declared Hay-on-Wye an independent kingdom and was duly crowned.
>
> Twenty-one years on, Hay-on-Wye is a thriving, vibrant town, and undoubtedly the world centre of the second-hand book trade, all due to his foresight and industry.
>
> Today he will be crowned by Stephen Davies, the first-born of his new kingdom.

May he survive the next twenty-one years and make them as successful as the last.

Declared this day, 4th April in the year of our Lord, 1998.

God bless King Richard and may God save Queen Elizabeth II.'

A shy youth placed the Imperial crown on my rain-splattered forehead. To the distant crowd, I was a motionless, glowing doll. Inebriated spectators hung around for a few hours, wondering if the event had yet taken place. Fireworks illuminated the words '21 YEARS' and golden sparks exploded into the sky. Hope and I left the festivities early. We drove into the night to watch the display from across the fields. Little impedes the view. Hay-on-Wye remains as it was in the fifteenth century – a tightly-walled medieval city...

*We publish a variety of of books of Welsh
and general interest. For a full list of
publications, send now for our free full-colour
Catalogue — or simply surf into our website!*

Talybont, Ceredigion, Cymru (Wales) SY24 5AP
tel (01970) 832 304
fax 832 782
isdn 832 813
e-mail ylolfa@ylolfa.com
website www.ylolfa.com